AN EASSAY ON THE EVILS OF POPULAR IGNORANCE

AN EASSAY ON THE EVILS OF POPULAR IGNORANCE

AND A DISCOURSE ON THE *COMMUNICATION OF CHRISTIANITY TO THE PEOPLE OF HINDOOSTAN*

JOHN FOSTER

GYAN

Published by

GYAN

Gyan Publishing House
5, Ansari Road
Daryaganj, New Delhi-110002
Phone: 011-47034999, 9811692060
E-mail: books@gyanbooks.com

Distribution Network
gyanbooks.com
India, USA, Canada, UK, Australia, France

ISBN: 978-81-212-8965-8 (PB)
First Published, 1895

2nd Impression 2023

Printed at: Gyan Press, Delhi.

AN EASSAY ON THE EVILLS OF POPULAR IGNORANCE

AUTHOR: JOHN FOSTER

AN ESSAY

ON THE EVILS OF

POPULAR IGNORANCE

JOHN FOSTER

GEORGE BELL & SONS

LONDON: YORK ST. COVENT GARDEN

AND NEW YORK: 66 FIFTH AVENUE

CAMBRIDGE: DEIGHTON BELL & CO.

AN ESSAY

ON THE EVILS OF

POPULAR IGNORANCE

AND A DISCOURSE ON THE

COMMUNICATION OF CHRISTIANITY TO THE PEOPLE OF HINDOOSTAN

BY

JOHN FOSTER

LONDON
GEORGE BELL AND SONS
1895

CONTENTS.

SECTION I.

SECTION II.

SECTION III.

SECTION IV.

SECTION V.

SECTION VI.

ESSAY ON POPULAR IGNORANCE

"*My people are destroyed for lack of knowledge.*"

HOSEA.

SECTION I.

IT may excite in us some sense of wonder, and perhaps of self-reproach, to reflect with what a stillness and indifference of the mind we can hear and repeat sentences asserting facts which are awful calamities. And this indifference is more than the accidental and transient state, which might prevail at seasons of peculiar heaviness or languor. The self-inspector will often be compelled to acknowledge it as a symptom and exemplification of the *habit* of his mind, that ideas of extensive misery and destruction, though expressed in the plainest, strongest language, seem to come with but a faint glimmer on his apprehension, and die away without awaking one emotion of that sensibility which so many comparatively trifling causes can bring into exercise.

Will the hearers of the sentence just now repeated from the sacred book, give a moment's attention to the effect it has on them? We might suppose them accosted with the question, Would you find it difficult to say what idea, or whether any thing distinct enough to deserve the name of an idea, has been impressed by the sound of words bearing so melancholy a significance? And would you have to confess, that they excite no interest which would not instantly give place to that of the smallest of your own concerns, occurring to your thoughts; or would not leave free the tendency to wander loose among casual fancies; or would not yield to feelings of the ludicrous, at the sight of any whimsical incident? It would not probably be unfair to suspect such faintness of apprehension, and such unfixedness and indifference of thought, in the majority of any large number of persons, though drawn together ostensibly to attend to matters of gravest concern. And perhaps many of the most serious of them would acknowledge it requires great and repeated efforts, to bring themselves to such a contemplative realization of an important subject, that it shall lay hold on the affections, though it should press on them, as in the present instance, with facts and reflections of a nature the most strongly appealing to a mournful sensibility.

That the "people are destroyed," is perceived to have the sound of a lamentable declaration. But its import loses all force of significance in falling on a state of feeling which, if resolvable into distinct sentiments, would be expressed to some such effect as this:—that the people's destruction, in whatever sense of the word, is, doubtless, a deplorable thing, but quite a customary and ordinary matter, the prevailing fact, indeed, in the general state of this world; that, in truth, it would seem as if they were made but to be destroyed, for that they have constantly been, in all imaginable ways, the subjects of destruction; that, subjected in common with all living corporeal beings to the doom of death, and to a fearful diversity of causes tending to inflict it, they have also appeared, through their long sad history, consigned to a spiritual and moral destruction, if that term be applicable to a condition the reverse of wisdom, goodness, and happiness; that, in short, such a sentence as that cited from the prophet, is too merely an expression of what has been always and over the whole world self-evident, to excite any particular attention or emotion.

Thus the destruction, in every sense of the word, of human creatures, is so constantly obvious, as mingled and spread throughout the whole system, that the mind has been insensibly wrought to that protective obtuseness which (like the thickness of the natural clothing of animals in rigorous climates) we acquire in defence of our own ease, against the aggrievance of things which inevitably continue in our presence. An instinctive policy to avoid feeling with respect to this prevailing destruction, has so effectually taught us how to maintain the exemption, by all the requisite sleights of overlooking, diverting, forgetting, and admitting deceptive maxims of palliation, that the art or habit is become almost mechanical. When fully matured, it appears like a wonderful adventitious faculty—a power of evading the sight, of *not seeing*, what is obviously and glaringly presented to view on all sides. There is, indeed, a dim general recognition that such things are; the hearing of a bold denial of their existence, would give an instant sense of absurdity, which would provoke a pointed attention to them, the more perfectly to verify their reality; and the perception how real and dreadful they are, might continue distinct as long as we were in the spirit of contradicting and exploding that absurd denial; but, in the ordinary state of feeling, the mind preserves an easy dulness of apprehension toward the melancholy vision, and sees it as if it saw it not.

This fortified insensibility may, indeed, be sometimes broken in upon with violence, by the sudden occurrence of some particular instance of human destruction, in either import of the word, some example of peculiar aggravation, or happening under extraordinary and striking circumstances, or very near us in place or interest. An emotion is excited of pity, or terror, or horror; so strong, that if the person so affected has been habitually thoughtless, and has no wish to be otherwise, he fears he shall never recover his state of careless ease; or, if of a more serious disposition, thinks it impossible he can ever cease to feel an awful and salutary effect. This more serious person perhaps also thinks it must be inevitable that henceforward his feelings will be more alive to the miseries of mankind. But how obstinate is an inveterate habitual state of the mind against any single impressions made in contravention to it! Both the thoughtless and the more reflective man may probably find, that a comparatively short lapse of time suffices, to relieve them from any thing more than slight momentary reminiscences of what had struck them with such painful force, and to restore, in regard to the general view of the acknowledged misery of the human race, nearly the accustomed tranquillity. The course of feeling resembles a listless stream of water, which, after being dashed into commotion, by a massive substance flung into it, or by its precipitation at a rapid, relapses, in the progress of a few fathoms and a few moments, into its former sluggishness of current.

But is it well that this should be the state of feeling, in the immediate presence of the spectacle exhibiting the people under a process of being destroyed? There must be a great and criminal perversion from what our nature ought to be, in a tranquillity to which it makes no material difference whether they be destroyed or saved; a tranquillity which would hardly, perhaps, have been awaked to an effort of intercession at the portentous sign of destruction revealed to the sight of Ornan; or which might at the deluge have permitted the privileged patriarch to sink in a soft slumber, at the moment when the ark was felt to be moving from its ground. If the original rectitude of that nature had been retained by any individual, he would be confounded to conceive how creatures having their lot cast in one place, so near together, so much alike, and under such a complication of connexions and dependences, can yet really be so insulated, as that some of them may behold, with immovable composure, innumerable companies of the rest in such a condition, that it had been better for them not to have existed.

To such a condition a vast multitude have been consigned by "the lack of knowledge." And we have to appeal concerning them to whatever there is of benevolence and conscience, in those who deem themselves happy instances of exemption from this deplorable consignment; and are conscious that their state of inestimable privilege is the result, under the blessing of heaven, of the reception of information, of truth, into their minds.

If it were suggested to the well instructed in our companies to take an account of the benefit they have received through the medium of knowledge, they would say they do not know where to begin the long enumeration, or how to bring into one estimate so ample a diversity of good. It might be something like trying to specify, in brief terms, what a highly improved portion of the ground, in a tract rude and sterile if left to itself, has received from cultivation; an attempt which would carry back the imagination through a progression of states and appearances, in which the now fertile spots, and picture-like scenes, and commodious passes, and pleasant habitations, may or must have existed in the advance from the original rudeness. The estimate of what has ultimately been effected, rises at each stage in this retrospect of the progress, in which so many valuable changes and additions still require to be followed by something more, to complete the scheme of improvement. In thus tracing backward the condition of a now fair and productive place of human dwelling and subsistence, it may easily be recollected, what a vast number of the earth's inhabitants there are whose places of dwelling are in all those states of worse cultivation and commodiousness, and what multitudes leading a miserable and precarious life amidst the inhospitableness of the waste howling wilderness. Each presented circumstance of fertility or shelter, salubrity or beauty, may be named as what is wanting to a much greater number of the occupants of the world, than those to whom the "lines are fallen in such pleasant places."

When, in like manner, a person richly possessed of the benefits imparted by means of knowledge, finds, in attempting to recount them, that they rise so fast on his view, in their variety, combinations, and gradations from less to greater, as to overpower his computing faculty, he may be reminded that this account of his wealth is, in truth, that of many other men's poverty. And if, while these benefits are coming so numerously in his sight, like an irregular crowd of loaded fruit-trees, one partially seen behind the offered luxury of another, and others still descried, through intervals, in the distance, he can imagine them all devastated and swept away from him, leaving him in a scene of mental desolation,—and if he shall then consider that nearly such is the state of the great multitude,—he will surely feel that a deep compassion is due to so depressed a condition of existence. And how strongly is its infelicity shown by the very circumstance, that a being who is himself but very imperfectly enlightened, and who is exposed to sorrow and doomed to death, is nevertheless in a state to be able to look down upon the victims of the "lack of knowledge" with profound commiseration. The degree of pity is the measure of a conscious superiority.

We may say to persons so favoured,—If knowledge has been made the cause that you are, beyond all comparison, better qualified to make the short sojourn on this earth to the greatest advantage, think what a fatal thing that must be which condemns so many, whose lot is contemporary and in vicinity with yours, to pass through the most precious possibilities of good unprofited, and at last to look back on life as a lost adventure. If through knowledge you have been introduced into a new and superior world of ideas and realities, and your intellectual being has there been brought into exercise among the highest interests, and into communication with the noblest objects, think of that condition of the soul to which this better economy has no existence. If knowledge rendered efficacious has become, in your minds, the light and joy of the christian faith and hope, look at the state of those, whose minds have never been cultivated to an ability to entertain the principles of religious truth, even as mere intellectual notions. You would not for the wealth of an empire consent to descend, were it possible, from the comparative elevation to which you have been raised by means of knowledge, into the melancholy region of spirits abandoned to ignorance.

But in this situation have the mass of the people been, from the time of the prophet whose words we have cited, down to this hour.

The prophets had their exalted privilege of dwelling amidst the illuminations of heaven effectually countervailed, as to any elation of feeling it might have imparted, by the grief of beholding the daily spectacle of the grossest manifestations and mischiefs of ignorance among the people, for the very purpose of whose exemption from that ignorance it was that they bore the sacred office. One of the most striking of the characteristics by which their writings so forcibly seize the imagination is, a strange continual fluctuation and strife of lustre and gloom, produced by the intermingling and contrast of the emanations from the Spirit of infinite wisdom with those proceeding from the dark debased souls of the people. We are tempted to pronounce that nation not only the most perverse, but the most unintelligent and stupid of all human tribes. The revealed law of God in the midst of them; the prophets and other organs of oracular communication; religious ordinances and emblems; facts, made and expressly intended to embody truths, in long and various series; the whole system of their superhuman government, constituted as a school—all these were ineffectual to create so much just thought in their minds, as to save them from the vainest and the vilest delusions and superstitions.

But, indeed, this very circumstance, that knowledge shone on them from Him who knows all things, may in part account for an intellectual perverseness that appears so peculiar and marvellous. The nature of man is in such a moral condition, that any thing is the less acceptable for coming directly from God; it being quite consistent, that the state of mind which is declared to be "enmity against him," should have a dislike to his coming so near, as to impart his communications by his immediate act, bearing on them the fresh and sacred impression of his hand. The supplies for man's temporal being are conveyed to him through an extended medium, through a long process of nature and art, which seems to place the great First Cause at a commodious distance; and those gifts are, on that account, more welcome, on the whole, than if they were sent as the manna to the Israelites. The manna itself might not have been so soon loathed, had it been produced in what we call the regular course of nature. And with respect to the intellectual communications which were given to constitute the light of knowledge in their souls, there can, on the same principle, be no doubt that the people would more willingly have opened their minds to receive them and exercise the thinking faculties on them, if they could have appeared as something originating in human wisdom, or at least as something which, though primarily from a divine origin, had been long surrendered by the Revealer, to maintain itself in the world by the authority of reason only, like the doctrines worked out from mere human speculation. But truth that was declared to them, and inculcated on them, through a continual immediate manifestation of the Sovereign Intelligence, had a glow of Divinity (if we may so express it) that was unspeakably offensive to their minds, which therefore receded with instinctive recoil. They were averse to look toward that which they could not see without seeing God; and thus they were hardened in ignorance, through a reaction of human depravity against the too luminous approach of the Divine presence to give them wisdom.

But in whatever degree the case might be thus, as to the cause, the fact is evident, that the Jewish people were not more remarkable for their pre-eminence in privilege, than for their grossness of mental vision under a dispensation specially and miraculously constituted and administered to enlighten them. The sacred history of which they are the subject, exhibits every mode in which the intelligent faculties may evade or frustrate the truth presented to them; every way in which the decided preference for darkness may avail to defy what might have been presumed to be irresistible irradiations; every perversity of will which renders men as accountable and criminal for being ignorant as for acting against knowledge; and every form of practical mischief in which the natural tendency of ignorance, especially wilful ignorance, is shown. A great part of what the devout teachers of that people had to address to them, wherever they appeared among them, was in reproach of their ignorance, and in order, if possible, to dispel it. And were we to indulge our fancy in picturing the forms and circumstances in which it was encountered by those teachers, we might be sure of not erring much by figuring situations very similar to what might occur in much later and nearer states of society. If we should imagine one of these good and wise instructors going into a promiscuous company of the people, and asking them, with a view at once to see into their minds and inform them, say, ten plain questions, relative to matters somewhat above the ordinary secular concerns of life, but essential for them to understand, it would be a quite probable supposition that he did not obtain from the whole company rational answers to more than three, or two, or even one, of those questions; notwithstanding that every one of them might be designedly so framed, as to admit of an easy reply from the most prominent of the dictates of the "law and the prophets," and from the right application of the memorable facts in the national history of the Jews. In his earlier experiments he might be supposed very reluctant to admit the fact, that so many of his countrymen, in one spot, could have been so faithfully maintaining the ascendency of darkness in their spirits, while surrounded by divine manifestations of truth. He might be willing to suspect he had not been happy in the form of words in which his queries had been conveyed. But it may be believed that all his changes and adaptations of expression, to elicit from the contents of his auditors' understandings something fairly answering to his questions, might but complete the proof that the thing sought was not there. And while he might be looking from one to another, with regret not unmingled with indignation at an ignorance at once so unhappy and so criminal, they probably might little care, excepting some slight feeling of mortified pride, that they were thus proved to be nearly pagans in knowledge within the immediate hearing of the oracles of God.

Or we may represent to ourselves this benevolent promoter of improvement endeavouring to instruct such a company, not in the way of interrogation, but in the ordinary manner of discourse, and *assuming* that they actually had in their minds those principles, those points of knowledge, which would, on the former supposition of a course of questions, have qualified them to make the proper replies. It may indeed be too much to imagine a discerning man to entertain such a presumption; but supposing he did, and proceeded upon it, you can well conceive what reception the reasonings, advices, or reproofs, would find among the hearers, according to their respective temperaments. Some would be content with knowing nothing at all about the matter, which they would perhaps say, might be, for aught they knew, something very wise; and, according to their greater or less degree of patience and sense of decorum, would wait in quiet and perhaps sleepy dulness for the end of the irksome lecture, or escape from it by a stolen retreat, or a bold-faced exit. To others it would all seem ridiculous absurdity, and they would readily laugh if any one would begin. A few possessed of some natural shrewdness, would set themselves to catch at something for exception, with unadroit aim but with good will for cavil. While perhaps one or two, of better disposition, imperfectly descrying at moments something true and important in what was said, and convinced of the friendly intention of the speaker, might feel a transient regret for what they would with honest shame call the stupidity of their own minds, accompanied with some resentment against those to whose neglect it was greatly attributable. The instructor also, as the signs grew evident to him of the frustration of his efforts upon the invincible grossness of the subjects before him, would become animated with indignation at the incompetence or wicked neglect in the system and office of public instruction, of which the intellectual condition of such a company of persons might be taken as a proof and consequence. And in fact there is no class more conspicuous in reprobation, in the solemn invectives of the prophets, than those whose special and neglected duty it was to instruct the Jewish people.

Now if such were the state of their intelligence, how would this friend of truth and the people find, how would he have *expected* to find, their piety, their morals, and their happiness affected by such destitution of knowledge? Do men gather grapes of thorns, or figs of thistles? We are supposing them to be in ignorance of four parts out of five, or perhaps of nine parts out of ten, of what the Supreme Wisdom was maintaining an extraordinary dispensation to declare to them. Why to declare, but because each particular in this divine promulgation was pointed to some circumstance, some propensity, some temptation, in their nature and condition, and was exactly fitted to be there applied as a rectifier and guard? The revelations and signs from heaven were the sum of what the Perfect Intelligence judged indispensable to be sent forth from him to his subjects, as seen by him liable to be wrong; and could there be one dictate or fact superfluous in such a communication? If not, consider the case of minds in which one, and a second, and the far greater number, of the points of information thus demonstrated to be necessary, had no place to shine or exist; of which minds, therefore, the estimates, passions, volitions, principles of action with the actions also, were in so many instances abandoned to take their chance for good or evil. But *had* they any chance for good in such an abandonment? What principle in their nature was to determine them to good, with an impulse that rendered needless the rational discrimination of it by the light of truth? It were an exceedingly probable thing truly, that some happy instinct, or some guiding star of good fortune, should have beguiled into an unknowing choice of what is right, that very nature which knowledge itself, including a recognition of the will of God, is so often insufficient to constrain to such a choice.

But further; the absence of knowledge is sure to be something more and worse than simple ignorance. Even were that absence but a mere negation, a vacancy of truth, (the terms truth and knowledge may be used for our present purpose as nearly synonymous, for what is not truth is not knowledge,) it would be by its effect as a *deficiency*, incalculably injurious. But it could not remain a mere deficiency: the vacancy of truth would commonly be found replenished with positive error. Not indeed replenished, (we are speaking of uncultivated persons,) with a comprehensive and arranged set of false notions; for there would not be thinking enough to form opinions in any sufficient number to be distinctly and specifically the opposites to the many truths that were absent; but a few false notions, such as could hardly fail to take the place of absent truth in the ignorant mind, however crude they might be, and however deficient for constituting a full system of error, would be sure to dilate themselves so as to have an operation at all the points where truth was wanting. It is frightful to see what a space in an ignorant mind one false notion can occupy, working nearly the same effect in many distinct particulars, as if there had been so many distinct wrong principles, each producing specifically its own bad effect. So that in that mind a few false notions, and those the ones most likely to establish themselves there, shall be virtually equivalent to a whole scheme of errors standing formally in place of so many truths of which they are the reverse. And thus the dark void of ignorance, instead of remaining a mere negation, becomes filled with agents of perversion and destruction; as sometimes the gloomy apartments of a deserted mansion have become a den of robbers and murderers.

Such a friend of the people, then, as we were supposing to expend his life and zeal on the object of rescuing them from their ignorance, would see in that ignorance not only the privation of all direction and impulsion to good, but a great positive force of determination toward evil.

But it may be alleged, that he would not find them *wholly* destitute of right information. True; but he would find that the small portion of knowledge which an ignorant people did really possess, could be of little avail. It is not only that, from the narrowness of its scope, knowledge so scanty as to afford no principles directly adapted for application to a vast number of matters of judgment and conduct, would of course be of small use, though it *were* efficient as far as it reached; —of small use though it *did* produce that very limited quantity of good which ought to be its proper share, in a due proportion to the larger amount of good to be produced by a larger knowledge. This is not the whole of the misfortune: it would not produce that proportionate share. For the fewer are the points to which there is knowledge that can be applied, the less availing is its application even to those few points. It shall be the kind of knowledge apposite to them, and yet be nearly useless; from the obvious cause, that a few just notions existing disconnected and confused among the mass of vain and false ones, which will, like noxious weeds, infest minds left in ignorance, are not *permitted* by those bad associates to do their duty. Weak by being few, insulated, unsupported, and dwelling among vicious neighbours, they not only cannot perform their own due service, but are liable to be seduced to that of the evil principles whose company they are condemned to keep. The *conjunction* of truths is of the utmost importance for preserving the genuine tendency, and securing the appropriate efficacy, of each. It is an unhappy "lack of knowledge" when there is not enough to preserve, to what there is of it, the honest beneficial quality of knowledge. How many of the follies, excesses, and crimes, in the course of the world, have taken their pretended warrant from some fragment of truth, dissevered from the connexion of truths indispensable to its right operation, and in that detached state easily perverted into coalescence with the most pernicious principles, which concealed and gave effect to their malignity under the falsified authority of a truth.

There were many and melancholy exemplifications of all we have said of ignorance, in the conduct of that ancient people at present in our view. Doubtless a sad proportion of the iniquities which, by their necessary tendency and by the divine vindictive appointment, brought plagues and destruction upon them, were committed in violation of what they knew. But also it was in no small part from blindness to the manifestation of truth and duty incessantly confronting them, that they were betrayed into crimes and consequent miseries. This is evident equally from the language in which their prophets reproached their intellectual stupidity, and from the surprise which they sometimes seem to have felt on finding themselves involved in retributive suffering, for what they could not conceive to be serious delinquencies. It appeared as if they had never so much as dreamed of such a consequence; and their monitors had to represent to them, that it had been through their thoughtlessness of divine dictates and warnings, if they did not *know* that such proceedings must provoke such an infliction.

How one portion of knowledge admitted, with the exclusion of other truths equally indispensable to be known, may not only be unavailing, but may in effect lend force to destructive error, is dreadfully illustrated in the final catastrophe of that favoured guilty nation. They were in possession of the one important point of knowledge, that a Messiah was to come. They held this assurance not slightly, but with strong conviction, and as a matter of the utmost interest. But then, that this knowledge might have its appropriate and happy effect, it was of essential necessity for them to know also the character of this Messiah, and the real nature of his great design. But this they closed up their understandings in a fatal contentment not to know. Literally the whole people, with a diminutive exception, had failed, or rather refused, to admit, as to that part of the subject, the inspired declarations. Now comes the consequence of knowing only one thing of several that require to be inseparable in knowledge. They formed to themselves a false idea of the Messiah, according to their own worldly imaginations; and they extended the full assurance which they justly entertained of his coming, to this false notion of what he was to be and to accomplish when he should come. From this it was natural and inevitable that when the true Messiah should come they would not recognise him, and that their hostility would be excited against a person who, while demanding to be acknowledged in that capacity, appeared without the characteristics pictured in their vain imagination, and with directly opposite ones. And thus they were placed in an incomparably worse situation for receiving him with honour when he did appear, than if they had had no knowledge that a Messiah was to come. For on that supposition they might have regarded him as a most striking phenomenon, with curiosity and admiration, with awe of his miraculous powers, and as little prejudice as it is possible in any case for depravity and ignorance to feel toward sanctity and wisdom. But this delusive pre-occupation of their minds formed a direct grand cause for their rejecting Jesus Christ. And how fearful was the final consequence of *this* "lack of knowledge!" How truly, in all senses, the people were destroyed! The violent extermination at length of multitudes of them from the earth, was but as the omen and commencement of a deeper perdition. And the terrible memorial is a perpetual admonition what a curse it is *not to know*. For He by the rejection of whom these despisers devoted themselves to perish, while he looked on their great city, and wept at the doom which he beheld impending, said, *If thou hadst known*, even thou in this thy day.——

So much for that selected people :—we may cast a glance over the rest of the ancient world, as exemplifying the pernicious effect of the want of knowledge.

The ignorance which pervaded the heathen nations, was fully equal to the utmost result that could have been calculated from all the causes contributing to thicken the mental darkness. The traditional glimmering of that knowledge which had been originally received by divine communication, had long since become nearly extinct, having gone out in the act, as it were, of lighting up certain fantastic inventions of doctrine, by ignition of an element exhaled from the corruptions of the human soul. In other words, the primary truths, imparted by the Creator to the early inhabitants of the earth, gradually losing their clearness and purity, had passed, by a transition through some delusive analogies, into the vanities of fancy and notion which sprang from the inventive depravity of man ; which inventions carried somewhat of an authority stolen from the grand truths they had superseded. And thus, if we except so much instruction as we may conceive that the extraordinary and sometimes dreadful interpositions of the Governor of the world might convey, unaccompanied with declarations in language, (and it was in but an extremely limited degree that these had actually the effect of illumination,) the human tribes were surrendered to their own understanding for all that they were to know and think. Melancholy predicament ! The understanding, the intellect, the reason, which had not sufficed for preserving the true light from heaven, was to be competent to give light in its absence. Under the disadvantage of this loss—after the setting of the sun—it was to exercise itself on an unlimited diversity of important things, inquiring, comparing, and deciding. All those things, if examined far, extended into mystery. All genuine thinking was a hard repellent labour. Casual impressions had a mighty force of perversion. The senses were not a medium through which the intellect could receive ideas foreign to material existence. The appetites and passions would infallibly occupy and actuate the whole man. When by these his imagination was put in activity, its gleams and meteors would be any thing rather than lights of truth. His interest, according to his gross apprehension of it, would in numberless instances require, and therefore would gain, false judgments for justification of the wrong manner of pursuing that interest. And all this while, there was no grand standard and test to which the notions of things could be brought. If there were some spirits of larger and purer thought, that went out in the honest search of truth, they must have felt an oppression of utter hopelessness in looking round on a world of doubtful things, on no one of which they could obtain the dictate of a supreme intelligence. There was no sovereign demonstrator in communication with the earth, to tell benighted man what to think in any of a thousand questions which arose to confound him. There were, instead, impostors, magicians, vain theorists, prompted by ambition and superior native ability to abuse the credulity of their fellow mortals, which they did with such success as to become their oracles, their dictators, or even their gods. The multitude most naturally surrendered themselves to all such delusions. If it may be conceived to have been possible that their feeble and degraded reason, in the absence of divine light and of sound human discipline, might by earnest exertion have attained in some small degree to judge better, that exertion was precluded by indolence, by the immediate wants and unavoidable employments of life, by sensuality, by love of amusement, by subjection, even of the mind, to superiors and national institutions, and by the tendency of human individuals to fall, if we may so express it, in dead conformity and addition to the lump.

The result of all these causes, the sum of all these effects, was, that unnumbered millions of beings, whose value was in their intelligent and moral nature, were, as to that nature, in a condition analogous to what their physical existence would have been under a total and permanent eclipse of the sun. It was perpetual night in their souls, with all the phenomena incident to night, except the sublimity. While the material economy, constituting the order of things which belonged to their temporal existence, was in conspicuous manifestation around them, pressing with its realities on their senses; while nature presented to them its open and distinctly-featured aspect; while there was a true light shed on them every morning from the sun; while they had constant experimental evidence of the nature of the scene; and thus they had a clear knowledge of one portion of the things connected with their existence—that portion which they were soon to leave, and look back upon as a dream when one awaketh;—all this while there was subsisting, present with them, unapprehended except in faint and delusive glimpses, another order of things involving their greatest interests, with no luminary to make that apparent to them, after the race had willingly forgotten the original instructions from their Creator.

The dreadful consequences of this "lack of knowledge," as appearing in the religion and morals of the nations, and through these affecting their welfare, equalled and even surpassed all that might by theory have been presaged from the cause.

This ignorance could not annihilate the *principle* of religion in the spirit of man ; but in taking away the awful repression of the idea of one exclusive sovereign Divinity, it left that spirit to fabricate its religion in its own manner. And as the creating of gods might be the most appropriate way of celebrating the deliverance from the most imposing idea of one Supreme Being, depraved and insane invention took this direction with ardour.* The mind threw a fictitious divinity into its own phantasms, and into the objects in the visible world. It is amazing to observe how, when one solemn principle was taken away, the promiscuous numberless crowd of almost all shapes of fancy and of matter became, as it were, instinct with ambition, and mounted into gods. They were alternately the toys and the tyrants of their miserable creator. They appalled him often, and often he could make sport with them. For overawing him by their supposed power, they made him a compensation by descending to a fellowship with his follies and vices. But indeed this was a condition of their creation; they *must* own their mortal progenitor by sharing his depravity, even amidst the lordly domination assigned to them over him and the universe. We may safely affirm, that the mighty artificer of deifications, the corrupt soul of man, never once, in its almost infinite diversification of device in their production, struck out a form of absolute goodness. No, if there

* Those who have read Goethe's Memoirs of Himself, may recollect the part where that late idolized "patriarch" of German literature tells of the lively interest he had at one time felt in shaping out of his imagination and philosophy a theology, beginning with the fabrication of a god (or gods), and amplified into a system of principles, existences, and relations.

were ten thousand deities, there should not be one that should be authorized by perfect rectitude in itself to punish *him;* not one by which it should be possible for him to be rebuked without having a right to recriminate.

Such a pernicious creation of active delusions it was that took the place of religion in the absence of knowledge. And to this intellectual obscuration, and this legion of pestilent fallacies, swarming like the locusts from the smoke of the bottomless pit in the vision of St. John, the fatal effect on morals and happiness corresponded. Indeed the mischief done there, perhaps even exceeded the proportion of the ignorance and the false theology; conformably to the rule, that anything wrong in the mind will be the *most* wrong where it comes the nearest to its ultimate practical effect—except when in this operation outward it is met and checked by some foreign counteraction.

The people of those nations (and the same description is applicable to modern heathens) did not know the essential nature of perfect goodness, or virtue. How should they know it? A depraved mind would not find in itself any native conception to give the bright form of it. There were no living examples of it. The men who held the pre-eminence in the community were generally, in the most important points, its reverse. It was for the *Divine* nature to have presented, in a manifestation of itself, the archetype of perfect rectitude, whence might have been derived the modified exemplar for human virtue. And so *would* the idea of perfect moral excellence have come to dwell and shine in the understanding, if it had been the True Divinity that men beheld in their contemplations of a superior existence. But when the gods of their heaven where little better than their own evil qualities, exalted to the sky to be thence reflected back upon them invested with Olympian charms and splendours, their ideas of deity would evidently combine with the causes which made it impossible for them to conceive a perfect model for human excellence. See the mighty labour of human depravity to confirm its dominion! It would translate itself to heaven, and usurp divinity, in order to come down thence with a sanction for man to be wicked,—in order, by a falsification of the qualities of the Supreme Nature, to preclude his forming the true idea of what would be perfect rectitude in his own.

A system which could thus associate all the modes of turpitude with the most lofty and illustrious forms of existence, would go far toward vitiating essentially the entire theory of moral good and evil. And it would in a great measure defraud of their practical efficacy any just principles that might, after all, maintain their place in the convictions of the understanding, and assert at times their claim with a voice which not even all this ruination could silence.

But, how small was the number of pure moral principles, (if indeed any,) that among the people of the heathen nations *did* maintain themselves in the convictions of the understanding. The privation of divine light gave full freedom, if there was any disposition to take such license, for every perverse speculation which could operate toward abolishing those principles in the natural reason of the species. What disposition there would be to take it may be imagined, when the abolishing of those principles was evidently to be also the destruction of all intrinsic authority in the practical rules founded on them, which destruction would confer an exemption infinitely desirable. The freedom for such thinking would infallibly be taken, in its utmost extent; and in fact the speculation was stimulated by so mighty a force of the depraved passions, that it went beyond the primary intention: it not only annulled the right principles and rules, but, not stopping at such negation, presumed to set forth opposite ones, so that the name and repute of virtues were given to iniquities without number. It is deplorable to consider how large a proportion of all the vices and crimes of which mankind were ever guilty, have actually constituted, in some or other of their tribes and ages, a part of the approved moral and religious system. It is questionable whether we could select from the worst forms of turpitude any one which has not been at least admitted among the authorized customs, if not even appointed among the institutes of the religion, of some portion of the human race. And depravities thus become licensed or sacred would have a fatal facility of communicating somewhat of their quality to all the other parts of the moral system. For this sanction both would reinforce their own power of infection, and would so beguile away all repugnance and counteraction, that the rest of the customs and institutes would readily admit the contamination, and become assimilated in evil; as the Mohammedans have no care to avoid contact with their neighbours who are ill of the plague, since the plague has the warrant of heaven. Wherever, therefore, in the imperfect notices afforded us of ancient nations, we find any one virulent iniquity holding an authorized place in custom or religion, we may confidently make a very large inference, though record were silent, as to the corresponding quality that would pervade the remainder of the moral system of those nations. Indeed the inference is equally justified whether we regard such a sanction and establishment of a flagrant iniquity as a cause, or as an effect. Suppose this sanction of some one enormity to *precede* the general and equal corruption of morals,—how powerfully would it tend to bear them all down to a conformity in depravation. Suppose it to be (the more natural order) the result and completion of that corruption—how vicious must have been the previous state which could go easily and consistently to such a consummation.

Every thing that, under the advantage given by this destitution of knowledge, operated to the destruction of the true morality, both in theory and practice, must have had a fatal augmentation of its power in that part especially of this ignorance which respected hereafter. The doctrine of a future existence and retribution did not, in any rational and salutary form, interfere in the adjustment of the economy of life. The shadowy notion of a future state which hovered about the minds of the pagans, a vague apparition which alternately came and vanished, was at once too fantastic and too little of a serious belief to be of any avail to preserve the rectitude, or to maintain the authority, of the distinction between right and wrong. It was not defined enough, or noble enough, or convincing enough, or of judicial application enough, either to assist the efficacy of such moral principles as might be supposed to be innate in a rational creature, and competent for prescribing to it some virtues useful and necessary to it even if its present brief existence were all; or to enjoin effectually those higher virtues to which there can be no adequate inducement but in the expectation of a future life.

Imagine, if you can, the withdrawment of this doctrine from the faith of those who have a solemn persuasion of it as a part of revealed truth. Suppose the grand idea either wholly obliterated, or faded into a dubious trace of what it had been, or transmuted into a poetic dream of classic or barbarian mythology,—and how many moral principles would be found to have vanished with it.

How many things, before rendered imperative by this great article of faith, would have ceased to be duties, or would continue such only on the strength, and to the extent of the requirement, of some very minor consideration which might remain to enforce them, and that probably in a most deteriorated practical form. The sense of obligation, if continuing to recognise the nature of duty in things which could then no longer retain any such quality, otherwise than as looking to the most immediate and tangible benefit or harm, the lowest of moral calculations, would be reduced to a vulgar and reptile principle. The best of its strength, and all its dignity, would be departed from it when it could refer no more to eternity, an invisible world, and a judgment to come. It would therefore have none of that emphasis of impression which can sometimes dismay and quell the most violent passions, as by the mysterious awe of the presence of a spirit. It would be deprived of that which forms the chief power of conscience. And it would be impotent in any attempt —if so absurd an attempt could be dreamed of—to uphold, in the more dignified character of *principle*, that care of what is right which would be constantly degenerating into mere policy, and rationally justifying itself in doing so.

The withdrawment, we said, of the grand truth in question, from a man's faith, (together with every thing of taste and *habit* which that faith might have created) would necessarily break up the government over his conscience. How evident then is it, that among the people of the heathen lands, under a disastrous ignorance of this and all the other sublime truths, that are the most fit to rule an immortal being during his sojourn on earth, no man could feel any peremptory obligation to be universally virtuous, or adequate motives to excite an endeavour to approach that high attainment, even were there not a perfect inability to form the true conception of it. And then how much of course it was that the general mass would be dreadfully depraved. Though a momentary surprise may at times have seized us on the occurrence, in their history, of some monstrous form of flagitiousness, we do not wonder at beholding a state of the people such in its general character as the sacred writers exhibit, in descriptions to which the other records of antiquity add their confirming testimony and ample illustrations. For while the immense aggregate is displayed to the mental view, as pervaded, agitated, and stimulated, by the restless forces of appetites and passions, and those forces operating with an impulse no less perverted than strong, let it be asked what kinds and measure of restraint there could be upon such a world of creatures so actuated, to keep them from rushing in all ways into evil. Conceive, if you can, the fiction of such a multitude, so actuated, having been placed under an adjustment of restraints competent to withhold them. And then take off, in your imagination, one after another of these, to see what will follow. Take off, at last, all the coercion that can be applied through the belief of a judgment to come, and a future state of retribution;—by doing which you would also empower the race to defy, if any recognition of him remained, the Supreme Governor, whose possible inflictions, being confined to the present life, might at any time be escaped by shortening it. All these sacred bonds being thus dissolved, behold this countless multitude abandoned to be carried or driven the whole length to which the impulses of their appetites and passions would go,—or could go before they were arrested by some obstruction opposed to them from a quarter foreign to conscience. And the main and final thing in reserve to limit their career, after all the worthier restraints were annihilated, would be only this,—the resistance which men's self-interest opposes to one another's bad inclinations. A gloomy and humiliating spectacle truly it is, to be offered by a world of rational and moral agents, if we see that, instead of a repression of the propensity to wickedness by reverence of the Sovereign Judge, and the anticipation of a future life, there is merely a restraint put on its external activity, and that by the force of men's fears of one another. But nearly to this it was, as the only strong restraint, that those heathens were left by their ignorance, or a notion so slight as to be little better, of a future existence and judgment.

Not but that it has been, in all nations and times, of infinite practical service that there is involved in the constitution of the world a law by which a coarse self-interest thus interposes to obstruct in a degree the violent propensity to evil; for it has prevented, under Providence, more actual mischief, beyond comparison more, than all other causes together. The man inclined to perpetrate an iniquity, of the nature of a wrong to his fellow-mortals, is apprised that he shall provoke a reaction, to resist or punish him; that he shall incur as great an evil as that he is disposed to do, or greater; that either a revenge regardless of all formalities of justice will strike him, or a process instituted in organized society will vindictively reach his property, liberty, or life. This defensive array, of all men against all men, compels to remain shut up within the mind an immensity of wickedness which is there burning to come out into action. But for this, Noah's flood had been rendered needless. But for this, our planet might have been accomplishing its circles round the sun for thousands of years past without a human inhabitant. Through the effect of this essential law in the social economy, it was possible for the race to subsist, notwithstanding all that ignorance of the Divine Being, of heavenly truth, and of uncorrupt morality, in which we are contemplating the heathen nations as benighted. But while thus it prevented utter destruction, it had no corrective operation on the depravity of the heart. It was not through a judgment of things being essentially evil that they were forborne; it was not by the power of conscience that wicked propensity was kept under restraint. It was only by a hold on the meaner principles of his nature, that the offender in will was arrested in prevention of the deed. And so the race were such virtually, as they would have hastened to become actually could they have ceased to be afraid of one another's strength and retaliation.*

But even this restraint imposed by mutual apprehension, important as its operation was in the absence of nobler influences, was yet of miserably partial efficacy. Men were continually breaking through this protective provision, and committed against one another a stupendous amount of crimes. And no wonder, when we consider that the evil passions, endowed as they seem to be with a portentous excess of vigour by the very circumstance of *being* evil, (as the demoniacs were the strongest of men,) are exasperated the more by a certain degree of awe impressed on them by the defensive attitude of their objects. When strength so great might thus be irritated to greater, and when there were no "powers of the world to come," to invade the dreadful cavern of iniquity in the mind, and there combat and subdue it, there would often be no want of the audacity

* It is not very uncommon to hear credit given to human nature apparently in sober simplicity, for the whole amount of the negation of bad actions *thus* prevented, as just so much genuine virtue, by some dealers in moral and theological speculations.

to send it forth into action at all hazards, and in defiance and contempt of the restraining force which operated through mutual fear of vindictive reaction.

But it may be said, perhaps, that in thus representing the people who were destitute of divine knowledge, as left with hardly any other control on their bad dispositions than one of a quality little more dignified than fetters literally binding the limbs, we are underrating what there still was among them to take effect in the way of *instruction*. Even this coarse principle of control itself, it may be alleged, this prudence of reciprocal fear, became refined into something worthier of moral agents. For it passed, by a compromise among the species, from the form of individual self-defence and revenge into that of institutions of *law;* and legislation, it will be said, is a teacher of morals. Retaining, indeed, the rough expedient of physical force, in readiness to coerce or punish where it cannot deter by warning, it yet strongly endeavours the repression of evil emotions by means of right *principles*, marked out, explained, and inculcated. It *teaches* these principles as dictates of reason and justice, while it embodies them in the menacing authority of enactments. There was therefore, it may be pleaded, as much *instruction* among the ancient heathen as there was legislation.

In answering this, we may forego any rigorous examination of the quality of principles and precepts enunciated by legislators who themselves, in common with the people, looked on human existence and duty through a worse than twilight medium; who had no divine oracles to impart wisdom, and were, some of them, reduced to begin their operations with the lie that pretended they had such oracles; from all which it was inevitable that some of their maxims and injunctions would even in their efficacy be noxious, as being at variance with eternal rectitude. It is enough to observe, on the claims of legislation to the character of a moral preceptor, that it retained so palpably, after all, the nature of the gross element from which it was a refinement or transfusion, that even what it might teach right, as to the matter, it was unable to teach with the right moral impression. With all its gravity, and phrases of wisdom, and show of homage to virtue, it was, and was plainly descried to be, that very same *Noli me tangere*, in a disguised form; a less provoking and hostile manner only of keeping up the state of preparation for defensive war. Every one knew right well that the pure approbation and love of goodness were not the source of law; but that it was an arrangement originating and deriving all its force from self-interest; a contrivance by which each man was glad to make the collective strength of society his guarantee against his neighbour's interest and wish to do him wrong. While pleased that others were under this restraint, he was often vexed at being under it also himself; but on the whole deemed this security worth the cost of suffering the interdict on his own inclinations,—perhaps as believing other men's to be still worse than his, or seeing their strength to be greater. We repeat that a preceptive system thus estimated could not, even had the principles to which it gave expression in the mandates of law been no other than those of the soundest morality, have impressed them with the weight of sanctity on the conscience. And all this but tends to show the necessity that the rules and sanctions of morality, to come with simplicity and power on the human mind, should primarily emanate, and be acknowledged as emanating, from a Being exalted above all implication and competition of interest with man.

Thus we see, that the pagan ignorance precluded one

grand requisite for crushing the dominion of iniquity; for there was nothing to insinuate or to force its way into the recesses of the soul, to apply *there* a repressive power to the depraved ardour which glowed in the passions. That was left, inaccessible and inextinguishable, as the subterranean fires in a volcanic region. And in the mighty impulse to evil with which it was continually operating as an energy of feeling, it compelled the subservience of the intellect; and thus combined the passions with a faculty skilful to guide their direction, to diversify their objects, to invent expedients, and to seize and create occasions. What was it that this intelligent depravity would stop short of accomplishing? Reflect on the extent of human genius, in its powers of invention, combination, and adaptation; and then think of all this faculty, in an immense number of minds, through many ages, and in every imaginable variety of situation, exerted with unremitting activity in aid of the wrong propensities. Reflect how many ideas, apt and opportune for this service, would spring up casually, or be suggested by circumstances, or be attained by the earnest study of beings goaded in pursuit of change and novelty. The simple modes of iniquity were put under an active ministry of art, to combine, innovate, and augment. And so indefatigable was its exercise, that almost all conceivable forms of immorality were brought to imagination, most of them into experiment, and the greater number into prevailing practice, in those nations: insomuch that the sated monarch would have imposed as difficult a task on ingenuity in calling for the invention of a new vice, as of a new pleasure. They would perhaps have been nearly identical demands when he was the person to be pleased.

Such are some of the most obvious illustrations that the absence of knowledge was a cause, and added in an unknown measure to the strength of all other causes, of the excessive corruption in the heathen nations. And if this depravity of a world of moral agents did not, contemplated simply as a destruction of their *rectitude*, appear equivalent to the gravest import of the terms "the people are destroyed," the *misery* inseparable from the depravity instantly comes in our view to complete their verification.

We are aware that the wickedness and misery of the ancient world, as asserted in illustration of the natural effect of estrangement from divine truth, are apt to be regarded as of the order of topics which have dwindled into insignificance, worn out by being repeated just because they have often been repeated before; a sort of exhausted quarries and dried-up wells. There is a certain class of vain and sneering mortals, in whose conceit nothing is such proof of superior sense as discarding the greatest number of topics and arguments as obsolete or impertinent. It is to be reckoned on that some of these, on hearing again the old maxims, that a people without divine instruction must be a vicious one, and that a vicious people must be an unhappy one,—and those maxims accompanied with a description of the old pagan world as illustrative evidence,—will be prompt to let forth their comments in some such strain as the following:—"The state of the ancient heathens, thus brought upon us in one cheap declamation more, is now a matter of trivial import, just fit to give some show and exaggeration to the stale common-place, that ignorance is likely to produce depravity, and that depravity and misery are likely enough to go together. The pagans might be wretched enough; and perhaps also the matter has been extravagantly magnified for the service of a favourite theme, or to make a rhetorical show. At any rate, it is not now worth while to go so far back to concern ourselves about it. The ancient heathens had their day and their destiny, and it is of little importance to us what they were or suffered."

It is fortunate, we may reply, to be "wiser than the ancients," without the trouble of *learning* any thing by means of them. It is fortunate, also, to have ascertained how much of all that ever existed can teach us nothing. We have a signal improvement in the fashion of wisdom, when that high endowment may be possessed as a thing distinct from compass of thought, from study of causes and effects as illustrated on the great scale, from aptitude to be instructed by the past, and from contemplation of the divine government as carried over a wide extent of time. But indeed this is not a privilege peculiar to this later day. In any former age there were men in sufficient number who were wise enough to be indifferent to all but immediate passing events, as knowing no lessons that persons like them had to learn from remoter views, looking either into the past or the future; who could even have before them the very monuments of awful events that were gone by, without perceiving inscribed on them any characters for contemplation to read. It is not impossible there might be persons who could plan their schemes, and debate their questions, and even follow their amusements, quite exempt from solemn reflections, within view of the ruins of Jerusalem, after the Roman legions had left it and its myriads of dead to silence. Any reference to that dreadful spectacle, as an example of the consequences of the ignorance and wickedness of a people, might have been heard with unconcern, and lightly passed off as foreign to the matters requiring their attention: it was all over with the people dead, and the people alive had their own concerns to mind. But would not exactly such as these have been the men most likely to fall into the vices and impieties which would provoke the next avenging visitation, and to perish in it? In all times, the triflers with the great exemplifications of the connexion of depravity with misery and ruin, who thought it but an impertinent moralizing that attempted to recall such funereal spectacles for admonition, were fools, whatever self-complacency they might feel in a habit of thinking more fitted, they would perhaps say, for making our best advantage of the world as we find it. And we of the present time are convicted of exceeding stupidity, if we think it not worth while to go a number of ages back to contemplate the mass of mankind, the wide world of beings such as ourselves, sunk in darkness and wretchedness, and to consider what it is that is taught by so melancholy an exhibition. What is to give fulness of evidence to an instruction, if a world be too narrow; what is to give it weight, if a world be too light?

It is to be acknowledged, that the mental darkness which we are representing as so greatly the cause of the wickedness and unhappiness of those nations of old, had the effect of protecting them, in a measure, from some kinds of suffering. They had not, as we have been observing, illumination enough, to have conscience enough, for inflicting the severest pains of remorse; and for oppressing them with a distinct alarming apprehension of a future account. But that they were unhappy, was practically acknowledged in the very quality of what they ardently and universally sought as the highest felicities of existence. Those delights were violent and tumultuous, in all possible ways and degrees estranged from reflection, and adverse to it. The whole souls of great and small, in the most barbarous and in the more polished state, were passionately set on revelry, on expedients for inflaming licentiousness to madness; or concourses of multitudes for pomps, celebrations, shows, games, combats; on the riots of exultation and revenge after victories. The ruder nations had, in their way, however pitiable on the score of magnificence, their grand festive, triumphal, and demoniac confluxes and revellings. To these joys of tumult, the people of the savage and the more cultivated nations sacrificed every thing belonging to the peaceful economy of life, with a desperate frantic fury. All this was the confession that there was little felicity in the heart or in the home. Nor was it found in these resources; if the wild elation might be mistaken for happiness while it lasted, it was brief in each instance, and it subsided in an aggravated dreariness of the soul.

The fact of their being unhappy had a still more gloomy attestation in the mutual enmity which seems to have been of the very essence of life, so vital a principle that it could not be spared for an hour. No, they could not live without this luxury drawn from the fountains of death! What is the most conspicuous material of ancient history, what is it that glares out the most hideously from that darkness and oblivion in which the old world is veiling its aspect, but the incessant furies of miserable mortals against their fellow-mortals, "hateful and hating one another?" We cannot look that way but we see the whole field covered with inflicters and sufferers, not seldom interchanging those characters. If that field widens to our view, it is still, to the utmost line to which the shade clears away, a scene of cruelty, oppression, and slavery; of the strong trampling on the weak, and the weak often attempting to bite at the feet of the strong; of rancorous animosities and murderous competitions of persons raised above the mass of the community; of treacheries and massacres; and of war, between hordes, and cities, and nations, and empires; war *never*, in spirit, intermitted, and suspended sometimes in act only to acquire renewed force for destruction, or to find another assemblage of hated creatures to cut in pieces. Powerful as "the spirit of the first-born Cain" has continued, down to our own age, and in the most improved divisions of mankind, there was nevertheless, in the ancient pagan race, (as there is in some portions of the modern,) a more complete, uncontrolled actuation of the all-killing, all-devouring fury, a more absolute possession of Moloch.

Now it is *as misery* that we are exhibiting all this depravity. To be thus, *was suffering*. The disease and the pain are inseparable in the description, and they were so in the reality. And both together, inevitably seizing on beings who had rejected or lost divine knowledge, maintained a hold as fatal and invincible as that of the intervolved serpents of Laocoon.

It is true, that a comprehensive estimate of the state of the people we are contemplating, would bring in view several minor circumstances which, though not availing to change materially the effect of the picture, are themselves of less gloomy colour. But at the same time such an estimate would include other forms also of infelicity, besides those which were at once the result and punishment of depravity, the stings with which sin rewarded the infatuation that loved it. If the design had been to exhibit any thing like a general view, we must have taken account of such particulars as these: the unhappiness of being without an assurance of an all-comprehending and merciful Providence, and of wanting therefore the best support in sorrow and calamity; the insuppressible impatience, or the deep melancholy, with which the more thoughtful persons must have seen departing from life, leaving them hopeless of ever meeting again in a life elsewhere, the relations or associates who were dear to them in spite of the prevailing effect of paganism to destroy philanthropy; and the gloomy sentiment with which they must have thought of their own continual approach toward death; a sentiment not always unaccompanied with certain intimidating hints and hauntings of possibilities in the darkness beyond that confine. But the more limited intention in the preceding description has been to illustrate their unhappiness as inflicted by their depravity, necessarily consequent on their ignorance. And what words so true, so irresistibly prompted at the view of such a scene, as those pronounced of a nation that at once despised the pagans and imitated them,—"The people are destroyed for lack of knowledge."

Let us not be suspected of having lost sight of the fact, that vice and misery have, in our nature, a deeper source than ignorance; or of being so absurd as to imagine that if the inestimable truths unknown to the heathen world had been, on the contrary, in all men's knowledge, but a slight portion of the depravity and wretchedness we have described could then have had an existence. To say, that under long absence of the sun any tract of terrestrial nature *must infallibly* be reduced to desolation, is not to say or imply, that under the benignant influence of that luminary the same region must, as necessarily and unconditionally, be a scene of beauty; but the only hope, for the only possibility, is for the field visited by much of that sweet influence. And it were an absurdity no less gross in the opposite extreme to the one just mentioned, to assert the uselessness, for rectifying the moral world, of a diffusion of the knowledge which shall compel men to see what is wrong; to deny that the impulses of the corrupt passions and will must suffer some abatement of their force and daring when encountered, like Balaam meeting the angel, by a clear manifestation of their bad and ruinous tendency, by a convinced judgment, a protesting conscience, and the aspect of the Almighty Judge,—instead of their being under the tolerance of a judgment not instructed to condemn them, or, (as ignorance is sure to quicken into error,) perverted to abet them.

SECTION II.

From this view of the prevalence and malignant effects of ignorance among the people of the ancient world, both Jews and Gentiles, we may come down, with a few brief notices in passing over the long subsequent periods, towards our own times. For any attempt to prosecute the object through the ages and regions of later heathenism, (with the infatuated Judaism still more destructive to its subjects), would be to lose ourselves in a boundless scene of desolation, an immense amplitude of darkness, frightfully alive throughout with the activity of all noxious and hideous things.

But by this time we are become aware how continually we are driven upon what will be in hazard of appearing an exaggerated phraseology; insomuch that we are almost afraid of accepting the epithets of description and aggravation which offer themselves as most appropriate to the subject. There are some self-complacent persons whose minds are so unapt to recognise the magnitude of a subject, or so averse perhaps to the contemplation of it if it be of tragical aspect, that strong terms accumulated to exhibit even what surpasses in its plain reality all the powers of language, offend them as declamatory exaggeration. Let it then be just observed, without one ambitious epithet, that since that period when ancient history, strictly so named, left off describing the state of mankind, more than a myriad of millions of our race have been on earth, and quitted it, without one ray of the knowledge the most important to spirits sojourning here, and going hence.

But while any attempt to carry the representation of the fatal effects of ignorance over the extent of so dreary a scene is declined, let it not be forgotten that they have been an awful reality; that they have actually existed, in time, and place, and number of victims; that there actually *were* the men, and so many men, who exemplified, and in so many ways, the truth we are illustrating. And a truth which has its demonstration in facts ought to come with the weight of all the facts that we believe ever *did* demonstrate it. When they are not presented in breadth and detail prominently in our view, we are apt to lose the due effect of our knowing them to have existed.

It will be enough to advert very briefly to the Mohammedan imposture, though that is perhaps the most signal instance within all time, of a malignant delusion maintained directly and immediately by ignorance, by an absolute determination and even a fanatic zeal not to receive one new idea. Tenets involving the most palpable impossibilities, and asserted in self-contradictory terms, must stand inviolable to all question or controversy; literature must be scouted as a profane folly; not a principle of true philosophy is to be admitted; hardly is an application of the plainest mechanics to improve a machine or implement to be tolerated; or an infidel is to be only *pardoned*, through contempt, for a successful obtrusion of science to render the most important service,—to save, for instance, a Mussulman ship with its proud besotted commander and crew from destruction,*—lest an acknowledgment made to science

* There is a very curious example of this related in Dr. Clarke's Travels.

should allow one momentary surmise of imperfection to insult the all-sufficiency and sanctity of the unalterable creed and institutes; lest any diminutive crevice should be made on any side of the temple of the vile superstition, for the passage of one glimpse of true light to annoy the foul fiend that dwells there, invested "in the dunnest smoke of hell." Not, however, that this is the policy of doubt and apprehension, the evading and repelling caution of men who suspect themselves to be wrong and dread being forced to meet the proof. For the subjects of this execrable usurpation on the human understanding have, in general, the firmest assurance that all things in the system are right: it has itself secured them against *knowing* anything that could discompose their sense of certainty. No fell savage, or serpent, or monster, ever had a more perfect instinct to avail itself of an impervious obscurity for its lurking place, than this imposture has shown to keep out all mental light from its realm. The delusion is so strong and absolute in ignorance, is so identified with it, and so systematically repels at all points the approach of knowledge, that it is difficult to conceive a mode of its extermination that shall not involve some fearful destruction, in the most literal sense, of the people whom it possesses. And such a catastrophe it is probable the great body of them, in the temper of mind prevailing among them at this hour, would choose to incur by preference, we do not say to a serious patient consideration of the true religion, but even to the admission among them of a system merely favouring knowledge in general, an order of measures which should urge upon the adults, and peremptorily enforce for the children, a discipline of intellectual improvement. There would be little national hesitation of choice, (at least in the central regions of the dominion of this hateful imposture,) between the introduction of any general system of expedients for driving them from their stupefaction into something like thinking and learning, and a general plague, to rage as long as any remained for victims.*

But let us now look, for a moment, at the intellectual state of the people denominated Christian, during the ages preceding the Reformation. The best of all the acquisitions by earth from heaven, Christianity, might have seemed to bring with it an inevitable necessity of a great and permanent difference soon to be effected, in regard to the competence of men's knowledge to prevent their destruction. It was as if, in the physical system, some one production, far more salutary to life than all the other things furnished from the elements, had been reserved by the Creator to spring up in a later age, after many generations of men had been languishing through life, and prematurely dying, from the deficient virtue of their sustenance and remedies. The image of the inestimable plant had been shown to the prophets in their visions, but the reality was now given to the world; it was of "wholly a right seed," "had the seed in itself," and claimed to be cultivated by the people, who in every land were suffering the maladies which it had the properties to heal. But, while by the greater part of mankind it was not accounted worth admission to a place on their blasted desolated soil, the manner in which its virtue was frus-

* In the interval since this was written, some change has taken place in favour of the admission of the elements of knowledge, in the capital, and in the second city of the Mohammedan regions; but with very slight alterative influence on the mass; and with respect to the faith, probably none at all. Within this interval, also, the central power has been hastening rapidly to its catastrophe.

trated among those who pretended to esteem it, as it was, the best gift of the divine beneficence, is recorded in eternal reproach of the Christian nations.

As the hostility of heathenism, in the direct endeavours to extirpate the Christian religion, became evidently hopeless, in the nations within the Roman empire, there was a grand change of the policy of evil; and all manner of reprobate things, heathenism itself among them, rushed as by general conspiracy into treacherous conjunction with Christianity, retaining their own quality under the sanction of its name, and by a rapid process reducing it to surrender almost every thing distinctive of it but that dishonoured name: and all this under protection of the "gross darkness covering the people." There were indeed in existence the inspired oracles, and these could not be essentially falsified. But there was no lack of expedients and pretexts for keeping them in a great measure secreted It might be done under a pretence that reverence for their sanctity required they should be secluded as within the recesses of a temple, nor be there consulted but by consecrated personages; a pretence excellently contrived, since it was its own security against exposure, the people being thus kept unaware that the sacred writings themselves expressly invited popular inspection, by declaring themselves addressed to mankind at large. The deceivers were not worse off for the other facilities. In the progress of translation, the holy Scriptures could be intercepted and stopped short in a language but little less unintelligible than the original ones to the bulk of the people, in order that this "profane vulgar" might never hear the very words of God, but only such report as it should please certain men, at their discretion, to give of what he had said; men, however, of whom the majority were themselves too ignorant to cite it in even a falsified import. But though the people had understood the language, in the usage of social converse, there was a grand security against them in keeping them so destitute of the knowledge of letters, that the Bible, if such a rare thing ever could happen to fall into any of their hands, would be no more to them than a scroll of hieroglyphics. When to this was added, the great cost of a copy of so large a book before the invention of printing, it remained perhaps just worth while, (and it would be a matter of no difficulty or daring,) to make it, in the maturity of the system, an offence, and sacrilegious invasion of sacerdotal privilege, to look into a Bible. If it might seem hard thus to constitute a new sin, in addition to the long list already denounced by the divine law, amends were made by indulgently rescinding some articles in that list, and qualifying the principles of obligation with respect to them all.

In this latency of the sacred authorities, withdrawn from all communication with the human understanding, there were retained still many of the terms and names belonging to religion. They remained, but they remained only such as they could be when the departing spirit of that religion was leaving them void of their import and solemnity, and so rendered applicable to purposes of deception and mischief. They were as holy vessels, in which the original contents might, as they were escaping, be clandestinely replaced by the most malignant preparations. And as crafty and wicked men had a direct interest in this substitution, the pernicious operation went on incessantly; and with an ability, and to an extent to evince that the utmost barbarism of the times cannot extinguish genius, when it is iniquity that sets it on fire. How prolific was the invention of the falsehoods and absurdities of notion, and of the vanities and corruptions of practice, which it was devised to make the terms and names of religion designate and sanction! while it was also managed, with no less sedulity and success, that the inventors and propagators should be held in submissive reverence by the community, as the oracular depositaries of truth. That community had not knowledge enough of any other kind, to create a resisting and defensive power against this imposition in the concern of religion. A sound exercise of reason on subjects out of that province, a moderate degree of instruction in literature and science rightly so called, might have produced, in the persons of superior native capacity, somewhat of a competency and a disposition to question, to examine, to call for evidence, and to detect some of the fallacies imposed for Christian faith. But in such completeness of ignorance, the general mind was on all sides pressed and borne down to its fate. All reaction ceased; and the people were reduced to exist in one huge, unintelligent, monotonous substance, united by the interfusion of a vile superstition, which permitted just enough mental life in the mass to leave it capable of being actuated to all the purposes of cheats, and tyrants,—a proper subject for the dominion of "our Lord God the Pope," as he was sometimes denominated; and might have been denominated without exciting indignation, in the hearing of millions of beings bearing the form of men and the name of Christians.

Reflect that all this took place under the nominal ascendency of the best and brightest economy of instruction from heaven. Reflect that it was in nations where even the sovereign authority professed homage to the religion of Christ, and adopted and enforced it as a grand national institution, that the popular mass was thus reduced to a material fit for all the bad uses to which priestcraft could wish to put the souls and bodies of its slaves. And then consider what *should* have been the condition of this great aggregate, wherever Christianity was acknowledged by all as the true religion. The people *should* have consisted of so many beings having each, in some degree, the independent beneficial use of his *mind;* all of them trained with a reference to the necessity of their being apprised of their responsibility to their Creator, for the exercise of their reason on the matters of belief and choice; all of them capacitated for improvement by being furnished with the rudiments and instrumental means of knowledge; and all having within their reach, in their own language, the Scriptures of divine truth, some by immediate possession, the rest by means of faithful readers, while the book existed only in manuscript; all of them after it came to be printed.

Can any doubt arise, whether there were in the Christian states resources competent, if so applied, to secure to all the people an elementary instruction, and the possession of the printed Bible? Resources competent! All nations, sufficiently raised above barbarism to exist as states, have consumed, in uses the most foreign and pernicious to their welfare, an infinitely greater amount of means than would have sufficed, after due provision for comfortable physical subsistence, to afford a moderate share of instruction to all the people. And in those popish ages, that expenditure alone which went to ecclesiastical use would have been far more than adequate to this beneficent purpose. Think of the boundless cost for supporting the magnificence and satiating the rapacity of the hierarchy, from its triple-crowned head, down through all the orders branded with a consecration under that head to maintain the delusion and share the spoil.

Recollect the immense system of policy for jurisdiction and intrigue, every agent of which was a devourer. Recollect the pomps and pageants, for which the general resources were to be taxed: while the general industry was injured by the interruption of useful employment, and the diversion of the people to such dissipation as their condition qualified and permitted them to indulge in. Think also of the incalculable cost of ecclesiastical structures, the temples of idolatry as in truth they were. One of the most striking situations for a religious and reflective Protestant is, that of passing some solitary hour under the lofty vault, among the superb arches and columns, of any one of the most splendid of these edifices remaining at this day in our own country. If he has sensibility and taste, the magnificence, the graceful union of so many diverse inventions of art, the whole mighty creation of genius that quitted the world without leaving even a name, will come with magical impression on his mind, while it is contemplatively darkening into the awe of antiquity. But he will be recalled,—the sculptures, the inscriptions, the sanctuaries enclosed off for the special benefit, after death, of persons who had very different concerns during life from that of the care of their salvation, and various other insignia of the original character of the place, will help to recall him,—to the thought, that these proud piles were in fact raised to celebrate the conquest, and prolong the dominion, of the Power of Darkness over the souls of the people. They were as triumphal arches, erected in memorial of the extermination of that truth which was given to be the life of men.

As he looks round, and looks upward, on the prodigy of design, and skill, and perseverance, and tributary wealth, he may image to himself the multitudes that, during successive ages, frequented this fane in the assured belief, that the idle ceremonies and impious superstitions, which they there performed or witnessed, were a service acceptable to heaven, and to be repaid in blessings to the offerers. He may say to himself, Here, on this very floor, under that elevated and decorated vault, in a "dim religious light" like this, but with the darkness of the shadow of death in their souls, they prostrated themselves to their saints, or their "queen of heaven;" nay, to painted images and toys of wood or wax, to some ounce or two of bread and wine, to fragments of old bones, and rags of cast-off vestments. Hither they came, when conscience, in looking back or pointing forward, dismayed them, to purchase remission with money or atoning penances, or to acquire the privilege of sinning with impunity in a certain manner, or for a certain time; and they went out at yonder door in the perfect confidence that the priest had secured, in the one case the suspension, in the other the satisfaction, of the divine law. Here they solemnly believed, as they were taught, that, by donatives to the church, they delivered the souls of their departed sinful relations from their state of punishment; and they went out at that door resolved, such as had possessions, to bequeath some portion of them, to operate in the same manner for themselves another day, in the highly probable case of similar need. Here they were convened to listen in reverence to some representative emissary from the Man of Sin, with new dictates of blasphemy or iniquity promulgated in the name of the Almighty; or to witness the trickery of some farce, devised to cheat or fright them out of whatever remainder the former impositions might have left them of sense, conscience, or property. Here, in fine, there was never presented to their understanding, from their childhood to their death, a comprehensive honest declaration of the laws of duty, and the pure doctrines of salvation. To think! that they should have mistaken for the house of God, and the very gate of heaven, a place where the Regent of the nether world had so short a way to come from his dominions, and his agents and purchased slaves so short a way to go thither. If we could imagine a momentary visit from Him who once entered a fabric of sacred denomination with a scourge, because it was made the resort of a common traffic, with what aspect and voice, with what infliction but the "rebuke with flames of fire," would he have entered this mart of iniquity, assuming the name of his sanctuary, where the traffic was in delusions, crimes, and the souls of men? It was even as if, to use the prophet's language, the very "stone cried out of the wall, and the beam out of the timber answered it," in denunciation; for a portion of the means of building, in the case of some of these edifices, was obtained as the price of dispensations and pardons.*

In such a hideous light would the earlier history of one of these mighty structures, pretendedly consecrated to Christianity, be presented to the reflecting Protestant; and then would recur the idea of its cost, as relative to what that expenditure might really have done for Christianity and the people. It absorbed in the construction, sums sufficient to have supplied, costly as they would have been, even manuscript Bibles, in the people's own language, (as a priesthood of truly apostolic character would have taken care the Scriptures should speak,) to all the families of a province; and in the revenues appropriated to its ministration of superstition, enough to

* That most superb Salisbury Cathedral, for example.

have provided men to teach all those families to read those Bibles.

In all this, and in the whole constitution of the Grand Apostasy, involving innumerable forms of abuse and abomination, to which our object does not require any allusion, how sad a spectacle is held forth of the people destroyed for lack of knowledge. If, as one of their plagues, an inferior one in itself, they were plundered as we have seen, of their worldly goods, it was that the spoil might subserve to a still greater wrong. What was lost to the accommodation of the body, was to be made to contribute to the depravation of the spirit. It supplied means for multiplying the powers of the grand ecclesiastical machinery, and confirming the intellectual despotism of the usurpers of spiritual authority. Those authorities enforced on the people, on pain of perdition, an acquiescence in notions and ordinances which, in effect, precluded their direct access to the Almighty, and the Saviour of the world; interposing between them and the Divine Majesty a very extensive, complicated, and heathenish mediation, which in a great measure substituted itself for the real and exclusive mediation of Christ, obscured by its vast creation of intercepting vanities the glory of the Eternal Being, and thus almost extinguished the true worship. But how calamitous was such a condition!—to be thus intercepted from direct intercourse with the Supreme Spirit, and to have the solemn and elevating sentiment of devotion flung downward, on objects to some of which even the most superstitious could hardly pay homage without a sense of degradation.

It was, again, a disastrous thing to be under a directory of practical life framed for the convenience of a corrupt system; a rule which enjoined many things wrong, allowed a dispensation from nearly every thing that was right, and abrogated the essential principle and ground-work of true morality. Still again, it was an unhappy thing, that the consolations in sorrow and the view of death should either be too feeble to animate, or should animate only by deluding. And it was the consummation of evil in the state of the people of those dark ages, it was, emphatically to be "destroyed," that the great doctrines of redemption should have been essentially vitiated or formally supplanted, so that multitudes of people were betrayed to rest their final hopes on a ground unauthorized by the Judge of the world. In this most important matter, the spiritual authorities might themselves be subjects of the fatal delusion in which they held the community; and well they deserved to be so, in judicial retribution of their wickedness in imposing on the people, deliberately and on system, innumerable things which they knew to be false.

We have often mused, and felt a gloom and dreariness spreading over the mind while musing, on descriptions of the aspect of a country after a pestilence has left it in desolation, or of a region where the people are perishing by famine. It has seemed a mournful thing to behold, in contemplation, the multitude of lifeless forms, occupying in silence the same abodes in which they had lived, or scattered upon the gardens, fields, and roads; and then to see the countenances of the beings yet languishing in life, looking despair, and impressed with the signs of approaching death. We have even sometimes had the vivid and horrid picture offered to our imagination, of a number of human creatures shut up by their fellow-mortals in some strong hold, under an entire privation of sustenance; and presenting each day their imploring, or infuriated, or grimly sullen, or more calmly woful countenances, at the iron and impregnable grates; each succeeding day more haggard, more perfect in the image of despair; and after awhile appearing each day one fewer, till at last all have sunk. Now shall we feel it as a *relief* to turn in thought, as to a sight of less portentous evil, from the inhabitants of a country, or from those of such an accursed prison-house, thus pining away, to behold the different spectacle of national tribes, or any more limited portion of mankind, on whose *minds* are displayed the full effects of knowledge denied; who are under the process of whatever destruction it is, that spirits can suffer from want of the vital aliment to the intelligent nature, especially from "a famine of the words of the Lord?"

To bring the two to a close comparison, suppose the case, that some of the persons thus doomed to perish in the tower were in the possession of the genuine light and consolations of Christianity, perhaps even had actually been adjudged to this fate, (no extravagant supposition) for zealously and persistingly endeavouring the restoration of the purity of that religion to the deluded community. Let it be supposed that numbers of that community, having conspired to obtain this adjudgment, frequented the precincts of the fortress to see their victims gradually perishing. It would be quite in the spirit of the popish superstition, that they should believe themselves to have done God service, and be accordingly pleased at the sight of the more and more deathlike aspect of the emaciated countenances. The while, they might be themselves in the enjoyment of "fulness of bread." We can imagine them making convivial appointments within sight of the prison gates, and going from the spectacle to meet at the banquet. Or they might delay the festivity, in order to have the additional luxury of knowing that the tragedy was consummated; as Bishop Gardiner would not dine till the martyrs were burnt.—Look at these two contemporary situations, that of the persons with truth and immortal hope in their spirits, enduring this slow and painful reduction of their bodies to dissolution,—and that of those who, while their bodies fared sumptuously, were thus miserably perishing in soul, through its being surrendered to the curse of a delusion which envenomed it with such a deadly malignity: and say which was the more calamitous predicament.

If we have no hesitation in pronouncing, let us consider whether we have ever been grateful enough to God for the dashing in pieces so long since, in this land, of a system which maintains, to this hour, much of its stability over the greater part of Christendom. If we regret that certain fragments of it are still held in veneration here, and that so tedious a length of ages should be required, to work out a complete mental rescue from the infatuation which possessed our ancestors, let us at the same time look at the various states of Europe, small and great, where this superstition continues to hold the minds of the people in its odious grasp; and verify to ourselves what we have to be thankful for, by thinking what reception *our* minds would give to an offer of subsistence on their mummeries, masses, absolutions, legends, relics, mediation of saints, and corruptions, even to complete reversal, of the evangelic doctrines.

It was, however, but very slowly that the people of our land realized the benefits of the Reformation, glorious as that event was, regarded as to its progressive and its ultimate consequences. Indeed, the thickness of the preceding darkness was strikingly manifested by the deep shade which still continued stretched over the nation, in spite of the newly risen luminary, whose beams lost their brightness in pervading it to reach the popular mind, and came with the faintness of an obscured and tedious dawn.

A long time there lingered enough of night for the evil spirit of popery to be at large and in power, not abashed, as Milton represents the Evil Angel on his being surprised by the guardians of paradise. Rather the case was that the vindicator itself of truth and holiness, the true Lucifer, shrunk at the rencounter and defiance of the old possessor of the gloomy dominion. The Reformation was not empowered to speak with a voice like that which said, "Let there be light—and there was light." Consider what, on its avowed national adoption in our land, were its provisions for acting on the community, and how slow and partial must have been their efficacy, for either the dissipation of ignorance in general, or the riddance of that worst part of it which had thickened round the Romish delusion, as malignant a pestilence as ever walked in darkness. There was an alteration of formularies, a curtailment of rites, a declaration of renouncing, in the name of the church and state, the most palpable of the absurdities; and a change, in some instances of the persons, but in very many others of the professions merely, of the hierarchy. Such were the appointments and instrumentality, for carrying an innovation of opinions and practices through a nation in which the profoundest ignorance and the most inveterate superstition fortified each other. And we may well imagine how fast and how far they would be effective, to convey information and conviction among a people whose reason had been just so much the worse, with respect to religion at least, as it had not been totally dormant; and who were too illiterate to be ever the wiser tor the volume of inspiration itself, had it been, in their native language, in every house, instead of being scarcely in one house in five thousand.

Doubtless some advantage was gained through this change of institutions, by the abolition of so much of the authority of the spiritual despotism as it possessed in virtue of being the imperative national establishment. And if, under this relaxation of its grasp, a number of persons declined and escaped into the new faith they hardly knew how or why, it was happy to make the transition on *any* terms, with however little of the exercise of reason, with however little competence to exercise it. Well was it to be on the right ground, though a man had come thither like one conveyed while partly asleep. To have grown to a state of mind in which he ceased and refused to worship relics and wafers, to rest his confidence on penance and priestly absolution, and to regard the Virgin and saints as in effect the supreme regency of heaven, was a valuable alteration *though* he could not read, and *though* he could not assign, and had not clearly apprehended, the arguments which justified the change. Yes, this would be an important thing gained; but not even thus much *was* gained to the passive slaves of popery but in an exceedingly limited extent, during a long course of time after it was supplanted as a national institution. It continued to maintain in the faith, feelings, and more private habits of the people, a dominion little enfeebled by the necessity of dissimulation in public observances. As far as to secure this exterior show of submission and conformity, it was an excellent argument that the state had decreed, and would resolutely enforce, a change in religion,—that is to say, till it should be the sovereign pleasure of the next monarch, readily seconded by a majority of the ecclesiastics, just to turn the whole affair round to its former position. But the argument would expend nearly its whole strength on this policy of saving appearances. For what was there conveyed in it that could strike inward to act upon the fixed tenets of the mind, to destroy there the effect of the earliest and ten thousand subsequent impressions, of inveterate habit and of ancient establishment? Was it to convince and persuade by authority of the maxim, that the government in church and state is wiser than the people, and therefore the best judge in every matter? This, as asserted generally, was what the people firmly believed: it has always, till lately, been the popular faith. But then, was the benefit of this obsequious faith to go exclusively to the government of just that particular time,—a government which, by its innovations and demolitions, was exhibiting a contemptuous dissent from all past government remembered in the land? Were the people not to hesitate a moment to take this innovating government's word for it that all their forefathers, up through a long series of ages, had been fools and dupes in reverencing, in their time, the wisdom and authority of *their* governors? The most unthinking and submissive would feel that this was too much: especially after they had proof that the government demanding so prodigious a concession might, on the substitution of just one individual for another at its head, revoke its own ordinances, and punish those who should contumaciously continue to be ruled by them. You summon us, they might have said to their governors, at your arbitrary dictate to renounce, as what you are pleased to call idolatries and abominations, the faith and rites held sacred by twenty generations of our ancestors and yours. We are to do this on peril of your highest displeasure, and that of God, by whose will you are professing to act; now who will ensure us that there may not be, some time hence, a vindictive inquisition, to find who among us have been the most ready of obedience to offer wicked insult to the Holy Catholic Apostolic Church?

This deficiency of the moral power of the government, to promote the progress of conviction in the mind of the nation, would be slenderly supplied by the authority of the class next to the government in the claim to deference, and even holding the precedence in actual influence,—that is, the families of rank and consequence throughout the country. For the people well knew, in their respective neighbourhoods, that many of these had never in reality forsaken the ancient religion, consulting only the policy of a time-serving conformity; and that some of them hardly attempted or wished to conceal from their inferiors that they preserved their fidelity. And then the substituted religion, while it came with a great diminution of the pomp which is always the delight of the ignorant, acknowledged,—proclaimed as one of its chief merits,—a still more fatal defect for attracting converts from among beings whose ignorance had never been suffered to doubt, till then, that men in ecclesiastical garb could modify, or suspend, or defeat for them the justice of God; it proclaimed itself unable to give any exemptions or commutations in matters of conscience.

When such were the recommendations which the new mode of religion had *not*, and when the recommendation which it *had* was simply, (the royal authority set out of the question,) an offer of evidence to the understanding *that it was true*, no wonder that many of a generation so insensate through ignorance should never become its proselytes. But even as to those who did, while it was a happy deliverance, as we have said, to escape almost any way from the utter grossness of popery, still they would carry into their better faith much of the unhappy effect of that previous mental debasement. How should a man in the rudeness of an intellect left completely ignorant of truth in general, have a luminous apprehension of its most important division? There could not be in men's minds a phenomenon similar to what we image to ourselves of Goshen in the preternatural night of Egypt, a space of perfect light, defined out by a precise limit amidst the general darkness.

Only consider, that the new ideas admitted into the proselyte's understanding as the true faith, were to take their situation there in nearly those very same encompassing circumstances of internal barbarism which had been so perfectly commodious to the superstition recently dwelling there; and that which had been favourable and adapted in the utmost degree, that which had afforded much of the sustenance of life, to the false notions, could not but be most adverse to the development of the true ones. These latter, so environed, would be in a condition too like that of a candle in the mephitic air of a vault. The newly adopted religion, therefore, of the uncultivated converts from popery, would be far from exhibiting, as compared with the renounced superstition, a magnitude of change, and force of contrast, duly corresponding to the difference between the lying vanities of priestcraft and a communication from the living God. The reign of ignorance combined with imposture had fixed upon the common people of the age of the Reformation, and of several generations downward, the doom of being incapable of admitting genuine Christianity but with an excessively inadequate apprehension of its attributes;—as in the patriarchal ages a man might have received with only the honours appropriate to a saint or prophet, the visitant in whom he was entertaining an angel unawares.

Happy for both that ancient entertainer of such a visitant, and the ignorant but honest adopter of the reformed religion, when that which they entertained rewarded them according to its own celestial quality, rather than in proportion to their inadequate reception. We may believe that the Divine Being, in special compassion to that ignorance to which barbarism and superstition had condemned inevitably the greater number of the early converts to the reformed religion, did render that faith beneficial to them beyond the proportion of their narrow and still half superstitious conception of it. And this is, in truth, the consideration the most consolatory in looking back to that tenebrious period in which popery was slowly retiring, with a protracted exertion of all the craft and strength of an able and veteran tyrant contending to the last for prolonged dominion.

It is, however, no consideration of a portion of the people sincere, inquiring, and emerging, though dimly enlightened, from the gloom of so dreary a scene, that is most apt to occur to our thoughts in extenuation of that gloom. Our unreflecting attention allows itself to be so engrossed by far different circumstances of that period of our history, that we are imposed upon by a spectacle the very opposite of mournful. For what is it but a splendid and animating exhibition that we behold in looking back to the age of Elizabeth?

And *was* not that, it may be asked, an age of the highest glory to our nation? Why repress our delight in contemplating it? How can we refuse to indulge an inspiring sympathy with the energy of those times, an elation of spirit at beholding the unparalleled allotment to her reign, of statesmen, heroes, and literary geniuses, but for whom, indeed, "that bright occidental star" would have left no such brilliant track of fame behind her?

Permit us to answer by inquiring, What should the intellectual condition of the *people,* properly so denominated, have been in order to correspond in a due proportion to the magnificence of these their representative chiefs, and complete the grand spectacle as that of a *nation?* Determine that; and then inquire what actually *was* the state of the people all this while. There is evidence that it was, what the fatal blight and blast of popery might be expected to have left it, generally and most wretchedly degraded. What it was is shown by the facts, that it was found impossible, even under the inspiring auspices of the learned Elizabeth, with her constellation of geniuses, orators, scholars, to supply the churches generally with officiating persons capable of going with decency through the task of the public service, made ready, as every part of it was, to their hands; and that to be able to read, was the very marked distinction of here and there an individual. It requires little effort but that of going low enough, to complete the general estimate in conformity to these and similar facts.

And here we cannot help remarking what a deception we suffer to pass on us from history. It celebrates some period in a nation's career as pre-eminently illustrious, for magnanimity, lofty enterprise, literature, and original genius. There was, perhaps, a learned and vigorous monarch, and there were Cecils and Walsinghams, and Shakspeares and Spensers, and Sidneys and Raleighs, with many other powerful thinkers and actors, to render it the proudest age of our national glory. And we thoughtlessly admit on our imagination this splendid exhibition as in some manner involving or implying the collective state of the people in that age! The ethereal summits of a tract of the moral world are conspicuous and fair in the lustre of heaven, and we take no thought of the immensely greater proportion of it which is sunk in gloom and covered with fogs. The general mass of the population, whose physical vigour, indeed, and courage, and fidelity to the interests of the country, were of such admirable avail to the purposes, and under the direction, of the mighty spirits that wielded their rough agency,—this great assemblage was sunk in such mental barbarism, as to be placed at about the same distance from their illustrious intellectual chiefs, as the hordes of Scythia from the finest spirits of Athens. It was nothing to this debased countless multitude spread over the country, existing in the coarsest habits, destitute, in the proportion of thousands to one, of cultivation, and still in a great degree enslaved by the popish superstition,—it was nothing to them, in the way of direct influence to draw forth their minds into free exercise and acquirement, that there were, within the circuit of the island, a profound scholarship, a most disciplined and vigorous reason, a masculine eloquence, and genius breathing enchantment. Both the actual possessors of this mental opulence, and the part of society forming, around them, the sphere immediately pervaded by the delight and instruction imparted by them, might as well, for any thing they diffused of this luxury and benefit among the general multitude, have been a Brahminical caste, dissociated by an imagined essential distinction of nature. While they were exulting in this elevation and free excursiveness of mental existence, the prostrate crowd were grovelling through a life on a level with the soil where they were at last to find their graves. But this crowd it was that constituted the substance of the *nation;* to which nation, in the mass, the historian applies the superb epithets, which a small proportion of the men of that age claimed by a striking *exception* to the general state of the community. History too much consults our love of effect and pomp, to let us see in a close and distinct manner any thing

> "On the low level of th' inglorious throng;"

and our attention is borne away to the intellectual splendour exhibited among the most favoured aspirants of the seats of learning, or in councils, courts, and camps, in heroic and romantic enterprises, and in some immortal works of genius. And thus we are gazing with delight at a fine public bonfire, while, in all the cottages round, the people are shivering for want of fuel.

Our history becomes very bright again with the intellectual and literary riches of a much later period, often denominated a golden age,—that which was illustrated by the talents of Addison, Pope, Swift, and their numerous secondaries in fame; and could also boast its philosophers, statesmen, and heroes. And in the lapse of four or five ages, according to the average term of human life, since the earlier grand display of mind, what had been effected toward such an advancement of intelligence in the community, that when this next tribe of highly endowed spirits should appear, they would stand in much less opprobrious contrast to the main body of the nation, and find a much larger portion of it qualified to receive their intellectual effusions. By this time, the class of persons who sought knowledge on a wider scale than what sufficed for the ordinary affairs of life, who took an interest in literature, and constituted the *Authors' Public*, had indeed extended a little, extremely little, beyond the people of condition, the persons educated in learned institutions, and those whose professions involved some necessity, and might create some taste, for reading. Still they *were* a *class*, and that with a limitation marked and palpable, to a degree very difficult for us now to conceive. They were in contact, on the one side, with the great thinkers, moralists, poets, and wits, but very slightly in communication with the generality of the people on the other. They received the emanations from the assemblage of talent and knowledge, but did not serve as conductors to convey them down indefinitely into the community. The national body, regarded in its intellectual character, had an inspirited and vigorous superior part, as constituted of these men of eminent talents and attainments, and this small class of persons in a measure assimilated to them in thinking and taste; but it was in a condition resembling that of a human frame in which, (through an injury in the spinal marrow,) some of the most important functions of vitality have terminated at some precise limit downward, leaving the inferior extremities devoid of sensation and the power of action.

It is on record, that works admirably adapted to find readers and to make them, had but an extremely confined and slowly widening circulation, according to *our* standard of the popular success of the productions of distinguished talents. Nor did the writers *reckon* on any such popular success. In the calculations of their literary ambition, it was a thing of course that the people went for nothing. It is apparent in allusions to the people occurring in these very works, that "the lower sort," "the vulgar herd," "the canaille," "the mob," "the many-headed beast," "the million," (and even these designations generally meant something short of the lowest classes of all,) were no more thought of in any relation to a state of cultivated intelligence than Turks or Tartars. The readers are habitually recognised as a kind of select community, conversed with on topics and in a language with which the vulgar have nothing at all to do,—a converse the more gratifying on that account. And any casual allusions to the bulk of the people are expressed in phrases unaffectedly implying, that they are a herd of beings existing on quite other terms and for essentially other ends, than we, fine writers, and you, our admiring readers. It is evident in our literature of that age, (a feature still more prominent in that of France, at the same and down to a much later period,) that the main national population, accounted as creatures to which souls and senses were given just to render their limbs mechanically serviceable, were regarded by the intellectual aristocracy with hardly so active a sentiment as contempt; they were not worth that; it was the easy indifference toward what was seldom thought of as in existence.

Wickedly wrong as such a feeling was, there is no doubt that the actual state of the people was quite such as would naturally cause it, in men whose large and richly cultivated minds did not contain philanthropy or christian charity enough to regret and pity the popular debasement as a calamity. For while they were indulging their pride in the elevation, and their taste in all the luxuries and varieties, of that ampler higher range of existence enjoyed by such men, in what light must they view the bulk of a nation, that knew nothing of their wit, genius, or philosophy, could not even read their writings, but as a coarse mass of living material, the mere earthy substratum of humanity, not to be accounted of in any comparison or even relation to what man is in his higher style? While they of that higher style were revelling in their mental affluence, the vast majority of the inhabitants of the island were subsisting, and had always subsisted, on the most beggarly pittance on which mind could be barely kept alive. Probably they had at that time still fewer ideas than the people of the former age which we have been describing. For many of those with which popery had occupied the faith and fancy of that earlier generation, had now vanished from the popular mind, without being replaced in equal number by better ideas, or by ideas of any kind. And then their vices had the whole grossness of vice, and their favourite amusements were at best rude and boisterous, and a large proportion of them savage and cruel. So that when we look at the shining wits, poets, and philosophers, of that age, they appear like gaudy flowers growing in a putrid marsh.

And to a much later period this deplorable ignorance, with all its appropriate consequences, continued to be the dishonour and the plague of the intellectual and moral condition of the inhabitants of England. Of England! which had through many centuries made so great a figure in Christendom; which has been so splendid in arms, liberty, legislation, science, and all manner of literature; which has boasted its universities, of ancient foundation and proudest fame, munificently endowed, and possessing, in their accumulations of literary treasure, nearly the whole results of all the strongest thinking there had been in the world; and which has had also, through the charity of individuals, such a number of minor institutions for education, that the persons entrusted to see them administered have, in very numerous instances, not scrupled to divert their resources to totally different purposes, lest, perchance, the cause of damage to the people should change from a lack of knowledge to a repletion of it. Of

England! so long after the Reformation, and all the while under the superintendence and tuition of an ecclesiastical establishment for both instruction and jurisdiction, co-extended with the entire nation, and furnished for its ministry with men from the discipline of institutions where every thing the most important to be known was professed to be taught. Thus endowed had England been, thus was she endowed at the period under our review, (the former part of the last century,) with the facilities, the provisions, the great intellectual apparatus, to be wielded in any mode her wisdom might devise, and with whatever strength of hand she chose to apply, for promoting her several millions of rational, accountable, immortal beings, somewhat beyond a state of mere physical existence. When therefore, notwithstanding all this, an awful proportion of them were under the continual process of destruction for want of knowledge, what a tremendous responsibility was borne by whatever part of the community it was that stood, either by office and express vocation, or by the general obligation inseparable from ability, in the relation of guardianship to the rest.

But here the voice of that sort of patriotism which is in vogue as well in England as in China, may perhaps interpose, to protest against malicious and exaggerated invective. As if it were a question of what might beforehand be reasonably expected, instead of an account of what actually exists, it may be alleged that surely it is a representation too much against antecedent probability to be true, that a civilized, christian, magnanimous, and wealthy state like that of England, can have been so careless and wicked as to tolerate, during the lapse of centuries, a hideously gross and degraded condition of the people.

But besides that the fact is plainly so, it were vain to presume, in confidence on any supposed consistency of character, that it *must* be otherwise. There is no saying *what* a civilized and christian nation, (so called,) may not tolerate. Recollect the Slave Trade, which, with the magnitude of a national concern, continued its abominations while one generation after another of Englishmen passed away; their intelligence, conscience, humanity, and refinement, as quietly accommodated to it, as if one portion of the race had possessed an express warrant from Heaven to capture, buy, sell, and drive another. This is but one of many mortifying illustrations how much the constitution of our moral sentiments resembles a Manichæan creation, how much of them is formed in passive submission to the evil principle, acting through prevailing custom; which determines that it shall but very partially depend on the real and most manifest qualities of things presented to us, whether we shall have any right perception of their characters of good and evil. The agency which works this mal-formation in our sentiments needs no greater triumph, than that the true nature of things should be disguised to us by the very effect of their being constantly kept in our sight. Could any malignant enchanter wish for more than this,—to make us insensible to the odious quality of things not only *though* they stand constantly and directly in our view, but *because* they do so? And while they do so, there may also stand as obviously in our view, and close by them, the truths which *expose* their real nature, and might be expected to make us instantly revolt from them; and these truths shall be no other than some of the plainest principles of reason and religion. It shall be as if men of wicked designs could be compelled to wear labels on their breasts wherever they go, to announce their character in conspicuous letters; or nightly assassins could be forced to carry torches before them, to reveal the murderer in their visages; or, as if, according to a vulgar superstition, evil spirits could not help betraying their dangerous presence by a tinge of brimstone in the flame of the lamps. Thus evident, by the light of reason and religion, shall have been the true nature of certain important facts in the policy of a christian nation; and nevertheless, even the cultivated part of that nation, during a series of generations, having directly before their sight an enormous nuisance and iniquity, shall yet never be struck with its quality, never be made restless by its annoyance, never seriously think of it. And so its odiousness shall never be decidedly apprehended till some individual or two, as by the acquisition of a new moral sense, receive a sudden intuition of its nature, a disclosure of its whole essence and malignity,—the essence and malignity of that very thing which has been exposing its quality, without the least reserve, by the most flagrant signs, to millions of observers.

Thus it has been with respect to the barbarous ignorance under which nine tenths of the population of our country have continued, through a number of ages subsequent to the Reformation, surrendered to every thing low, vicious, and wretched. This state of national debasement and dishonour lay spread out, a wide scene of moral desolation, in the sight of statesmen, of dignified and subordinate ecclesiastics, of magistrates, of the philosophic speculators on human nature, and of all those whose rank and opulence brought them hourly proofs what great influence they might have, in any way in which they should choose to exert it, on the people below them. And still it was all right that the multitudes, constituting the grand living agency through the realm, should remain in such a condition that, when they died, the country should lose nothing but so much animated body, with the quantum of vice which helped to keep it in action. When at length some were beginning to apprehend and proclaim that all this was wrong, these classes were exceedingly slow in their assent to the reformed doctrine. A large proportion of them even declared, on system, against the speculations and projects for giving the people, at last, the use and value of their souls as well as their hands. The earnest and sanguine philanthropists might be pardoned the simplicity of not foreseeing such an opposition, though they ought, perhaps, to have known better than to be surprised at the phenomenon. They were to be made wiser by force, with respect to men's governing prejudices and motives. And from credulity mortified is a short transit to suspicion. So ungracious a manner of having the insight into motives sharpened, does not tend to make its subsequent exercise indulgent, when it comes to inspect the altered appearances assumed by persons and classes who have previously been in decided opposition. What arguments have prevailed with you, (the question might be,) since you have never frankly retracted your former contempt of those which convinced *us*? May any sinister thought have occurred, that you might defeat our ends by a certain way of managing the means? Or do you hope to determine and limit to some subordinate purposes, what we wish to prosecute for the most general good? Or would you rather impose on yourselves the grievance of promoting an object which you dislike, than that we should have the chief credit of promoting it? Do you sometimes accompany your working in the vineyard with maledictions on those who have reduced you to such a necessity? Would you have been glad to be saved the unwelcome service by *their* letting it alone?

Those friends of man and their country who were the earliest to combine in schemes for enlightening the people and who continue to prosecute the object on the most liberal and comprehensive principle, have to acknowledge surmises like these. Nevertheless, they are willing to forego any shrewd investigation into the causes of the later silence and apparent acquiescence of former opposers; and into the motives which have induced some of them, though in no very amicable mood, to take a part in measures tending in their general effect to the same end. Whatever were their suspicion of those motives, they would be reminded of an example, not altogether foreign to the nature of their business, and quite in point to their duty,—that of the magnanimous principle through which the great Apostle disappointed his adversaries, by finding his own triumph in that of his cause, while he saw that cause availing itself of these foes after the manner of some consummate general, who has had the art to make those who have come into the field as but treacherous auxiliaries, cooperate effectually in the battle which they never intended he should gain. Some preached Christ of envy, and strife, and contention, supposing to add affliction to his bonds; but, says he, What then? notwithstanding every way, whether in pretence or truth, Christ is preached—*the thing itself is done*—and I therein rejoice, yea, and will rejoice. When animated by this high principle, this ambition absolutely *for the cause itself*, its servant is a gainer, because *it* is a gainer, by all things convertible into tribute, whatever may be the temper or intention of the offerers, either as towards the cause or towards himself. He may say to them, I am more pleased by what you are actually doing, be the motive what it will, in advancement of the object to which I am devoted, than it is possible for you to aggrieve me by letting me see that you would not be sorry for the frustration of *my* schemes and exertions for its service; or even by betraying, though I should lament such a state of your minds, that you would be content to sacrifice *it* if that might be the way to defeat *me*.

We revert but for a moment to the review of past times.——We said that long after the brilliant show of talent, and the creation of literary supplies for the national use, in the early part of the last century, the deplorable mental condition of the people remained in no very great degree altered. To pass from beholding that bright and sumptuous display, in order to see what there was corresponding to it in the subsequent state of the popular cultivation, is like going out from some magnificent apartment with its lustres, music, refections, and assemblage of elegant personages, to be beset by beggars in the gloom and cold of a winter night.

Take a few hours' indulgence in the literary luxuries of Addison, Pope, and their secondaries, and then turn to some authentic plain representation of the attainments and habits of the mass of the people, at the time when Whitefield and Wesley commenced their invasion of the barbarous community. But the benevolent reader, (or let him be a patriotically proud one,) is quite reluctant to recognise his country, his celebrated christian nation, "the most enlightened in the world," (as song and oratory have it,) in a populace for the far greater part as perfectly estranged from the page of knowledge, as if printing, or even letters, had never been invented; the younger part finding their supreme delight in rough frolic and savage sports, the old sinking down into impenetrable stupefaction with the decline of the vital principle.

If he would eagerly seek to fix on something as a counterbalance to this, and endeavour to modify the estimate and relieve the feeling, by citing perhaps the courage, and a certain rudimental capacity of good sense, in which the people are deemed to have surpassed the neighbouring nations, he will be compelled to see how these native endowments were overrun and befooled by a farrago of contemptible superstitions;—contemptible not only for their stupid absurdity, but also as having in general nothing of that pensive, solemn, and poetical character which superstition is capable of assuming.—It is an exception to be made with respect to the northernmost part of the island, that superstition did there partake of this higher character. It seems to have had somewhat of the tone imitated, but in a softer mode, in the poetry, denominated of Ossian.

As to religion, there is no hazard in saying, that several millions had little further notion of it than that it was an occasional, or, in the opinion of perhaps one in twenty, a regular appearance at church, hardly taking into the account that they were to be taught any thing there. And what *were* they taught—those of them who gave their attendance and attention? What kind of notions it was that had settled in their minds under such ministration, would be, so to speak, brought out, it would be made apparent what they were or were not taught, when so strong and general a sensation was produced by the irruption among them of the two reformers just named; proclaiming, as they both did, (notwithstanding very considerable differences of secondary order), the principles which had been authoritatively declared to be of the essence of Christianity, in that model of doctrine which had been appointed to prescribe and conserve the national faith. If such doctrine *had* been imparted to a portion of the popular mind, even though with somewhat less positive statement, less copiousness of illustration, and less cogency of enforcement, than it ought; if it had been but in crude *substance* fixed in the people's understanding, by the ministry of the many thousand authorized instructors, who were by their institute solemnly enjoined and pledged not to teach a different sort of doctrine, and not to fail of teaching this; if, we repeat, this faith, so conspicuously declared in the articles, liturgy, and homilies, had been in any degree in possession of the people, they would have recognised its main principles, or at least a similarity of principles, in the addresses of these two new preachers. They would have done so, notwithstanding a peculiarity of phraseology which Whitefield and Wesley carried to excess; and notwithstanding certain specialities which the latter did not, even supposing them to be truths, keep duly subordinate in exhibiting the prominent essentials of Christianity. The preaching, therefore, of these men was a test of what the people had been previously taught or allowed to repose in as christian truth, under the tuition of their great religious guardian, the national church. What it was or was not would be found, in their having a sense of something like what they had been taught before, or something opposite to it, or something altogether foreign and unknown, when they were hearing these loud proclaimers of the old doctrines of the Reformation. Now then, as carrying with them this quality of a test, how were those men received in the community? Why, they were generally received, on account of the import of what they said, still more than from their zealous manner of saying it, with as strong an impression of novelty, strangeness, and contrariety to everything hitherto heard of, as any of our voyagers and travellers of discovery have been by the barbarous tribes who had never before seen civilized man, or as the Spaniards on their arrival in Mexico or Peru. They might, as the voyagers have done, experience every local difference of moral temperament, from that which hailed them with acclamations, to that which often exploded in a volley of mud and stones; but through all these varieties of greetings, there was a strong sense of something then brought before them for the first time. "Thou bringest certain strange things to our ears," was an expression not more unaffectedly uttered by any hearer of an apostle, preaching in a heathen city. And to many of the auditors, it was a matter of nearly as much difficulty as it would to an inquisitive heathen, and required as new a posture of the mind, to attain an understanding of the evangelical doctrines, though they were the very same which had been held forth by the fathers and martyrs of the English Church.

We have alluded to the violence, which sometimes encountered the endeavour to restore these doctrines to the knowledge and faith of the people. And if any one should have thought that, in the descriptions we have been giving, too frequent and willing use has been made of the epithet "barbarous," or similar words, as if we could have a perverse pleasure in degrading our nation, we would request him to select for himself the appropriate terms for characterizing that state of the people, in point of sense and civilization, to say nothing of religion, which could admit such a fact as this to stand in their history—namely, that, in a vast number of instances and places, where some person unexceptionable in character as far as known, and sometimes well known as a worthy man, has attempted to address a number of the inhabitants, under a roof or under the sky, on what it imported them beyond all things in the world to know and consider, a multitude have rushed together, shouting and howling, raving and cursing, and accompanying, in many of the instances, their furious cries and yells with loathsome or dangerous missiles; dragging or driving the preacher from his humble stand, forcing him, and the few that wished to encourage and hear him, to flee for their lives, sometimes not without serious injury before they could escape. And that such a history of the people may show how deservedly their superiors were denominated their "betters," it has to add, that these savage tumults were generally instigated or abetted, sometimes under a little concealment, but often avowedly, by persons of higher condition, and even by those consecrated to the office of religious instruction; and this advantage of their station was lent to defend the perpetrators against shame, or remorse, or just punishment, for the outrage.

There would be no hazard in affirming, that since Wesley and Whitefield began the conflict with the heathenism of the country, there have been in it hundreds of occurrences answering in substance to this description. From any one, therefore, who should be inclined to accuse us of harsh language, we may well repeat the demand in what terms *he* would think he gave the true character of a mental and moral condition, manifested in such uproars of savage violence as the Christian missionaries among eastern idolaters never had the slightest cause to apprehend. These outrages were so far from uncommon, or confined to any one part of the country, some time before, and for a very long while after, the middle of the last century, that they might be fairly taken as indicating the depth at which the greatest part of the nation lay sunk in ignorance and barbarism. Yet the good and zealous men whose lot it was to be thus set upon by a depraved infuriate rabble, the foremost of them active in direct assault, and the rest venting their ferocious delight in a hideous blending of ribaldry and execration, of joking and cursing, were taxed with a canting hypocrisy, or a fanatical madness, for speaking of the prevailing ignorance and barbarism in terms equivalent to our sentence from the Prophet, "The people are destroyed for lack of knowledge," and for deploring the hopelessness of any revolution in this empire of darkness by means of the existing institutions, which seemed indeed to have become themselves its strong holds.

But they whom serious danger could not deter from renewing and indefinitely repeating such attempts at all hazards, were little likely to be appalled by these contumelies of speech. To the persons so abusing them they might coolly reply, "Now really you are inconsiderately wasting your labour. Don't you know, that on the account of this same business we have sustained the battery of stones, brickbats, and the contents of the ditch? And can you believe we can much care for mere *words* of insult, after that? Albeit the opprobrious phrases *have* the fetid coarseness befitting the bluster of property without education, or the more highly inspirited tone of railing learnt in a college, they are quite another kind of thing to be the mark for, than such assailments as have come from the brawny arms of some of your peasants, set on probably by broad hints or plain expressions how much you would be pleased with such exploits."—It is gratifying to see thus exemplified, in the endurance of evil for a good cause, that provision in our nature for economizing the expense of feeling, through which the encountering of the greater creates a hardihood which can despise the less.

That our descriptive observations do not exaggerate the popular ignorance, with its natural concomitants, as prevailing at the middle of the last century and far downward, many of the elderly persons among us can readily confirm, from what they remember of the testimony of their immediate ancestors. It will be recollected what pictures they gave of the moral scene spread over the country when they were young. They could convey lively images of the situations in which the vulgar notions and manners had their free display, by representing the assemblages, and the fashion of discourse and manners, at fairs, revels, and other rendezvous of amusement; or in the field of rural employment, or on the village green, or in front of the mechanic's workshop. They could recount various anecdotes characteristic of the times; and repeat short dialogues, or single sayings, which expressed the very essence of what was to the population of the township or province instead of law and prophets, or sages or apostles. They could describe how free from all sense of shame whole families would seem to be, from grandsires down to the third rude reckless generation, for not being able to read; and how well content, when there was some one individual in the neighbourhood who could read an advertisement, or ballad, or last dying speech of a malefactor, for the benefit of the rest. They could describe the desolation of the land, with respect to any enlightening and impressive religious instruction in the places of worship; in the generality of which, indeed, the whole spirit and manner of the service tended to what we just now described as the fact—that religion, in its proper sense, was absolutely *a thing not recognised* *at all.* To most of the persons there the forms attended to were *representative* of literally nothing—they were *themselves* the all.* And as to those who really did in the course of their attendance acquire something assignable as their creed, our supposed reporters could tell what wretched and delusive notions of religion, or rather instead of religion, they were permitted and authorized, by their appointed spiritual guides, to carry with them to their last hour. At which hour, some ceremonial form was to be a passport to heaven: a little bread and wine, converted into a mysterious object of superstition, by receiving an ecclesiastical name of unknown import, accompanied with some sentences regarded much in the nature of an incantation—and all was safe! The sinner expiring believed so, and the sinners surviving were left to go on in their thoughtless way of life, on a calculation of the same final resource.

* None of the anecdotes, that have come down in traditions now fading away, are more illustrative of those times, than those which show both people and priest satisfied with the observances at church as *constituting* religion, never thinking of them as but the means to *teach* and *inspire* it. Such anecdotes must have been heard by every one who has conversed much with such aged persons as remember the most of former times. Some traditions of this kind may be recalled to mind, through similarity of character, by hearing such an instance as the following. A friend of the writer mentions, that he heard his father, whose veracity was above all question, relate as one of the recollections of the time when he was a young man, that in the parish church where he attended, the service was one Sunday morning performed with a somewhat unusual despatch, and every abbreviation that depended on the discretion of the minister; who at the conclusion explained the circumstance publicly, by saying, that as neighbour such-a-one (mentioning the name) was going to bait his bull in the afternoon, he had been as short as possible that the congregation might have good time for the sport.—It is on the same principle that the Catholics on the continent, having attended mass in the morning, never think of doubting their license for every frivolity the rest of the day.

Thus the past age has left an image of its character in the minds of the generation now themselves grown old, received by immediate tradition from persons who lived in it. Here and there, indeed, there still lingers, so long after the departure of the great company to which he belonged, an ancient who retains a trace of this image immediately from the reality, as having become of an age to look at the world, and take a share in its activities, about the middle of the last century.* And it might be an employment of considerable though rather melancholy interest, for a person visiting many parts of the land, to put in requisition, in each place, for a day or two, the most faithful of the memories of the most narrative of the oldest people, for materials toward forming an estimate of the mental and moral state of the main body of the inhabitants, of town or country, in the period of which they themselves saw the latter part, and remember it in combination with what their progenitors related of the former. After these few retainers of the original picture from the life shall have left the world, it will be comparatively a faint conception that can be formed of that age from written memorials, which exist but in a very imperfect and scattered state.

But supposing the scene could be brought back to the mental eye, in full verity and distinctness, as in a vision supernaturally imparted, are we sure we should not have the mortification of perceiving that the change, from the condition of the people then to their condition now, has been in but poor proportion to the amount of the advantages, which we are apt to be elated in recounting as the boast and happiness of later times? To assume that we should *not*, is to impute to that former

* They are here supposed to be looking back from about the year 1820.

age still more ignorance and debasement than appear in the above description. For what could, what must that condition have been, if it was worse than the present by anything near the difference made by what would be a tolerably fair improvement of the additional means latterly afforded? An estimate being made of the measure of intelligence and worth found among the descendants, let so much be taken out as we would wish to attribute to the effect of the additional means, and what will that remainder be which is to represent the state of the ancestors, formed under a system of means wanting all those which we are allowing ourselves to think important enough to warrant the frequent expression, "This new era?"

The means wanting to the former generation, and that have sprung into existence for the latter, may be briefly noted; and those of a religious nature may be named first. It is the most obvious of public expedients, that good men who wish to make others so should *preach* to them. And there has been a wonderful extension of this practice since the zealous exertions of Whitefield, Wesley, and their co-operators awakened other good men to a sense of their capacity and duty. The spirit actuating the associated followers of the latter of those two great agitators, has impelled forth their whole disposable force (to use a military phrase) to this service; and they have sent preachers into many parts of the land where preaching itself, in any fair sense of the term, was wholly a novelty; and where there was roused as earnest a zeal to crush this alarming innovation, as the people of Iceland are described to feel on the occasion of the approach of a white bear to invade their folds or poorly stocked pastures.* To a confederacy of

* The writer had just been reading that description.

Christians so well aware of their own strength and progress, it may seem a superfluous testimony that they are doing incalculable good among our population, more good probably than any other religious sect. This tribute is paid not the less freely for a material difference in theological opinion; nor for a wish, a quite friendly one, that they may admit some little modification of a spirit perhaps rather too sectarian in religion, and rather less than independent in politics.

An immense augmentation has been brought to the sum of public instruction, by the continually enlarging numbers of dissenters of other denominations. Whatever may be thought of some of the consequences of the great extension of dissent, it will hardly be considered as a circumstance tending to prolong the reign of *ignorance* that thus, within the last fifty years, there have been put in activity to impart religious ideas to the people not fewer (exclusively of the Wesleyans) than several thousand minds that would, under a continuance of the former state of the nation, have been doing no such service; that is to say, the service would not have been done at all. Let it be considered, too, that the doctrines inculcated as of the first importance, in the preaching of far the greatest number of them, were exactly those which the Established Church avowed in its formularies and disowned in its ministry,—one of the circumstances which contributed the most to *make* dissenters of the more seriously disposed among the people.—It is to be added, that so much public activity in religious instruction could not be unaccompanied by an increase of exertion in the more private methods of imparting it.

It is another important accession to the enlarged system of operations against religious ignorance, that a proportion of the Established Church itself has been recovered to the spirit of its venerable founders, by the progressive formation in it of a zealous evangelical ministry; dissenters within their own community, if we may believe the constant loud declarations of the bulk of that community, and especially of the most dignified, learned, and powerful classes in it. But in spite of whatever discredit they may suffer from being thus disowned, these worthy and useful men have still, in their character of clergymen, a material advantage above other faithful teachers, for influence on many of the people, by being invested with the credentials of the ancient institution, from which the popular mind has been slow and reluctant in withdrawing its veneration; and for which that sentiment, when not quite extinct, is ready to revive at any manifestation in it of the quickening spirit of the Gospel. We say, if the sentiment be not quite extinct; for we are aware what a very large proportion of the people are gone beyond the possibility of feeling it any more. But still the number is great of those who experience, at this new appearance, a reanimation of their affection for the Church; and so fondly identify the partial change with the whole institution, that they feel as if a parent, who had for a long while neglected or deserted them, but for whom they could never cease to cherish a filial regard, were beginning to be restored to them, with a renewal of the benignant qualities and cares of the parental character.

Thus far the account of the means which England was not to furnish for its people till the latter part of the eighteenth century, relates to their better instruction in religion. This will not be thought beside the purpose of an enumeration of expedients for lessening their *ignorance*, by any one who can allow that religion, regarded as a subject of the understanding, is the most important part of knowledge, and who has observed the fact that religion, when it begins to *interest* uncultivated minds, works surprisingly in favour of the intellectual faculties; an effect exactly the reverse of that of superstition, and produced by the contrary operation; for while superstition represses, and even curses any free action of the intellect, genuine religion both requires and excites it. Though it is too true that the great Christian principles, when embraced with conviction and seriousness by a very uneducated man, must greatly partake, by contractedness of apprehension, the ill fortune which has confined his mental growth, yet they will often do more than any other thing within the same space of time to avenge him of it.

In addition to the great extension of instruction in a form specifically religious, there have been various causes and means contributing to the increase of knowledge among the people. After it had been seen for centuries in what manner the children of the poor were suffered to spend the Sunday, it struck one observer at last, that they might on that day be taught to read!—a possibility which had never been suspected; a disclosure as of some hitherto hidden power of nature. And then the schools which taught the children to read made some of the parents so much better pleased with their children for their first steps in so new an attainment, that they could not be indifferent to the opening of other schools of a humble order to continue that instruction through the week. It was within the same period that there was a large circulation of tracts, by some of which many who might be little desirous of instruction, were beguiled into it by the amusing vehicle ingeniously contrived to convey it; and the most popular of which will remain a monument of the talent, knowledge, and benevolence, of that distinguished benefactor of her country and age, Mrs. H. More, perhaps even pre-eminent above her many excellent works in a higher strain. Later and continual issues of this class of papers, of every diversity of composition, and diffused by the activity of numberless hands, have solicited perhaps a fourth part of the thoughtless beings in the nation to make at least one short effort to think.

The enormous flight of periodical miscellanies, and of newspapers, must be taken as both the indication and the cause that hundreds of thousands of persons were giving some attention to the matters of general information, where their grandfathers had been, during the intervals of time allowed by their employments, prating, brawling, sleeping, or drinking their hours away.*

It is perhaps an item of some small value in the account, that a new class of ideas was furnished by the many wonderful effects of science, in the application of the elements and mechanical powers. The people saw human intelligence so effectually inspiriting inanimate matter, as to create a new and mighty order of agency, appearing in a certain degree independent of man himself, and in its power immensely surpassing any simple immediate exertion of *his* power. They saw wood and iron, fire, water, and air, actuated to the production of effects which might vie with what their rude ancestors had been accustomed to believe, (those of them who had heard of such beings,) of giants, magicians,

* Since this was written there has been a prodigious augmentation of all such means of general excitement; and happily a diversified multiplication of a class of them calculated to benefit the inferior people, at once by giving them a new and enlarged range of ideas, and by bringing them on some tracts of common ground with the liberally educated; thus abating the former almost total incapacity, on the part of those inferiors, for intelligent intercommunication.

alchymists, and monsters; effects, the dream of which, if any one could so have dreamed, would have been scoffed at by even the more intelligent of the former race.

It is true, that very ignorant persons can wonder at such things without deriving much instruction from them; and that much sooner than the more cultivated ones they become so familiarized with them as not to think of them. All *effects*, however astonishing, are apt, if they be but regular in their recurrence, to become soon insignificant to those who have never learnt to inquire into *causes*. But still, it would be some little advantage to the people's understanding to see what prodigious effects could be produced without any preternatural interference. Though not comprehending the science employed, they could comprehend that what they saw *was* purely a matter of science, and that the cause and the effect were natural and definite; unlike the present race of Egyptians, who not long since regarded the very mechanics of an European as an operation of magic; and were capable of expecting that a machine constructed by a man from England, for raising water from the Nile, should inundate the country in an hour. These wonders of science and art must therefore have contributed somewhat to rid our people of the impressions of being at every turn beset by occult powers, under the name perhaps of witchcraft, and to expel the notions of a vague and capricious agency interfering and sporting with events throughout the system around them. Their rationality thus obtained an improvement, which may be set against the injury undoubtedly done them through that diminished exercise of the understanding which accompanied the progressive division of labour; an alteration rendered inevitable, and in other respects so advantageous.

When we come down to a comparatively recent time, we see the Bible "going up on the breadth of the land." In passing by any given number of houses of the inferior class, we may presume there are in them four or five times as many copies of that sacred book as there were in the same number thirty or forty years since. And when we consider how many more persons in those houses can read, and that in some of them the book may be *more* read for having come there as a novelty, than it is in many others where it has been an old article of the furniture, we may fairly presume that the increased reading is in a greater proportion than the increased number of Bibles.—This late period has also brought into action, a new expedient, worthy to stand, in the province of education, parallel and rival to the most useful modern inventions in the mechanical departments; an organization for schools, by which, instead of one or two overlaboured agents upon a mass of reluctant subjects, that whole mass itself shall be animated into a system of reciprocal agency. It has all the merit of a contrivance which associates with mental labour a pleasure never known to young learners before.

One more distinction of our times has been, that effect which missionary and other philanthropic societies have had, to render familiar to common knowledge, by means of their meetings and publications, a great number of such interesting and important facts, in the state of other countries and our own, as were formerly quite beyond the sphere of ordinary information.

In aid of all these means at work in the trial to raise the people from the condition in which they had been so many ages sunk and immovable, there has been of late years the unpretending but important ministration of an incessant multifarious inventiveness in making almost every sort of information offer itself in brief, familiar, and attractive forms, adapted to youth or to adult ignorance; so that knowledge, which was formerly a thing to be searched and dug for "as for hid treasures," has seemed at last beginning to effloresce through the surface of the ground on all sides of us.

The statement of what recent times have produced for effecting an alteration among the people, must include the prodigious commotion in the political world. It were absurd, it is true, to name this in the simple character of a *cause*, when we speak of the rousing of the popular mind from a long stagnation; it being itself a proof and result of some preceding cause beginning to pervade and disturb that stagnation. But whatever may be assigned as the true and sufficient explanation of its origin, we have to look on the mighty operation of its progress, forcing a restlessness, instability, and tendency to change, into almost every part of the social economy. In the whole compass of time there has been no train of events, that has within so short a period stirred to the very bottom the mind of so vast a portion of the race. And the power of this great commotion has less consisted in what may be termed its physical energy, evinced in grand exploits and catastrophes, than in its being an intense activity of *principles*. It was as different from other convulsions in the moral world, as would be a tempest attributed to the direct intervention of a mighty spirit, whether believed celestial or infernal, from one raised in the elements by mere natural causes. The people were not, as in other instances of battles, revolutions, and striking alternations of fortune, gazing at a mere show of wonderful events, but regarded these events as the course of a great practical debate of questions affecting their own interests.

And now, when we have put all these things together, we may well pause to indulge again our wonder what *could* have been the mental situation of a majority of the inhabitants of this country, antecedently to this creation and conjunction of so many means and influences for awaking them to something of an intelligent existence.

SECTION III.

THE review of the past may here be terminated And how welcome a change it would be if we might here completely emerge from the gloom which has overspread it. How happy were it if in proceeding to an estimate of the people of the present times, we found so rich a practical result of the means for forming a more enlightened race, that we should have no further recollection of that sentence from the Prophet, which has hitherto suggested itself again at every step in prosecution of the survey. But we are compelled to see how slow is the progress of mankind toward thus rendering obsolete any of the darker lines of the sacred record. So completely, so desperately, had the whole popular body and being been pervaded by the stupifying power of the long reign of ignorance, with such heavy reluctance, at the best, does the human mind open its eyes to admit light,—and so incommensurate as yet, even on the supposition of its having much less of this reluctance, has been in quantity the whole new supply of means for a happy change,—that a most melancholy spectacle still abides before us. Time, in sweeping away successive generations, has preserved, in substance, the sad inheritance to that which is as yet the latest.

Even that portion of beneficial effect which actually has resulted from this co-operation of new forces, has served to make a more obvious exposure of the unhappiness and offensiveness of what is still the condition of the far greater part of our population; as a dreary waste is made to give a more sensible impression how dreary it is, by the little inroads of cultivation and beauty in its hollows, and the faint advances of an unwonted green upon its borders. The degradation of the main body of the lower classes is exposed by a comparison with the small reclaimed portion within those classes themselves. It is not with the philosophers, literati, and most accomplished persons in higher life, that we should think of placing in immediate comparison the untutored rustics and workmen in stones and timber, for the purpose of showing how much is wanting to them. These extreme orders of society would seem less related in virtue of their common nature, than separated by the wide disparity of its cultivation. They would appear so immeasurably asunder, such antipodes in the sphere of human existence, that the state of the one could afford no standard for judging of the defects or wants of the other. It was not in a speculation which amused itself, as with a curious fact, in seeing that the same material can be made into scholars, legislators, sages, and models of elegance—and also into helots; and then went into a fanciful question of how near they might possibly be brought together: it was in a speculation which, instead of dwelling on the view of what was impossible to the common people in a comparative reference to the highest classes of their fellow men, considered what was left practicable to them within their own narrow allotment, that the schemes originated which have actually imparted to a proportion of them an invaluable share of the benefits of knowledge. There has thus been formed a small improved order of people amidst the multitude; and it is the contrast between these and the general state of that multitude that most directly exposes the popular debasement. It certainly were ridiculous enough to fix on a labouring man and his family, and affect to deplore that he is doomed not to behold the depths and heights of science, not to expatiate over the wide field of history, not to luxuriate among the delights, refinements, and infinite diversities of literature; and that his family are not growing up in a training to every high accomplishment, after the pattern of some family in the neighbourhood, favoured by fortune, and high ability and cultivation in those at their head. But it is a quite different thing to take this man and his family, hardly able, perhaps, even to read, and therefore sunk in all the grossness of ignorance,—and compare them with another man and family in the same sphere of life, but who have received the utmost improvement within the reach of that situation, and are sensible of its value; who often employ the leisure hour in reading, (sometimes socially and with intermingled converse,) some easy work of instruction or innocent entertainment; are detached, in the greatest degree that depends on their choice, from society with the absolute vulgar; have learnt much decorum of manners; can take an intelligent interest in the great events of the world; and are prevented, by what they read and hear, from forgetting that there is another world. It is, we repeat, after thus seeing what may, and in particular instances does exist, in a humble condition, that we are compelled to regard as really a dreadful spectacle the still prevailing state of our national population.

We shall endeavour to exhibit, though on a small scale, and perhaps not with a very strict regularity of proportion and arrangement, a faithful representation of the most serious of the evils conspicuous in an uneducated state of the people. Much of the description and reflections must be equally applicable to other countries; for spite of all their mutual antipathies and hostilities, and numberless contrarieties of customs and fashions, they have been wonderfully content to resemble one another in the worst national feature, a deformed condition of their people. But it is here at home that this condition is the most painfully forced on our attention; and here also of all the world it is, that such a wretched exhibition is the severest reproach to the nation for having suffered its existence.

The subject is to the last degree unattractive, except to a misanthropic disposition; or to that, perhaps, of a stern theological polemic, when tempted to be pleased with every superfluity of evidence for overwhelming the opposers of the doctrine which asserts the radical corruption of our nature. As spread over a coarse and repulsive moral and physical scenery, it is a subject in the extreme of contrast with that susceptibility of magnificent display, on account of which some of the most cruel evils that have preyed on mankind have ever been favourite themes with writers ambitious to shine in description. Nor does it present a wild and varying spectacle, where a crowd of fantastic shapes, (as in a view of the pagan superstitions,) may stimulate and beguile the imagination though we know we are looking on a great evil. It is a gloomy monotony; Death without his dance. Moreover, the representation which exhibits one large class degraded and unhappy, reflects ungraciously, and therefore repulsively, by an imputation of neglect of duty, on the other classes who are called upon to look at the spectacle. There is, besides, but little power of arresting the attention in a description of familiar matter of fact, plain to every one's observation. Yet ought it not to be so much the better, when we are pleading for a certain mode of benevolent exertion, that every one can see, and that no one can deny, the sad reality of all that forms the object, and imposes the duty, of that exertion?

Look, then, at the neglected ignorant class in their childhood and youth. One of the most obvious circumstances is *the perfect non-existence in their minds of any notion or question what their life is for, taken as a whole.* Among a crowd of trifling and corrupting ideas that soon find a place in them, there is never the reflective thought,—For what purpose am I alive? What is it that I should be, more than the animal that I am? Does it signify *what* I may be?—But surely, it is with ill omen that the human creature advances into life without such a thought. He should in the opening of his faculties receive intimations, that something more belongs to his existence than what he is about to-day, and what he may be about to-morrow. He should be made aware that the course of activity he is beginning ought to have a leading principle of direction, some predominant aim, a general and comprehensive purpose, paramount to the divers particular objects he may pursue. It is not more necessary for him to understand that he must in some way be employed in order to live, than to be apprised that life itself, that existence itself, is of no value but as a mere capacity of something which he should realize, and of which he may fail. He should be brought to apprehend that there is a something essential for him to *be*, which he will not *become* merely by passing from one day into another, by eating and sleeping, by growing taller and stronger, seizing what share he can of noisy sport, and performing appointed portions of work; and that if he do *not* become that which he *cannot* become without a general and leading purpose, he will be worthless and unhappy.

We are not entertaining the extravagant fancy that

it is possible, except in some rare instances of premature thoughtfulness, to turn inward into deep habitual reflection, the spirit that naturally goes outward, in these vivacious, active, careless beings, when we assert that it *is* possible to teach many of them with a degree of success, in very juvenile years, to apprehend and admit somewhat of such a consideration. We have many times seen this exemplified in fact. We have found some of them appearing apprised that *life is for some thing as a whole;* and that, to answer this general purpose, a mere succession of interests and activities, each gone into for its own sake, will not suffice. They could comprehend, that the multiplicity of interests and activities in detail, instead of constituting of themselves the purpose of life, were to be regarded as things subordinate and subservient to a general scope, and judged of, selected, and regulated, in reference and amenableness to it.—By the presiding comprehensive purpose, we do not specifically and exclusively mean a direction of the mind to the *religious* concern, viewed as a separate affair, and in *contradistinction* to other interests; but a purpose formed upon a collective notion of the person's interests, which shall give one general right bearing to the course of his life; an aim proceeding in fulfilment of a scheme, that comprehends and combines with the religious concern all the other concerns for the sake of which it is worth while to dispose the activities of life into a *plan* of conduct, instead of leaving them to custom and casualty. The scheme will look and guide toward ultimate felicity: but will at the same time take large account of what must be thought of, and what may be hoped for, in relation to the present life.

Now, we no more expect to find any such idea of a presiding purpose of life, than we do the profoundest philosophical reflection, in the minds of the uneducated children and youth. They think nothing at all about their existence and life in any moral or abstracted or generalizing reference whatever. They know not any good that it is to have been endowed with a rational rather than a brute nature, excepting that it affords more diversity of action, and gives the privilege of tyrannizing over brutes. They think nothing about what they shall become, and very little about what shall become of them. There is nothing that tells them of the relations for good and evil, of present things with future and remote ones. The whole energy of their moral and intellectual nature goes out as in brute instinct on present objects, to make the most they can of them for the moment, taking the chance for whatever may be next. They are left totally devoid even of the thought, that what they are doing is the beginning of a life as an important adventure for good or evil; their whole faculty is engrossed in the doing of it; and whether it signify anything to the next ensuing stage of life, or to the last, is as foreign to any calculation of theirs, as the idea of reading their destiny in the stars. Not only, therefore, is there an entire preclusion from their minds of the faintest hint of a monition, that they should live for the grand final object pointed to by religion, but also, for the most part, of all consideration of the attainment of a reputable condition and character in life. The creature endowed with faculties for "large discourse, looking before and after," capable of so much design, respectability, and happiness, even in its present short stage, and entering on an endless career, is seen in the abasement of snatching, as its utmost reach of purpose, at the low amusements, blended with vices, of each passing day; and cursing its privations and tasks, and often also the sharers of those privations, and the exactors of those tasks.

When these are grown up into the mass of mature population, what will it be, as far as their quality shall go toward constituting the quality of the whole? Alas! it will be, to that extent, just a continuation of the ignorance, debasement, and misery, so conspicuous in the bulk of the people now. And to *what* extent? Calculate *that* from the unquestionable fact, that hundreds of thousands of the human beings in our land, between the ages, say of six and sixteen, are at this hour thus abandoned to go forward into life at random, as to the use they shall make of it,—if, indeed, it can be said to be at random, when there is strong tendency and temptation to evil, and no discipline to good. Looking at this proportion, does any one think there will be, on the whole, wisdom and virtue enough in the community to render this black infusion imperceptible or innoxious?

But are we accounting it absolutely inevitable that the sequel must be in full proportion to this present fact,—*must* be every thing that this fact threatens, and *can* lead to,—as we should behold persons carried down in a mighty torrent, where all interposition is impossible, or as the Turks look at the progress of a conflagration or an epidemic? It is in order to "frustrate the tokens" of such melancholy divination, to arrest something of what a destructive power is in the act of carrying away, to make the evil spirit find, in the next stages of his march, that all his enlisted host have not followed him, and to quell somewhat of the triumph of his boast, "My name is Legion, for we are many;" —it is for this that the friends of improvement, and of mankind, are called upon for efforts greatly beyond those which are requisite for maintaining in its present extent of operation the system of expedients for intercepting, before it be too late, the progress of so large a portion of the youthful tribe toward destruction.

Another obvious circumstance in the state of the untaught class is, *that they are abandoned, in a direct unqualified manner, to seize recklessly whatever they can of sensual gratification.* The very narrow scope to which their condition limits them in the pursuit of this, will not prevent its being to them the most desirable thing in existence, when there are so few other modes of gratification which they either are in a capacity to enjoy, or have the means to obtain. By the very constitution of the human nature, the mind seems half to belong to the senses, it is so shut within them, affected by them, dependent on them for pleasure, as well as for activity, and impotent but through their medium. And while, by this necessary hold which they have on what would call itself a spiritual being, they absolutely will engross to themselves, as of clear right, a large share of its interest and exercise, they will strive to possess themselves of the other half too. And they will have it, if it has not been carefully otherwise claimed and pre-occupied. And when the senses have thus usurped the whole mind for their service, how will you get any of it back? Try, if you will, whether this be a thing so easy to be done. Present to the minds so engrossed with the desires of the senses, that their main action is but in these desires and the contrivances how to fulfil them,—offer to their view nobler objects, which are appropriate to the spiritual being, and observe whether that being promptly shows a sensibility to the worthier objects, as congenial to its nature, and, obsequious to the new attraction, disengages itself from what has wholly absorbed it.

Nor would we require that the experiment be made by presenting something of a precisely religious nature, to which there is an innate aversion on account of its *divine* character, separately from its being an intellectual thing,—an aversion even though the mental faculties *be* cultivated. It may be made with something that ought to have power to please the mind as simply a being of intelligence, imagination, and sentiment,—a pleasure which, in some of its modes, the senses themselves may intimately partake; as when, for instance, it is to be imparted by something beautiful or grand in the natural world, or in the works of art. Let this refined solicitation be addressed to the grossly uncultivated, in competition with some low indulgence—with the means, for example, of gluttony and inebriation. See how the subjects of your experiment, (intellectual and moral natures though they are,) answer to these respective offered gratifications. Observe how these more dignified attractives encounter and overpower the meaner, and reclaim the usurped, debased spirit. Or rather, observe whether they can avail for more than an instant, so much as to divide its attention. But indeed you can foresee the result so well, that you may spare the labour. Still less could you deem it to be of the nature of an experiment, (which implies uncertainty,) to make the attempt with ideal forms of nobleness or beauty, with intellectual, poetical, or moral captivations.

Yet this addiction to sensuality, beyond all competition of worthier modes and means of interest, does not altogether refuse to admit of some division and diversion of the vulgar feelings, in favour of some things of a more mental character, provided they be vicious. A man so neglected in his youth that he cannot spell the names of Alexander, Cæsar, or Napoleon, or read them if he see them spelt, may feel the strong incitement of ambition. This, instead of raising him, may only propel him forward on the level of his debased condition and society; and it is a favourable supposition that makes him "the best wrestler on the green," or a manful pugilist; for it is probable his grand delight may be, to indulge himself in an oppressive insolent arrogance toward such as are unable to maintain a strife with him on terms of fair rivalry, making his will the law to all whom he can force or frighten into submission.

Coarse sensuality admits, again, an occasional competition of the gratifications of cruelty; a flagrant characteristic, generally, of uncultivated degraded human creatures, both where the whole community consists of such, as in barbarian and savage tribes, and where they form a large portion of it, as in this country.—It is hardly worth while to put in words the acknowledgment of the obvious and odious fact, that a considerable share of mental attainment is sometimes inefficient to extinguish, or even repress, this infernal principle of human nature, by which it is gratifying to witness and inflict suffering, even separately from any prompting of revenge. But why do we regard such examples as peculiarly hateful, and brand them with the most intense reprobation, but *because* it is judged the fair and natural tendency of mental cultivation to repress that principle, insomuch that its failure to do so is considered as evincing a surpassing virulence of depravity? Every one is ready with the saying of the ancient poet, that liberal acquirements suppress ferocious propensities. But if the whole virtue of such discipline may prove insufficient, think what must be the consequence of its being almost wholly withheld, so that the execrable propensity may go into action with its malignity unmitigated, unchecked, by any remonstrance of feeling or taste, or reason or conscience.

And such a consequence is manifest in the lower ranks of our self-extolled community; notwithstanding a diminution, which the progress of education and religion has slowly effected, in certain of the once most favourite and customary practices of cruelty; what we might denominate the classic games of the rude populace. These very practices, nevertheless, still keep their ground in some of the more heathenish parts of the country; and if it were possible, that the more improved notions and taste of the more respectable classes could admit of any countenance being given to their revival in the more civilized parts, it would be found that, even there, a large portion of the people is to this hour left in a disposition which would welcome the return of savage exhibitions. It may be, that some of the most atrocious forms and degrees of cruelty would not please the greater number of them; there have been instances in which an English populace has shown indignation at extreme and *unaccustomed* perpetrations, sometimes to the extent of cruelly revenging them; very rarely, however, when only brute creatures have been the sufferers. Not many would be delighted with such scenes as those which, in the *Place de Grève*, used to be a gratification to a multitude of all ranks of the Parisians. But how many odious facts, characteristic of our people, have come under every one's observation.

Who has not seen numerous instances of the delight with which advantage is taken of weakness or simplicity, to practise upon them some sly mischief, or inflict some open mortification; and of the unrepressed glee with which the rude spectators can witness or abet the malice? And if, in such a case, an indignant observer has hazarded a remark or expostulation, the full stare, and the quickly succeeding laugh and retort of brutal scorn, have thrown open to his revolting sight the state of the recess within, where the moral sentiments are; and shown how much the perceptions and notions had been indebted to the cares of the instructor. Could he help thinking what was deserved somewhere, by individuals or by the local community collectively, for suffering a being to grow up to quite or nearly the complete dimensions and features of manhood, with so vile a thing within it in substitution for what a soul should be? We need not remark, what every one has noticed, how much the vulgar are amused by seeing vexatious or injurious incidents, (if only not quite disastrous or tragical,) befalling persons against whom they can have no resentment; how ferocious often their temper and means of revenge when they *have* causes of resentment; or how intensely delighted, (in company, it is true, with many that are called their betters,) in beholding several of their fellow-mortals, whether in anger or athletic competition, covering each other with bruises, deformity, and blood.

Our institutions, however, protect, in some considerable degree, man against man, as being framed in a knowledge of what would else become of the community. But observe a moment what are the dispositions of the vulgar as indulged, and with no preventive interference of those institutions, on the inferior animals. To a large proportion of this class it is, in their youth, one of the most vivid exhilarations to witness the terrors and anguish of living beings. In many parts of the country it would be no improbable conjecture in explanation of a savage yell heard at a distance, that a company of rationals may be witnessing the writhings, agonies, and cries, of some animal struggling for escape or for life, while it is suffering the infliction, perhaps, of stones, and kicks, or wounds by more directly fatal means of violence. If you hear in the clamour a sudden burst of fiercer exultation, you may surmise that just then a deadly blow has been given. There is hardly an animal on the whole face of the country, of size enough, and enough within reach to be a marked object of attention, that would not be persecuted to death if no consideration of ownership interposed. The children of the uncultivated families are allowed, without a check, to exercise and improve the hateful disposition, on flies, young birds, and other feeble and harmless creatures; and they are actually encouraged to do it on what, under the denomination of vermin, are represented in the formal character of enemies, almost in such a sense as if a moral responsibility belonged to them, and they were therefore not only to be destroyed as a nuisance, but deserving to be punished as offenders.

The hardening against sympathy, with the consequent carelessness of inflicting pain, combined as this will probably be, with the *love* of inflicting it, must be confirmed by the horrid spectacle of slaughter; a spectacle sought for gratification by the children and youth of the lower order; and in many places so publicly exhibited that they cannot well avoid seeing it, and its often savage preliminary circumstances, sometimes directly wanton aggravations; perhaps in revenge of a struggle to resist or escape, perhaps in a rage at the awkward manner in which the victim adjusts itself to a convenient position for suffering. Horrid, we call the prevailing practice, because it is the infliction, on millions of sentient and innocent creatures every year, in what calls itself a humane and christian nation, of anguish unnecessary to the purpose. Unnecessary—what proof is there to the contrary?—To *what* is the present practice necessary?—Some readers will remember the benevolent (we were going to say *humane*, but that is an equivocal epithet,) attempt made a number of years since by Lord Somerville to introduce, but he failed, a mode of slaughter, without suffering; a mode in use in a foreign nation with which we should deem it very far from a compliment to be placed on a level in point of civilization. And it is a flagrant dishonour to such a country, and to the class that virtually, by rank, and formally, by official station, have presided over its economy, one generation after another, that so hideous a fact should never, as far as we know, have been deemed by the highest state authorities worth even a question whether a mitigation might not be practicable. An inconceivable daily amount of suffering, inflicted on unknown thousands of creatures, dying in slow anguish, when their death might be without pain as being instantaneous, is accounted no deformity in the social system, no incongruity with the national profession of religion of which the essence is charity and mercy, nothing to sully the polish, or offend the refinement, of what demands to be accounted, in its higher portions, a preeminently civilized and humanized community. Precious and well protected polish and refinement, and humanity, and christian civilization! to which it is a matter of easy indifference to know that, in the neighbourhood of their abode, those tortures of butchery are unnecessarily inflicted, which could not be actually witnessed by persons in whom the pretension to these fine qualities is any thing better than affectation, without sensations of horror; which it would ruin the character of a fine gentleman or lady to have voluntarily witnessed in a single instance.

They are known to be inflicted, and yet this is a rifle not worth an effort toward innovation on inveterate custom, on the part of the influential classes; who nay be far more worthily intent on a change in the fashion of a dress, or possibly some new refinement in the cookery of the dead bodies of the victims. Or the *living* bodies; as we are told that the most delicious preparation of an eel for exquisite palates is to thrust the fish alive into the fire: while lobsters are put into water *gradually* heated to boiling. The latter, indeed, is an old practice, like that of *crimping* another fish. Such things are allowed or required to be done by persons pretending to the highest refinement. It is a matter far below legislative attention; while the powers of definition are exhausted under the stupendous accumulation of regulations and interdictions for the good order of society. So hardened may the moral sense of a community be by universal and continual custom, that we are perfectly aware these very remarks will provoke the ridicule of many persons, including, it is possible enough, some who may think it quite consistent to be ostentatiously talking at the very same time of christian charity and benevolent zeal.* Nor will that ridicule be repressed by the notoriety of the fact, that the manner of the practice referred to steels and depraves, to a dreadful degree, a vast number of human beings immediately employed about it; and, as a spectacle, powerfully contributes to confirm, in a greater number, exactly that which it is, by eminence, the object of moral tuition to counteract—men's disposition to make light of all suffering but their own. This one thing, this not caring for what may be endured by other beings made liable to suffering, is the very essence of the depravity which is so fatal to our race in their social constitution. This selfish hardness is moral plague enough even in an inactive state, as a mere carelessness what other beings may suffer; but there lurks in it a malignity which is easily stimulated to delight in seeing or causing their suffering. And yet, we repeat it, a civilized and christian nation feels not the slightest self-displacency for its allowing a certain unhappy but necessary part in the

* This was actually done in a religious periodical publication.

economy of the world to be executed, (by preference to a harmless method,) in a manner which probably does as much to corroborate in the vulgar class this essential principle of depravity, as all the expedients of melioration yet applied are doing to expel it.

Were it not vain and absurd to muse on supposable new principles in the constitution of the moral system, there is one that we might have been tempted to wish for, namely, that, of all suffering *unnecessarily* and wilfully inflicted by man on any class of sentient existence, a bitter intimation and participation might be conveyed to him through a mysterious law of nature, enforcing an avenging sympathy in severe proportion to that suffering, on all the men who were really accountable for its being inflicted.

After children and youth are trained to behold with something worse than hardened indifference, with a gratifying excitement, the sufferings of creatures dying for the service of man, it is no wonder if they are barbarous in their treatment of those that serve him by their life. And in fact nothing is more obvious as a prevailing disgrace to our nation, than the cruel habits of the lower class toward the labouring animals committed to their power. These animals have no security in their best condition and most efficient services; but generally the hateful disposition is the most fully exercised on those that have been already the greatest sufferers. Meeting, wherever we go, with some of these starved, abused, exhausted figures, we shall not unfrequently meet with also another figure accompanying them—that of a ruffian, young or old, who with a visage of rage, and accents of hell, is wreaking his utmost malevolence on a wretched victim for being slow in performing, or quite failing to perform, what the excess of loading, and perhaps the feebleness of old age, have rendered difficult or absolutely impracticable; or for shrinking from an effort to be made by a pressure on bleeding sores, or for losing the right direction through blindness, and that itself perhaps occasioned by hardship or savage violence. Many of the exacters of animal labour really seem to resent it as a kind of presumption and insult in the slave, that it would be anything else than a machine, that the living being should betray under its toils that it suffers, that it is pained, weary, or reluctant. And if, by outrageous abuse, it should be excited to some manifestation of resentment, that is a crime for which the sufferer would be likely to incur such a fury and repetition of blows and lacerations as to die on the spot, but for an interfering admonition of interest against destroying such a piece of property, and losing so much service. When that service has utterly exhausted, often before the term of old age, the strength of those wretched animals, there awaits many of them a last short stage of still more remorseless cruelty; that in which it is become a doubtful thing whether the utmost efforts to which the emaciated diseased sinking frame can be forced by violence, be worth the trouble of that violence, the delays and accidents, and the expense of the scanty supply of subsistence. As they must at all events very soon perish, it has ceased to be of any material consequence, on the score of interest, how grossly they may be abused; and their tormentors seem delighted with this release from all restraint on their dispositions. Those dispositions, as indulged in some instances, when the miserable creatures are formally consigned to be destroyed, cannot be much exceeded by any thing we can attribute to fiends. Some horrid exemplifications were adduced, not as single casual circumstances, but as usual practices, by a patriotic senator some years since, in endeavouring to obtain a legislative enactment in mitigation of the sufferings of the brute tribes. The design vanished to nothing in the House of Commons, under the effect of argument and ridicule from a person distinguished for intellectual cultivation; whose resistance was not only against that specific measure, but avowedly against the principle itself on which *any* measure of the same tendency could ever be founded.* Nor could any victory have pleased him better, probably, than one which contributed to prolong the barbarism of the people, as the best security, he deemed, for their continuing fit to labour at home and fight abroad. It might have added to his gratification to hear (as was the fact) his name pronounced with delight by ruffians of all classes, who regarded him as their patron saint.

If any one should be inclined to interpose here with a remark, that after *such* a reference, we have little right to ascribe to those classes, as if it were peculiarly one of their characteristics, the insensibility to the sufferings of the brute creation, and to number it formally among the results of the "lack of knowledge," we can only reply, that however those of higher order may explode any attempt to make the most efficient authority of the nation bear repressively upon the evil, and however it may in other ways be abetted by them, it is, at any rate, in those inferior classes chiefly that the actual perpetrators of it are found. It is something to say in favour of cultivation, that it does, generally speaking, render those who have the benefit of it

* Lord Erskine's memorable Bill, triumphantly scouted by the late Mr. Windham.—Undoubtedly there are considerable difficulties in the way of legislation on the subject; but an equal share of difficulty attending some other subjects—an affair of revenue, for instance, or a measure for the suppression (at that time) of political opinion—would soon have been overcome.

incapable of practising, *themselves*, the most palpably flagrant of those cruelties which they may be virtually countenancing, by some things which they do, and some things which they omit or refuse to do. Mr. Windham would not himself have practised a wanton barbarity on a poor horse or ass, though he scouted any legislative attempt to prevent it among his inferiors.

The proper place would perhaps have been nearer the beginning of this description of the characteristics of our uneducated people, for one so notorious, and one entering so much into the essence of the evils already named, as that we mention next; *a rude, contracted, unsteady, and often perverted, sense of right and wrong in general.*

It is curious to look into a large volume of religious casuistry, the work of some divine of a former age, (for instance Bishop Taylor's *Ductor Dubitantium,*) with the reflection what a conscience disciplined in the highest degree might be; and then to observe what this regulator of the soul actually is where there has been no sound discipline of the reason, and where there is no deep religious sentiment to rectify the perceptions in the absence of an accurate intellectual discrimination of things. This sentiment being wanting, dispositions and conduct cannot be taken account of according to the distinction between holiness and sin; and in the absence of a cultivated understanding, they cannot be brought to the test of the distinguishing law between propriety and turpitude; nor estimated upon any comprehensive notion of utility. The evidence of all this is thick and close around us; so that every serious observer has been struck and almost shocked to observe, in what a very small degree conscience is a *necessary* attribute of the human creature; and how nearly a nonentity the whole system of moral principles may be, as to any recognition of it by an unadapted spirit. While that system is of a substance veritable and eternal, and stands forth in its exceeding breadth, marked with the strongest characters and prominences, it has to these persons hardly the reality or definiteness of a shadow, except in a few matters, if we may so express it, of the grossest bulk. There must be glaring evidence of something bad in what is done, or questioned whether to be done, before conscience will come to its duty, or give proof of its existence. There must be a violent alarm of mischief or danger before this drowsy and ignorant magistrate will interfere. And since occasions thus involving flagrant evil cannot be of very frequent occurrence in the life of the generality of the people, it is probable that many of them have considerably protracted exemptions from any interference of conscience at all; it is certain that they experience no such pertinacious attendance of it, as to feel habitually a monitory intimation, that without great thought and care they will inevitably do something wrong. But what may we judge and presage of the moral fortunes of a sojourner, of naturally corrupt propensity, in this bad world, who is not haunted, sometimes to a degree of alarm, by this monitory sense, through the whole course of his life? What is likely to become of him, if he shall go hither and thither on the scene exempt from all sensible obstruction of the many interdictions, of a nature too refined for any sense but the vital tenderness of conscience to perceive?

Obstructions of a more gross and tangible nature he is continually meeting. A large portion of what he is accustomed to see presents itself to him in the character of boundary and prohibition; on every hand there is something to warn him what he must not do. There are high walls, and gates, and fences, and brinks of torrents and precipices; in short, an order of things on all sides signifying to him, with more or less of menace, —Thus far and no further. And he is in a general way obsequious to this arrangement. We do not ordinarily expect to see him carelessly transgressing the most decided of the artificial boundaries, or daring across those dreadful ones of nature. But, nearly destitute of the faculty to perceive, (as in coming in contact with something charged with the element of lightning,) the awful interceptive lines of that other arrangement which he is in the midst of as a subject of the laws of God, we see with what insensibility he can pass through those prohibitory significations of the Almighty will, which are to devout men as lines streaming with an infinitely more formidable than material fire. And if we look on to his future course, proceeding under so fatal a deficiency, the consequence foreseen is, that those lines of divine interdiction which he has not conscience to perceive as meant to deter him, he will seem as if he had acquired, through a perverted will, a recognition of in another quality—as temptations to attract him.

But to leave these terms of generality, and advert to a few particulars of illustration:—Recollect how commonly persons of the class described are found utterly violating truth, not in hard emergencies only, but as a habitual practice, and apparently without the slightest reluctance or compunction, their moral sense quite at rest under the accumulation of a thousand deliberate falsehoods. It is seen that by far the greater number of them think it no harm to take little unjust advantages in their dealings, by deceptive management; and very many would take the greatest but for fear of temporal consequences; would do it, that is to say, without inquietude of conscience, in the proper sense. It is the testimony of experience, from persons who have had the most to transact with them, that the indispensable rule of proceeding is to assume generally their want of principle, and leave it to time and prolonged trial to establish, rather slowly, the individual exceptions. Those unknowing admirers of human nature, or of English character, who are disposed to exclaim against this as an illiberal rule, may be recommended to act on what they will therefore deem a liberal one—at their cost.

That power of established custom, which is so great, as we had occasion to show, on the moral sense of even better instructed persons, has its dominion complete over that of the vulgar; insomuch that the most unequivocal iniquity of a practice long suffered to exist, shall hardly bring to their mere recollection the common acknowledged rule not to do as we would wish not done to us. From recent accounts it appears, that the entire coast of our island is not yet clear of those people called *wreckers*, who felt not a scruple to appropriate whatever they could seize of the lading of vessels cast ashore, and even whatever was worth tearing from the personal possession of the unfortunate beings who might be escaping but just alive from the most dreadful peril. The cruelty we have so largely attributed to our English vulgar, never recoils on them in self-reproach. The habitual indulgence of the irascible, vexatious, and malicious tempers, to the plague or terror of all within reach, scarcely ever becomes a subject of judicial estimate, as a character hateful in the abstract, with them a reflection of that estimate on the man's own self. He reflects but just enough to say to himself that it is all right and deserved, and unavoidable too, for he is unpardonably crossed and provoked; nor will he be driven from this self-approval, when it may be evident to every one else that the provocations are comparatively slight, and are only taken as offences by a disposition habitually seeking occasions to vent its spite. The inconvenience and vexation incident to low vice, may make the offenders fret at themselves for having been so foolish, but it is in general with an extremely trifling degree of the sense of guilt. Suggestions of reprehension, in even the discreetest terms, and from persons confessedly the best authorized to make them, would not seldom be answered by a grinning defying carelessness, in some instances by abusive retort; instead of any betrayed signs of an internal acknowledgment of deserving reproof.

And while thus the censure of a fellow-mortal meets no internal testimony to own its justice, this insensate self-complacency is undisturbed also on the side toward heaven. A mere philosopher, that should make little account of religion, otherwise than as capable of being applied to enforce and aggravate the sense of obligation with respect to rules of conduct, and would not, provided it may have this effect, care much about its truth or falsehood,—might be disposed to assert, that the ignorant and debased part of the population, of this Christian and Protestant country, are but so much the worse for the riddance of some parts of the superstitions of former ages. He might allege, with plausibility, that the system which imposed so many falsehoods, vain observances, and perversions of moral principles, acknowledging nevertheless *some* correct rules of morality, as an external practical concern, had the advantage of enjoining them, as far as it chose to do so, with the force of superstition, a stronger authority with a rude conscience than that of plain simple religion. That system exercised a mighty complexity and accumulation of authority, all avowedly divine; by which it could artificially augment, or rather supersede, the mere divine prescription of such rules, making *itself* the authority and prescriber; and thus could infix them in the moral sense of the people with something more, or something else, than the simply divine sanction. Whereas, now, when those superstitions which held the people so powerfully in awe, are gone, and have taken away with them that spurious sanction, there remains nothing to exert the same power of moral enforcement; since the people have not, in their exemption from the superstitions of their ancestors, come under any solemn and commanding effect of the true idea of the Divine Majesty. And it is undeniable that this is the state of conscience among them. The vague faint notion, as they conceive it, of a being who is said to be the creator, governor, lawgiver, and judge, and who dwells perhaps somewhere in the sky, has not, to many of them, the smallest force of intimidation from evil, at least when they are in health and daylight. One of the large sting-armed insects of the air does not alarm them less. A certain transitory fearfulness that occasionally comes upon them, points more to the Devil, and perhaps (in times now nearly gone by) to the ghosts of the dead, than to the Almighty. It may be, indeed, that this feeling is in its ultimate principle, if it were ever followed up so far, an acknowledgment of justice and power in God, reaching to wicked men through these mysterious agents; who though intending no service to him, but actuated by dispositions of their own, malignant in the greatest of them, and supposed inauspicious in the others, are yet carrying into effect his hostility. But it is little beyond such proximate objects of apprehension that many minds extend their awe of invisible spiritual existence. Even the notion really entertained by them of the greatness of God, may be entertained in such a manner as to have but slight power to restrain the inclinations to sin, or to impress the sense of guilt after it is committed. He is too great, they readily say, to mind the little matters that such creatures as we may do amiss; they can do *him* no harm. The idea, too, of his bounty, is of such unworthy consistence as to be a protection against all conscious reproach of ingratitude and neglect of service toward him;—he has made us to need all this that it is said he does for us; and it costs him nothing, it is no labour, and he is not the less rich; and besides, we have toil, and want, and plague enough, notwithstanding any thing that he gives.

It is probable this unhappiness of their condition, oftener than any other cause, brings God into their thoughts, and that as a being against whom they have a complaint approaching to a quarrel on account of it. And this strongly assists the reaction against whatever would enforce the sense of guilt on the conscience. When he has done so little for us, (something like this is the sentiment), he cannot think it any such great matter if we *do* sometimes come a little short of his commands. There is no doubt that their recollections of him as a being to murmur against for their allotment, are more frequent, more dwelt upon, and with more of an excited feeling, than their recollections of him as a being whom they ought to have loved and served, but have offended against. The very idea of such offence, as the chief and essential constituent of wickedness, is so slightly conceived, (because he is invisible, and has his own felicity, and is secure against all injury,) that if the thoughts of one of these persons *should*, by some rare occasion, be forced into the direction of unwillingly seeing his own faults, it is probable his impiety would appear the most inconsiderable thing in the account; that he would easily forgive himself the negation of all acts and feelings of devotion towards the Supreme Being, and the countless multiplications of insults to him by profane language.

To conclude this part of the melancholy statement; it may be observed of the class in question, that they have but very little notion of guilt, or possible guilt, in any thing but external practice. That busy interior existence, which is the moral person, genuine and complete; the thoughts, imaginations, volitions; the motives, projects, deliberations, devices, the indulgence of the ideas of what they cannot or dare not practically realize,—all this, we have reason to believe, passes nearly exempted from jurisdiction, even of that feeble and undecisive kind which *may* occasionally attempt an interference with their actions. They do indeed take such notice of the quality of these things within, as to be aware that some of them are not to be disclosed in their communications; which prudential caution has of course little to do with conscience, when the things so withheld are internally cherished in perfect disregard of the Omniscient Observer, and with hardly the faintest monition that the essence of the guilt is the same, with only a difference in degree, in intending or deliberately desiring an evil, and in acting it.

It is not natural obtuseness of mental faculty that we are attributing, all this while, to the uneducated class of our people, in thus exposing the defectiveness of their discernment between right and wrong. If it were, there might arise somewhat of the consolation afforded in contemplating some of the very lowest of the savage tribes of mankind, by the idea that such outcasts of the rational nature must stand very nearly exempt from accountableness, through absolute natural want of mind. But in the barbarians of our country we shall often observe a very competent, and now and then an abundant, share of native sense. We may see it evinced in respect to the very questions of morality, in cases where they are quite compelled, as will occasionally happen, to feel themselves brought within the cognizance of one or other of its plainest rules. In such cases we have witnessed a sharpness and activity of intellect claiming almost our admiration. What contrivance of deception and artful evasion. What dexterity of quibble, and captious objection, and petty sophistry. What vigilance to observe how the plea in justification or excuse takes effect, and, if they perceive it does not succeed, what address in sliding into a different one. What quickness to avail themselves of any mistake, or apparent concession, in the examiner or reprover. What copious rhetoric in exaggeration of the cause which tempted to do wrong, or of the great good hoped to be effected by the little deviation from the right,—a good surely enough to excuse so trifling an impropriety. What facility of placing between themselves and the censure, the recollected example of some good man who has been "overtaken in a fault."

Here *is* mind, after all, we have been prompted to exclaim; mind educating itself to evil, in default of that discipline which should have educated it to good. How much of the wisdom of evil, (if we may be allowed the expression,) there is faculty enough in the neglected corrupt popular mass of this nation to attain, by the exercise into which the individual's mind is carried by its own impulse, and in which he may every where and every hour find ample cooperation. Each of these self-improvers in depraved sense has the advantage of finding himself among a great tribe of similar improvers, forming an immense school, as if for the promotion of this very purpose; where they all teach by a competition in learning; where the rude faculty which is not expanded into intelligence is, however, sharpened into cunning; where the spirit which cannot grow into an eagle, may take the form and action of a snake. This advantage,—that there should not be a diminution of the superabundant plenty of associates always at hand, to assist each man in making the most of his native intellect for its least worthy use,—has been from age to age secured to our populace, as if it had been the most valuable birthright of Englishmen. Whatever else the person born to the inheritance of low life was destined to find in it, the national state had made as sure to him as it had before made the same privilege to his ancestors, that the generality of his equals should be found fit and ready to work with him in the acquirement of a depraved shrewdness.

But while the bulk of the people have been, in every period, abandoned to such a process of educating themselves and one another, where has been that character of parental guardianship, which seems to be ascribed when poets, orators, and patriots, are inspired with tropes, and talk of England and her children? This imperial matron of their rhetoric seems to have little cared how much she might be disgraced in the larger portion of her progeny, or how little cause they might have to all eternity to remember her with gratitude. She has had far other concern about them, and employment for them, than that of their being taught the value of their spiritual nature, and carefully trained to be enlightened, good, and happy. Laws against crime, it is true, she has enacted for them in liberal quantity; appointed her quorums of magistrates; and not been sparing of punishments. She has also maintained public sabbath observances to remind them of religion, of which observances she cared not that they little understood the very terms; except when the reading of a Book of Sports was appointed an indispensable part at one time long after her adoption of the Reformation. But she might plainly see what such provisions did *not* accomplish. It was a glaring fact before her eyes, that the majority of her children had far more of the mental character of a colony from some barbarian nation, than of that which an enlightened and Christian state might have been expected to impart. She had most ample resources indeed for supplying the remedy; but, provided that the productions of the soil and the workshop were duly forthcoming, she thought it of no consequence, it should seem, that the operative hands belonged to degraded minds. And then, too, as at all times her lofty ambition destined a good proportion of them to the consumption of martial service, she perhaps judged that the less they were trained to think, the more fit they might be to be actuated mechanically, as an instrument of blind impetuous force. Or perhaps she thought it would be rather an inconsistency, to be making much of the inner existence of a thing which was to be, in frequent wholesale lots, sent off to be cut or dashed to pieces.* And besides, a certain measure of instruction to think, especially if consisting, in a considerable part, of the inculcation of religion, might have done something to disturb that notion, (so worthy to have been transferred from the Mohammedan creed,) which she was by no means desirous to expel from her fleets and armies, that death for "king and country" clears off all accounts for sin.

* "Killed off," was the sentimental phrase emitted in parliament, in easy unconsciousness of offence, by the accomplished senator named in a former page. He probably was really unaware that the creatures were made for any thing better.

Let our attention be directed a little while to the effects of the privation of knowledge, as they may be seen conspicuous in the several parts of the economy of life, in the uneducated part of the community. Observe those people in their daily occupations. None of us need be told that, of the prodigious diversity of manual employments, some consist of, or include, operations of such minuteness or complexity, and so much demanding nicety, arrangement, or combination, as to necessitate the constant and almost entire attention of the mind; nor that all of them must require its full attention at times, at particular stages, changes, and adjustments, of the work. We allow this its full weight, to forbid any extravagant notion of how much it is possible to think of other things during the working time. It is however to be recollected, that persons of a class superior to the numerous one we have in view, take the chief share of those portions of the arts and manufactures which require the most of mental effort, —those which demand extreme precision, or inventive contrivance, or taste, or scientific skill. We may also take into the account of the allotment of employments to the uncultivated multitude, how much facility is acquired by habit, how much use there is of instrumental mechanism, (a grand exempter from the responsibility that would lie on the mind,) and how merely general and very slight an attention is exacted in the ordinary course of some of the occupations. These things considered, we may venture perhaps to assume, on an average of those employments, that the persons engaged in them might be, as much at least as one third part of the time, without detriment to the manual performance, giving the thoughts to other things with attention enough for such interest as would involve improvement. This is particularly true of the more ordinary parts of the labours of agriculture, when not under any critical circumstances, or special pressure owing to the season.

But as the case at present is, what does become, during such portion of the time, of the ethereal essence which inhabits the corporeal labourer, this spirit created, it is commonly said and without contradiction, for thought, knowledge, religion, and immortality? If we be really to believe this doctrine of its nature and destiny, (for we are not sure that politicians think so,) can we know without regret, that in very many of the persons in the situations supposed, it suffers a dull absorption, subsides into the mere physical nature, is sunk and sleeping in the animal warmth and functions, and lulled and rocked, as it were, in its lethargy, by the bodily movements, in the works which it is not necessary for it to keep habitually awake to direct? And its obligation to keep just enough awake to see to the right performance of the work, seems to give a licensed exemption from any other stirring of its faculties. The employment *is something to be minded*, in a general way, though but now and then requiring a pointed attention ; and therefore this said intellectual being, if uninformed and unexercised, will feel no call to mind anything else: as a person retained for some service which demands but occasionally an active exercise, will justify the indolence which declines taking in hand any other business in the intervals, under the pretext that he has his appointment; and so, when not under the immediate calls of that appointment, he will trifle or go to sleep, even in the full light of day, with an easy conscience.

But here we are to beware of falling into the inadvertency of appearing to say, that the labouring classes, in this country and age, have actually this full exemption, during their employments, from all exercise of thought beyond that which is immediately requisite for the right performance of their work. It is true that there is little enough of any such mental activity directed to the instructive uses we were supposing. But while such partial occupation of the thoughts (of course it is admitted, in an irregular and discontinuous, but still a beneficial manner) with topics and facts of what may be called intellectual and moral interest as we are assuming to be compatible with divers of the manual operations, is a thing to which most among the labouring classes are strangers, many of them are equally strangers to an easy vacancy of mind; experiencing amidst their employments a severe arrest of those thoughts which the mere employment itself may leave free. During the little more than mechanical action of their hands and eyes, the circumstances of their condition press hard into their minds. The lot of many of those classes is placed in a melancholy disproportion between what *must* be given to the cares and toils for a bare subsistence, and what *can*, at most, be given to the interests of the nobler part of their nature, either during their work or in its intervals. It is a sad spectacle to behold so many myriads of spiritual beings, (proviso, again, that we may call them so without being suspected to forget that their proper calling is to work with their hands,) doomed to consume a proportion so little short of the whole of their vigour and time, in just merely supporting so many bodies in the struggle to live.

When it is in special relation to the present times that we speak of this struggle to live, we of course mean by it something more than that circumstance of the general lot of humanity which is expressed in the sentence, "In the sweat of thy brow thou shalt eat thy bread." We put the emphasis on the peculiar aggravation of that circumstance in this part of the world in this and recent times, by the adventitious effect of some dreadful disorder of the social economy, in consequence of which the utmost exertions of the body and mind together but barely suffice in so many cases, in some hardly do suffice, for the mere protraction of life; comfortable life being altogether out of the question. The course of the administration of the civilized states, and the recent dire combustion into which they have almost unanimously rushed, as in emulation which of them should with the least reserve, and with the most desperate rapidity, annihilate the resources that should have been for the subsistence and competence of their people, have resulted in such destitution and misery in this country as were never known before, except as immediately inflicted by the local visitation of some awful calamity. The state of very many of our people, at this hour, is nearly what might be conceived as the consequence of a failure of the accustomed produce of the earth.*

There is no wish to deny or underrate the additions made to the evil by the intervention of causes, whose operation admits of being traced in some measure distinctly from the effect of this grand one. They may be traced in an operation which is *distinguishable;* and referable to each respectively; but it were most absurd to represent them as working out of connexion, or otherwise than subordinately concurring, with that cause which has invaded with its pernicious effects everything that has an existence or a name in the

* No exaggeration at the time when it was written. The condition of the working classes during the subsequent years does not admit of any comprehensive uniform description. It has suffered successive harassing fluctuations, and been probably at all times severely distressing in one part of the country or another.

social system. And it were simply monstrous to attribute the main substance of so wide and oppressive an evil to causes of any debateable quality, while there is glaring in sight a cause of stupendous magnitude, which *could not possibly do otherwise* than produce immense and calamitous effects. It would be as if a man were prying about for this and the other cause of damage, to account for the aspect of a region which has recently been devastated by inundations or earthquakes. It has become much a fashion to explain the distresses of a country on any principles rather than those that are taught by all history, and prominently manifest in the nature of things. And airs of superior intelligence shall be assumed on hearing a plain man fix the main charge of national exhaustion and distress on the nation's consuming its own strength in an unquenchable fury to destroy that of others; just as if such madness had never been known to result in poverty and distress, and it were perfectly inexplicable how it should. This is partly an affectation of science, accompanied, it is likely, by somewhat of that sincere extravagance with which some newly developed principle is apt to be accounted the comprehension of all wisdom, a nostrum that will explain everything. But we suspect that in many instances this substitution of subordinate causes for a great substantial one, proceeds from something much worse than such affectation or self-duped extravagance. It is from a resolute determination that ambition shall be the noblest virtue of a state; that martial glory shall maintain its ground in human idolatry; and that wars and their promoters shall be justified at all hazards.

We were wishing to show how the labouring people's thoughts might be partly employed, during their daily task, and consistently with industry and good workmanship. But what a state of things is exhibited where the very name of industry, the virtue universally honoured, the topic of so many human and divine inculcations, cannot be spoken without offering a bitter insult; where the heavy toil, denounced on man for his transgression, in the same sentence as death, is in vain implored as the greatest privilege; or thought of in despair, as a blessing too great to be attainable; and when the reply of the artisan to an unwitting admonition, that even amidst his work he might have some freedom for useful thinking, may be, "Thinking! I have no work to confine my thinking; I may, for that, employ it all on other subjects; but those subjects are, whether I please or not, the plenty and luxury in which many creatures of the same kind as myself are rioting, and the starvation which I and my family are suffering."

We hope in Providence, more than in any wisdom or disposition shown by men, that this melancholy state of things will be alleviated, otherwise than by a reduction of number through the diseases generated by utter penury.* We trust the time will come when the christian monitor shall no longer be silenced by the apprehension of such a reply to the suggestion he wishes to make to the humble class, that they should strive against being reduced to mere machines amidst their manual employments; that it is miserable to have the whole mental existence shrunk and shrivelled as it were to the breadth of the material they are working upon; that the noble interior agent, which lends itself to maintain the external activity, and direct the operations required of the bodily powers for the body's welfare, has eminently a right and claim to have

* It *has* been alleviated; but not till after a considerable duration. In England it has; but look at Ireland!

employments on its own account, during such parts of those operations as do not of necessity monopolize its attention. It may claim, in the superintendence of these, a privilege analogous to that possessed in the general direction of subordinate agents by a man of science, who will interfere as often as it is necessary, but will not give up all other thought and employment to be a constant mere looker on, during such parts of the operations as are of so ordinary a nature that he could not really fix his attention on them.

But how is the mind of the labourer or artisan to be delivered from the blank and stupified state, during the parts of his employment that do not necessarily engross his thoughts? How, but by its having within some store of subjects for thought; something for memory, imagination, reflection; in a word, by the possession of knowledge? How can it be sensibly alive and active, when it is placed fully and decidedly out of communication with all things that are friendly to intellectual life, all things that apply a beneficial stimulus to the faculties, all things, of this world or another, that are the most inviting or commanding to thought and emotion? We can imagine this ill-fated spirit, especially if by nature of the somewhat finer temperament, thus detached from all vital connexion, secluded from the whole universe, and inclosed as by a prison wall,—we can imagine it sometimes moved with an indistinct longing for its appropriate interests; and going round and round by this dark dead wall, to seek for any spot where there might be a chance of escape, or any crevice where a living element for the soul transpires; and then, as feeling it all in vain, dejectedly resigning itself again to its doom. Some ignorant minds have instinctive impulses of this kind; though far more of them are so deeply stupified as to be habitually safe from any such inquietude. But let them have received, in their youth and progressively afterwards, a considerable measure of interesting information, respecting, for instance, the many striking objects on the globe they inhabit, the memorable events of past ages, the origin and uses of remarkable works within their view, remaining from ancient times; the causes of effects and phenomena familiar to their observation as now unintelligible facts; the prospects of man, from the relation he stands in to time, and eternity, and God, explained by the great principles and facts of religion. Let there be fixed in their knowledge so many ideas of these kinds, as might be imparted by a comparatively humble education, (one quite compatible with the destination to a life of ordinary employment,) and even involuntarily the thoughts would often recur to these subjects, in those moments and hours when the manual occupation can, and actually will, be prosecuted with but little of exclusive attention. Slight incidents, casual expressions, would sometimes suggest these subjects; by association they would suggest one another. The mere re-action of a somewhat cultivated spirit against invading dulness, might recall some of the more amusing and elating ones; and they would fall like a gleam of sunshine on the imagination. An emotion of conscience, a self-reflection, an occurring question of duty, a monitory sensation of defective health, would sometimes point to the serious and solemn ones. The mind might thus go a considerable way, to recreate or profit itself, and, on coming back again, find all safe in the processes of the field or the loom. The man would thus come from these processes with more than the bare earnings to set against the fatigue. There would thus be scattered some appearances to entertain, and some sources and productions to refresh, over what were else a dead and barren flat of existence.

There is no romancing in all this; we have known instances of its verification to a very pleasing and exemplary extent. We have heard persons of the class in question tell of the exhilarating imaginations, or solemn reflections, which, through the reminiscences of what they had read in youth or more advanced years, had visited their minds; and put them, as it were, in communication for a while with diversified, remote, and elevated objects, while in their humble employments under the open sky or the domestic roof. And is not this, (if it be true, after all, that the intellectual immortal nature is by emphasis the man,) is not this vastly better than that this mind should lie nearly as dormant, during the labourer's hours of business, as his attendant of the canine species shall be sometimes seen to do in the corner of the field where he is at work?

But perhaps it will be said, that the minds of the uncultivated order are not generally in this state of utter inanity during their common employments; but are often awake and busy enough in recollections, fancies, projects, and the tempers appropriate; and that they abundantly show this when they stop sometimes in their work to talk, or talk as they are proceeding in it. So much the stronger, we answer, the argument for supplying them with useful knowledge; for it were better their mental being *were* sunk in lethargy, than busy among the reported, recollected or imagined transactions, the wishes, and the schemings, which will be the most likely to occupy the minds of persons abandoned to ignorance, vulgarity, and therefore probably to low vice.

We may add to the representation, the manner in

which they spend the part of their time not demanded for the regular, or the occasional, exercise of their industry. It is not to be denied that many of them have too much truth in their pleading that, with the exception of Sunday, they have little remission of their toils till they are so weary that the remainder of the time is needed for complete repose. This is particularly the case of the females, especially those who have the chief cares and the actual work of a family. Nevertheless, it is within our constant observation that a considerable proportion of the men, a large one of the younger men, in the less heavily oppressed divisions of our population, do in fact include, for substance, their manual employments within such limits of time, as often to leave several hours in the day to be spent nearly as they please. And in what manner, for the most part, is this precious time expended by those of no mental cultivation? It is true, again, that in many departments of labour, a diligent exertion during even this limited space of the day, occasions such a degree of lassitude and heaviness as to render it almost inevitable, especially in certain seasons of the year, to surrender some moments of the spare time, beyond what is necessary for the humble repast, to a kind of listless subsidence of all the powers of both body and mind. But after all these allowances fully conceded, a great number in the class under consideration have in some days several hours, and in the whole six days of the week, on an average of the year, very many hours, to be given, as they choose, to useful purposes or to waste; and again we ask, where the mind itself has been left waste how *is* that time mostly expended?

If the persons are of a phlegmatic temperament, we shall often see them just simply annihilating those portions of time. They will for an hour, or for hours together, if not disturbed by some cause from without, sit on a bench, or lie down on a bank or hillock, or lean on a wall, or fill the fire-side chair; yielded up to utter vacancy and torpor, not asleep perhaps, but more lost to mental existence than if they were; since the dreams, that would probably visit their slumbers, would be a more lively train of ideas than any they have awake. Of a piece with this is the habit, among many of this order of people, of giving formally to sleep as much as one-third part, sometimes considerably more. of the twenty-four hours. Certainly there are innumerable cases in which infirmity, care, fatigue, and the comfortlessness and penury of the humble dwelling, effectually plead for a large allowance of this balm of oblivion. But very many surrender themselves to this excess from destitution of any thing to keep their minds awake, especially in the evenings of the winter. What a contrast is here suggested to the imagination of those who have read Dr. Henderson's, and other recent descriptions, of the habits of the people of Iceland!

These, however, are their most harmless modes of wasting the time. For, while we might think of the many hours merged by them in apathy and needless sleep, with a wish that those hours could be recovered to the account of their existence, we might well wish that the hours could be struck out of it which they may sometimes give, instead, to conversation; in parties where ignorance, coarse vulgarity, and profaneness, are to support the dialogue, on topics the most to their taste; always including, as the most welcome to that taste, the depravities and scandals of the neighbourhood; while all the reproach and ridicule, expended with good will on those depravities, have the strange result of making the censors the less disinclined themselves to practise them, and only a little better instructed how to do it with impunity. In many instances there is the additional mischief, that these assemblings for corrupt communication find their resort at the public-house, where intemperance and ribaldry may season each other, if the pecuniary means for the former ingredient can be afforded, even at the cost of distress at home.—But without including depravity of this degree, the worthlessness of the communications of a number of grossly ignorant associates is easy to be imagined; besides that most of us have been made judges of their quality by numberless occasions of unavoidably hearing samples of them.

In the finer seasons of the year, much of these leisure spaces of time can be expended out of doors; and we have still only to refer to every one's own observation of the account to which they are turned, in the lives of beings whose lot allows but so contracted a portion of time to be, at the best, applied directly to the highest purposes of life.—Here the hater of all such schemes of improvement, as would threaten to turn the lower order into what that hater may probably call Methodists, (a term we venture to interpret for him as meaning thoughtful beings and Christians,) comes in with a ready cant of humanity and commiseration. And why, he says, with an affected indignation of philanthropy, why should not the poor creatures enjoy a little fresh air and cheerful sunshine, and have a chance of keeping their health, confined as many of them are, for the greatest part of the time, in narrow squalid rooms, unwholesome workshops, and every sort of disagreeable places and employments? Very true, we answer; and why should not numbers of them be collected in groups by the road side, in readiness to find in whatever passes there occasions for gross jocularity; practising some impertinence, or uttering some jeering scurrility, at the expense of persons going by; shouting with laughter at the success of the annoyance, or to *make* it successful, and all this blended with language of profaneness and imprecation, as the very life of the hilarity? Or why should not the boldest spirits among them form a little conventicle for cursing, blaspheming, and blackguard obstreperousness in the street, about the entrance of one of the haunts of intoxication; where they are perfectly safe from that worse mischief of a gloomy fanaticism, with which they might have been smitten if seduced to frequent the meeting-house twenty paces off? Or why should not the children, growing into the stage called youth, be turned loose through the lanes, roads, and fields, to form a brawling impudent rabble, trained by their association to every low vice, and ambitiously emulating, in voice, visage, and manners, the ruffians and drabs of maturer growth? Or why should not the young men and women collect in clusters, or range about or beyond the neighbourhood in bands, for revel, frolic, and all kinds of coarse mirth; to come back late at night to quarrel with their wretched elders, who perhaps envy them their capacity for such wild gaieties and strollings, while rating them for their disorderly habits? We say, where can be the harm of all this? What reasonable and benevolent man would think of making any objection to it? Reasonable and benevolent,—for these have been among the qualities boasted for the occasion by the opposers of any materially improved education of the people; while in such opposition they virtually avowed their willing tolerance of all that is here described.

We have allowed most fully the plea of how little time, *comparatively*, could be afforded to the concern o mental improvement by the lower classes from their indispensable employments; and also that of the consequent fatigue, causing a temporary incapacity of effort in any other way. But this latter plea cannot be admitted without great abatement in the case of our neglected *young* people of the working classes; for when we advert to their actual habits, we see that, nevertheless, time, strength, and wakefulness, and spring and spirit for exertion, *are* found for a vast deal of busy diversion, much of it blended with such folly as tends to vice.

If such is the manner in which the spare time of the week-days goes to waste and worse, the Sunday is welcomed as giving scope for the same things on a larger scale. It is very striking to consider, that several millions, we may safely assert, of our English people, arrived at what should be years of discretion, are almost completely destitute of any manner of conscience respecting this seventh part of time; not merely as to any required consecration of it to religion, but as to its being under any claim or of any worth at all, otherwise than for amusement. It is actually regarded by them as a section of time far less under obligation than any other. They take it as so absolutely at their free disposal, by a right so exclusively vested in their taste and will, that a demand made even in behalf of their own most important interests, is contemptuously repelled as a sanctimonious impertinence. If the idea occurs at all (with multitudes it never does) of claims which they have heard that God should make on the hours, it is dismissed with the thought that it really cannot signify to him how creatures, condemned by his appointment to toil all the rest of the week, may wish to spend this one day, on which the secular taskmaster manumits them, and He, the spiritual one, might surely do as much. An immense number pay no attention whatever to any sort of religious worship; and many of those that do give an hour or two to such an observance, do so, some of them as merely a diversification of amusement, and the others by way of taking a license of exemption from any further accountableness for the manner in which they may spend the day. It is the natural consequence of all this, that there is more folly, if not more crime, committed on this than on all the other six days together.

Thus man, at least *ignorant* man, is unfit to be trusted with anything under heaven; since a remarkable appointment for raising the general tenour of moral existence, has with these persons the effect of sinking it. There is interposed, at frequent regular intervals throughout the series of their days, a richer vein, as it were, of time. The improvement of this, in a manner by no means strained to the austerity of exercise prescribed in the Puritan rules, might diffuse a worth and a grace over all the time between, and assist them against the tendency there may be in its necessary habits and employments, to depress the intelligent nature into meanness or debasement. The space which they are passing over is marked, at near intervals, with broad lines of a benignant light, which might spread an appearance of mild lustre over the whole extent as contemplated in retrospect; but how many, in looking back when near the end of their progress, have to perceive its general shade rendered darker by the very spaces where that light had been shed from heaven.

The Sundays of those who do not improve them to a good purpose, will infallibly be perverted to a bad one. But it were still a melancholy account if we could regard them as merely standing for nothing, as a blank in the life of this class of the people. It is a deeply unhappy spectacle and reflection, to see a man of perhaps more than seventy, sunk in the grossness and apathy of an almost total ignorance of all the most momentous subjects, and then to consider, that, since he came to an age of some natural capacity for the exercise of his mind, there have been more than three thousand Sundays. In their long succession they were *his time.* That is to say, he had the property in them which every man has in duration; they were present to him, he had them, he spent them. Perhaps some compassionate friend may have been pleading in his behalf,—Alas! what opportunity, what time, has the poor mortal ever had? His lot has been to labour hard through the week throughout almost his whole life. Yes, we answer, but he has had three thousand Sundays; what would not even the most moderate improvement of so vast a sum of hours have done for him? But the ill-fated man, (perhaps rejoins the commiserating pleader,) grew up from his childhood in utter ignorance of any use he ought to make of time which his necessary employment would allow him to waste. There, we reply, you strike the mark. Sundays are of no value, nor Bibles, nor the enlarged knowledge of the age, nor heaven nor earth, to beings brought up in estrangement from all right discipline. And therefore we are pleading for the schemes and institutions which will not *let* human beings be thus brought up.

In so pleading, we happily can appeal to one fact in evidence that the intellectual and religious culture, in the introductory stages of life, tends to secure that the persons so trained shall be, when they are come to maturity, marked off from the neglected barbarous mass, by at least an external respect, but accompanied, we trust, in many of them, by a still better sentiment, to the means for keeping truth and duty constantly in their view. Observe the numbers now attending, with a becoming deportment, public worship and instruction, as compared with what the proportion is remembered or recorded to have been half a century since, or any time previous to the great exertions of benevolence to save the children of the inferior classes from preserving the whole mental likeness of their forefathers.

It can be testified also, by persons whose observation has been the longest in the habit of following children and youth from the instruction of the school institutions into mature life, that, in a gratifying number of instances, they have been seen permanently retaining too much love of improvement, and too much of the habit of an useful employment of their minds, to sink, in their ordinary daily occupations, into that wretched inanity we were representing; or to consume the free intervals of time in the listlessness, or worthless gabble, or vain sports, of which their neighbours furnished plenty of example and temptation.

These representations have partly included, what we may yet specify distinctly as one of the unhappy effects of gross ignorance—*a degraded state of domestic society*.

Whatever is of a nature to render individuals uninteresting or offensive to one another, has a specially bad effect among them as members of a family; because there is in that form of community itself a peculiar tendency to fall below the level of dignified and complacent social life.—A number of persons cannot be placed in a state of social communication, without having a certain sense of claiming from one another a conduct meant and adapted to please. It is expected that a succession of efforts should be made for this purpose, with a willingness of each individual to forego, in little things, his own inclination or convenience. This is all very well when the society is *voluntary*, and the parties can separate when the cost is felt to be greater than the pleasure. Under this advantage of being able soon to separate, even a company of strangers casually assembled will often recognise the claim and conform to the law; with a certain indistinct sentiment partaking of reciprocal gratitude for the disposition which is so accommodating But the members of the domestic community also have each this same feeling which demands a mutual effort and self-denial to please, while the condition of their association is adverse to their *yielding* what they thus respectively claim. Theirs, when once it is formed, is not exactly a voluntary companionship, and it is one of undefinable continuance. The claim therefore seems as if it were to be of a prolongation interminable, while the grateful feeling for the concession is the less for the more compulsory bond of the association. And to be thus required, in a community which must not be dissolved, and in a series that reaches away beyond calculation, to exercise a self-restraint on their wills and humours in order to please one another, goes so hard against the great principle of human feeling—namely, each one's preference of pleasing himself—that there is an habitual impulse of reaction against the claim. This shows itself in their deportment, which has the appearance of a practical expression of so many individuals that they *will* maintain each his own freedom. Hence the absence, very commonly, in domestic society, of the attentiveness, the tone of civility, the promptitude of compliance, the habit of little accommodations, voluntary and supernumerary, which are so observable in the intercourse of friends, acquaintance, and often, as we have said, even of strangers.

And then consider, in so close a kind of community, what near and intimate witnesses they are of all one another's faults, weaknesses, tempers, perversities; of whatever is offensive in manner, or unseemly in habit.

of all the irksome, humiliating, or sometimes ludicrous circumstances and situations. And also, in this close association, the bad moods, the strifes, and resentments, are pressed into immediate lasting corrosive contact with whatever should be the most vital to social happiness. If there be, into the account, the wants, anxieties, and vexations of severe poverty, they will generally aggravate all that is destructive to domestic complacency and decorum.

Now add gross ignorance to all this, and see what the picture will be. How many families have been seen where the parents were only the older and stronger animals than their children, whom they could teach nothing but the methods and tasks of labour. They naturally could not be the mere companions, for alternate play and quarrel, of their children, and were disqualified by mental rudeness to be their respected guardians. There were about them these young and rising forms, containing the inextinguishable principle, which was capable of entering on an endless progression of wisdom, goodness, and happiness! needing numberless suggestions, explanations, admonitions, brief reasonings, and a training to attend to the lessons of written instruction. But nothing of all this from the parent. Their case was as hopeless for receiving these necessaries of mental life, as the condition, for physical nutriment, of infants attempting to draw it, (we have heard of so affecting and mournful a fact,) from the breast of a dead parent. These unhappy heads of families possessed no resources for engaging youthful attention by mingled instruction and amusements; no descriptions of the most wonderful objects, or narratives of the most memorable events, to set, for superior attraction, against the idle stories of the neighbourhood; no assemblage of admirable examples, from the sacred or other records of human character, to give a beautiful real form to virtue and religion, and promote an aversion to base companionship.

Requirement and prohibition must be a part of the domestic economy habitually in operation of course; and in such families you will have seen the government exercised, or attempted to be exercised, in the roughest, barest shape of will and menace, with no aptitude or means of imparting to injunction and censure a convincing and persuasive quality. Not that the seniors should allow their government to be placed on such a ground that, in every thing they enforce or forbid, they may be liable to have their reasons demanded by the children, as an understood condition of their compliance. Far from it; they will sometimes have to require a prescribed conduct for reasons not intelligible, or which it may not be discreet to explain, to those who are to obey. But their authority becomes odious, and as a moral force worse than inefficient, when the natural shrewdness of the children can descry that they really *have* no reasons better than an obstinate or capricious will; and infallibly makes the inference, that there is no obligation to submit, but that necessity which dependence imposes. But this must often be the unfortunate condition of such families.

Now imagine a week, month, or year, of the intercourse in such a domestic society, the course of talk, the mutual manners, and the progress of mind and character; where there is a sense of drudgery approaching to that of slavery, in the unremitting necessity of labour; where there is none of the interest of imparting knowledge or receiving it, or of reciprocating knowledge that has been imparted and received; where there is not an acre, if we might express it so, of intellectual space around them, clear of the thick universal fog of ignorance; where, especially, the luminaries of the spiritual heaven, the attributes of the Almighty, the grand phenomenon of redeeming mediation, the solemn realities of a future state and another world, are totally obscured in that shade; where the conscience and the discriminations of duty are dull and indistinct, from the youngest to the oldest; where there is no genuine respect on the one side, nor affection unmixed with vulgar petulance and harshness, expressed perhaps in language of imprecation, on the other; where a mutual coarseness of manners and words has the effect, without their being aware of it as a cause, of debasing their worth in one another's esteem, all round; and where, notwithstanding all, they absolutely must pass a great deal of time together, to converse, to display their dispositions toward one another, and exemplify the poverty of the mere primary relations of life, as divested of the accessories which give them dignity, endearment, and conduciveness to the highest advantage of existence.

Home has but little to please the young members of such a family, and a great deal to make them eager to escape out of the house; which is also a welcome riddance to the elder persons, when it is not in neglect or refusal to perform allotted tasks. So little is the feeling of a peaceful cordiality created among them by their seeing one another all within the habitation, that, not unfrequently, the passer-by may learn the fact of their collective number being there, from the sound of a low strife of mingled voices, some of them betraying youth replying in anger or contempt to maturity or age. It is wretched to see how early this liberty is boldly taken. As the children perceive nothing in the *minds* of their parents that should awe them into deference, the most important difference left between them is that of physical strength. The children, if of hardy disposition, to which they are perhaps trained in battles with their juvenile rivals, soon show a certain degree of daring against this superior strength. And as the difference lessens, and by the time it has nearly ceased, what is so natural as that they should assume equality, in manners and in following their own will? But equality assumed where there should be subordination, inevitably involves contempt toward the party in defiance of whom it is asserted.

The relative condition of such parents as they sink in old age, is most deplorable. And all that has preceded, leads by a natural course to that consequence which we have sometimes beheld, with feelings emphatically gloomy,—the almost perfect indifference with which the descendants, and a few other relations, of a poor old man of this class, could consign him to the grave. A human being was gone out of the world, a being they had been with or near all their lives, some of them sustained in their childhood by his labours, and yet perhaps not one heart, at any moment, felt the sentiment—I have lost——. They never could regard him with respect, and their miserable education had not taught them humanity enough to regard him in his declining days as an object of pity. Some decency of attention was perhaps shown him, or perhaps hardly that, in his last hours. His being now a dead, instead of a living man, was a burden taken off; and the insensibility and levity, somewhat disturbed and repressed at the sight of his expiring struggle, and of his being lowered into the grave, recovered by the day after his interment, if not on the very same evening, their accustomed tone, never more to be interrupted by the effect of any remembrance of him. Such a closing scene one day to be repeated is foreshown to us, when we look at an ignorant and thoughtless father surrounded by his untaught children. In the silence of thought we thus accost him,—The event which will take you finally from among them, perhaps after forty or fifty years of intercourse with them, will leave no more impression on their affections, than the cutting down of a decayed old tree in the neighbourhood of your habitation.

There are instances, of rare occurrence, when such a man becomes, late in life, far too late for his family to have the benefit of the change, a subject of the only influence which could awake him to earnest thoughtfulness and the full sensibility of conscience. When the sun thus breaks out toward the close of his gloomy day, and when, in the energy of his new life, he puts forth the best efforts of his untaught spirit for a little divine knowledge, to be a lamp to him in entering ere long the shades of death, with what bitter regrets he looks back to the period when a number of human beings, some perhaps still with him, some now scattered from him, and here and there pursuing their separate courses in careless ignorance, were growing up under his roof, within his charge, but in utter estrangement from all discipline adapted to ensure a happier sequel. His distressing reflection is often representing to him what they might now have been if they had grown up under such discipline. And gladly would he lay down his life to redeem for them but some inferior share of what the season for imparting to them is gone for ever.

Another thing is to be added, to this representation of the evils attendant on an uncultivated state of the people, namely—that *this mental rudeness puts them decidedly out of beneficial communication with the superior and cultivated classes.*

We are assuming (with permission) that a national community should be constituted for the good of all its parts, not to be obtained by them as detached independent portions, but adjusted and compacted into one social body; an economy in which all the parts shall feel they have the benefit of an amicable combination; in other words, that they are the better for one another. But it can be no such constitution when the most palpable relations between the two main divisions of society consist of such direct opposites as refinement and barbarism, dignity and gross debasement, intelligence and ignorance; which are the distinctions asserted by the higher classes as putting a vast distance between them and the lower. If so little of the correct understanding, the information, the liberalized feeling, and the propriety of deportment, which we are to ascribe to the higher and cultivated portion, goes downward into the lower, it should seem impossible but there must be more of repulsion than of amicable disposition and communication between them. We may suspect, perhaps, that those more privileged classes are not generally desirous that the interval were much less wide, provided that without cultivation of the lower orders the nuisance of their annoying and formidable temper could be abated. But however that may be, it is exceedingly desirable, for the good of both, that the upper and inferior orders *should* be on terms of communication and mutual good will, and therefore that there should be a diminution of that rudeness of mind and habits which must contribute to keep them alienated and hostile.

If it were asked what communication, at all of a nature to be described by epithets of social and friendly import, we can be supposing by possibility to subsist between classes so different and distant, we may exemplify it by such an instance as we have now and then the pleasure of seeing. Each reader also, of any moderate compass of observation, may probably recollect an example, in the case of some man in humble station, but who has had (for his condition) a good education; having been well instructed in his youth in the elements of useful knowledge; having had good principles diligently inculcated upon him; having subsequently instructed himself, to the best of his very confined means and opportunity, through a habit of reading; and being in his manners unaffectedly observant of all the decorums of a respectable human being. It has been seen, that such a man has not found in some of his superiors in station and attainment any disposition to shun him; and has not felt in himself or his situation any reason why he should seek to shun them. He would occasionally fall into conversation with the wealthy and accomplished proprietor, or the professional man of learning, in the neighbourhood. His intelligent manner of attending to what they said, his perfect understanding of the language naturally used by cultivated persons, the considerateness and pertinence of his replies, and the modest deference, combined with an honest freedom in making his observations on the matters brought in question, pleased those persons of superior rank, and induced various friendly and useful attentions, on their part to him and his family. He and his family thus experienced a direct benefit of superior sense, civility, and good principle, in a humble condition; and were put under a new responsibility to preserve a character for those distinctions.—Now think of the incalculable advantage to society, if any thing approaching to this were the general state of social relation between the lower and the higher orders.

On the contrary, there is no medium of complacent communication between the classes of higher condition and endowment, and an ignorant coarse populace. Except on occasion of giving orders or magisterial rebukes, the gentleman will never think of such a thing as converse with the clowns in his vicinity. They, on their part, are desirous to avoid him; excepting when any of them may have a purpose to gain, by arresting his attention, with an ungainly cringe; or when some of those who have no sort of present dependence on him, are disposed to cross his way with a look and strut of rudeness, to show how little they care for him. The servility, and the impudence, almost equally repress in him all friendly disposition toward a voluntary intercourse with the class. There is thus as complete a dissociation between the two orders, as mutual dislike, added to every imaginable dissimilarity, can create. And this broad ungracious separation intercepts all modifying influence that might otherwise have passed, from the intelligence and refinement of the one, upon the barbarism of the other.

But there is in human nature a pertinacious disposition to work disadvantages, in one way or other, into privileges. The people, in being thus consigned to a low and alien ground, in relation to the cultivated part of society, are put in possession, as it were, of a territory of their own; where they can give their disposition freer play, and act out their characters in their own manner; exempt equally from the voluntary and the involuntary influence of the cultivated superiors; that is to say, neither insensibly modified by the attraction of what is the most laudable in them as a pattern, nor swayed through policy to a studied accommodation to their understood opinion and will. This is a great emancipation enjoyed by the inferiors. And however injurious it may be, it is one of which they will not fail to take the full license. For in all things and situations, it is one of the first objects with human beings, to verify experimentally the presumed extent of their liberty and privilege. In this dissociation, the people are rid of the many salutary restraints and incitements which they would have been made to feel, if on terms of friendly recognition with the respectable part of the community; they have neither honour nor disgrace, from that quarter, to take into their account; and this contributes to extinguish all sense and care of respectability of character,—a care to which there will be no motive in any consideration of what they may, as among themselves, think of one another; for, with the low estimate which they mutually and justly entertain, there is a conventional feeling among them that, for the ease and privilege of them all, they are systematically to set aside all high notions and nice responsibilities of character and conduct. There is a sort of recognised mutual *right* to be no better than they are. And an individual among them affecting a high conscientious principle would be apt to incur ridicule, as a man foolishly divesting himself of a privilege;—unless, indeed, he let them understand that hypocrisy was his way of maintaining that privilege, and turning it to account.

The people are thus, by their ignorance, and what inseparably attends it, far removed and estranged from the more cultivated part of their fellow-countrymen; and consequently from every beneficial influence under which a state of friendly contiguity, if we may so express it, would have placed them. Let us now see what, in this abandonment to themselves, are their growing dispositions toward the superior orders and the existing arrangements of the community; dispositions which are promoted by causes more definite than this estrangement considered merely as the negation of benevolent intercourse, but to which it mightily contributes.

Times may have been when the great mass, while

placed in such decided separation from the upper orders, combined such a quietude with their ignorance, that they had little other than submissive feelings toward these superiors, whose property, almost, for all service and obsequiousness, they were accustomed to consider themselves; when no question would occur to them why there should be so vast a difference of condition between beings of the same race; when no other proof was required of the right appointment of their lot, however humble it might be, than their being, and their forefathers having been, actually in it; and when they did not presume, hardly in thought, to make any inferences from the fact of the immense disproportion of numbers and consequent physical strength between them and their superiors.* But the times of this perfect, unquestioning, unmurmuring succumbency under the actual allotment, have passed away; except in such regions as the Russian empire, where they have yet long to continue. In other states of Europe, but especially in our own, the ignorance of the people has nowhere prevented them from acquiring a sense of their strength and importance; with a certain ill-conceived, but stimulant notion, of some change which they think ought to take place in their condition. How, indeed, should it have been possible for them to remain unaware of this strength and importance, while the whole civilized world was shaken with a practical and tremendous controversy between the two grand opposed orders of society, concerning their respective rights; or

* Here, however, it should be observed that in the former age, when there was far less of jealous invidious feeling between the upper and lower classes than has latterly intervened, there was a more amicable manner of intercommunication. The settled and perfectly recognised state of subordination precluded on the one side, all apprehension of encroachment, and on the other the disposition to it.

that they should not have taken a strong, and from the rudeness of their mental condition, a fierce interest, in the principle and progress of the strife? And how should they have failed to know that, during this controversy, innumerable persons raised from the lower rank by talent and spirit, had left no place on earth except in courts (and hardly even there) for the dotage of fancying some innate difference between the classes distinguished in the artificial order of society?

The effect of all this is gone deep into the minds of great numbers who are not excited, in consequence, to any worthy exertion for raising themselves, individually, from their degraded condition, by the earnest application and improvement of their means and faculties. The feeling of many of them seems to be, that they must and will sullenly abide by the ill-starred fate of their order, till some great comprehensive alteration in their favour shall absolve them from that bond of hostile sentiment, in which they make common cause against the superior classes; and shall create a state of things in which it shall be worth while for the individual to make an effort to raise himself. We can at best, (they seem to say,) barely maintain, with the utmost difficulty, a miserable life; and you talk to us of cultivation, of discipline, of moral respectability, of efforts to come out from our degraded rank! No, we shall even stay where we are; till it is seen how the question is to be settled between the people of our sort, and those who will have it that they are of a far worthier kind. There may then, perhaps, be some chance for such as we; and if not, the less we are disturbed about improvement, knowledge, and all those things, the better, while we are bearing the heavy load a few years, to die like those before us.

We said they are banded in a hostile sentiment. It

is true, that among such a degraded populace there is very little kindness, or care for one another's interests. They all know too well what they all are not, to feel mutual esteem or benevolence. But it is infinitely easier for any set of human beings to maintain a community of feeling in hostility to something else, than in benevolence toward one another; for here no sacrifice is required of any one's self-interest. And it is certain, that the subordinate portions of society have come to regard the occupants of the tracts of fertility and sunshine, the possessors of opulence, splendour, and luxury, with a deep, settled, systematic aversion; with a disposition to contemplate in any other light than that of a calamity an extensive downfal of the favourites of fortune, when a brooding imagination figures such a thing as possible; and with but very slight monitions from conscience of the iniquity of the most tumultuary accomplishment of such a catastrophe. In a word, so far from considering their own welfare as identified with the stability of the existing social order, they consider it as something that would spring from the ruin of that order. The greater number of them have lost that veneration by habit, partaking of the nature of a superstition, which had been protracted downward, though progressively attenuated with the lapse of time, from the feudal ages into the last century. They have quite lost, too, in this disastrous age, that sense of competence and possible well-being, which might have harmonized their feelings with a social economy that would have allowed them the enjoyment of such a state, even as the purchase of great industry and care. Whatever the actual economy may have of wisdom in its institutions, and of splendour, and fulness of all good things, in some parts of its apportionment, they feel that what is allotted to most of *them* in its arrangements is pressing hardship, unremitting poverty, growing still more hopeless with the progress of time, and of what they hear trumpeted as national glory, nay, even "national prosperity and happiness unrivalled." This bitter experience, which inevitably becomes associated in their thoughts with that frame of society under which they suffer it, will naturally have a far stronger effect on their opinion of that system than all that had ever rendered them acquiescent or reverential toward it. That it brings no relief, or promise of relief, is a circumstance preponderating in the estimate, against all that can be said of its ancient establishment, its theoretical excellences, or the blessings in which it may be pretended to have once abounded, or still to abound. What were become of the most essential laws of human feeling, if such experience *could* leave those who are undergoing its discipline still faithfully attached to the social order on the strength of its consecration by time, and of the former settled opinions in its favour,—however tenacious the impressions so wrought into habit are admitted to be? And the minds of the people thus thrown loose from the former ties, are not arrested and recovered by any substitutional ones formed while those were decaying. They are not retained in a temper of patient endurance and adherence, by the bond of principles which a sedulous and deep instruction alone could have enforced on them. The growth of sound judgment under such instruction, might have made them capable of understanding how a proportion of the evil may have been inevitable, from uncontrollable causes; of perceiving that it could not fail to be aggravated by a disregard of prudence in the proceedings in early life among their own class, and that so far it were unjust to impute it to their superiors or to the order of society; of admitting that national calamities are visitations of divine judgment, of which they were to reflect whether they had not deserved a heavy share; of feeling it to be therefore no impertinent or fanatical admonition that should exhort them to repentance and reformation, as an expedient for the amendment of even their temporal condition; and of clearly comprehending that, at all events, rancour, violence, and disorder, cannot be the way to alleviate any of the evils, but to aggravate them all. But, we repeat it, there are millions in this land, and if we include the neighbouring island politically united to it, very many millions, who have received no instruction adequate, in the smallest degree, to counteract the natural effect of the distresses of their condition; or to create a class of moral restraints and mitigations in prevention of a total hostility of feeling against the established order, after the ancient attachments to it have been worn down by the innovations of opinion, and the pressure of continued distress.

Thus uninstructed to apprehend the considerations adapted to impose a moral restraint, thus unmodified by principles of mitigation, there is a large proportion of human strength and feeling not in vital combination with the social system, but aloof from it, looking at it with "gloomy and malign regard;" in a state progressive toward a fitness to be impelled against it with a dreadful shock, in the event of any great convulsion, that should set loose the legion of daring, desperate, and powerful spirits, to fire and lead the masses to its demolition. There have not been wanting examples to show with what fearful effect this hostility may come into action, in the crisis of the fate of a nation's ancient system; where this alienated portion of its own people, rushing in, have revenged upon it the neglect of their tuition; that neglect which had abandoned them to so utter a "lack of knowledge," that they really understood no better than to expect their own solid advantage in general havoc and disorder. But how bereft of sense the *State* too must be, that would thus *let* a multitude of its people grow up in a condition of mind to believe, that the sovereign expedient for their welfare is to be found in spoliation and destruction! It might easily have comprehended what it was reasonable to expect from the matured dispositions and strength of such of its children as it abandoned to be nursed by the wolf.

While this principle of ruin was working on by a steady and natural process, this supposed infatuated State was, it is extremely possible, directing its chief care to maintain the splendour of a court, or to extort the means for prosecuting some object of vain and wicked ambition, some project of conquest and military glory. And probably nothing could have appeared to many of its privileged persons more idle and ridiculous, or to others of them more offensive and ill-intentioned, than a remonstrance founded on a warning of such a consequence. The despisers would have been incomparably the greater number; and, "Go (they would have said) with your mock-tragical fortune-telling, to whoever can believe, too, that one day or other the quadrupeds of our stalls and meadows may be suddenly inspirited by some supernatural possession to turn their strength on us in a mass, or those of our kennels to imitate the dogs of Actæon."

SECTION IV.

There may be persons ready to make a question here, whether it be so certain that giving the people of the lower order more knowledge, and sharpening their faculties, will really tend to the preservation of good order. Would not such improvement elate them, to a most extravagant estimate of their own worth and importance; and therefore result in insufferable arrogance, both in the individuals and the class? Would they not, on the strength of it, be continually assuming to sit in judgment on the proceedings and claims of their betters, even in the most lofty stations; and demanding their own pretended rights, with a troublesome and turbulent pertinacity? Would they not, since their improvement cannot, from their condition in life, be large and deep, be in just such a half taught state, as would make them exactly fit to be wrought upon by all sorts of crafty schemers, fierce declaimers, empirics, and innovators? Is it not, in short, too probable that, since an increase of mental power is available to bad uses as well as good, the results would greatly preponderate on the side of evil?

It would be curious to observe how objections so plausible, so decisive in the esteem of those who advance them, would sound if expressed in other terms. Let them be put in the form of such sentences and propositions as the following:—Though understanding is to be men's guide to right conduct, the less of it they possess the more safe are we against their going wrong. The duty of a human being has many branches; there are connected with all of them various general and special considerations, to induce and regulate the performance; it must be well for these to be defined with all possible clearness; and it is also well for the great majority of men to be utterly incapable of apprehending them with any such definiteness. It is desirable that the rule, or set of rules, by which the demeanour of the lower orders toward those above them is to be directed, should appear to them *reasonable* as well as distinctly defined; but let us take the greatest care that their reason shall be in no state of fitness to perceive this rectitude of the rules. It would be a noble thing to have a competent understanding of all that belongs to human interest and duty; and therefore the next best thing is to be retained very nearly in ignorance of all. It would be a vast advantage to proceed a hundred degrees on the scale of knowledge; but the advantage is no where in the progress; each of the degrees is in itself worth nothing; nay, less than nothing; for unless a man could attain all, he had better stop at two or one, than advance to four, six, or ten. Truths support one another; by the conjunction of several each is kept the clearer in the understanding, the more efficient for its proper use, and the more adequate to resist the pressure of the surrounding ignorance and delusion; therefore let there be the greatest caution that we do not give to three truths in a man's understanding the aid of a fourth, or four the aid of a fifth; let the garrison be so diminutive that its successful resistance to the siege must be a miracle.——The reader will be in little danger of excess in shaping into as many forms of absurdity as he pleases a notion which goes to the depreciation of the desire and use of truth, of all that has been venerated as wisdom, of the divine revelation of knowledge, and of our rational nature itself.

If it *be* a rational nature that the lower ranks possess as well as the superior, one should have imagined it must be in the highest degree important that they, as well as their superiors, should habitually make their duty and conduct *a matter of thought*, of intelligent consideration, instead of going through it mechanically, or with little more than a brute accommodation of what they do to a customary and imposed manner of doing it; but this thoughtful way of acting will never prevail among them, while they are unexercised in that thinking which (generally speaking) men will never acquire but in the exercise of gaining knowledge. It were, again, better, one would think, that they should be capable of seeing some reason and use in gradations and unequal distributions in the community, than be left to regard it as all a matter of capricious or iniquitous fortune, to their allotment under which there is no reason for submission but a bare necessity. The improvement of understanding by which we are wishing to raise them in this humble allotment, without carrying them from the ground where it is placed, will explain to them the best compensations of their condition, will show them it is no essential degradation, and point them to the true respectability which may be obtained in it. And even if they *should* be a little too much elated with the supposed attainments, (while the flattering possession is yet new, and far from general in their class,) what taste would it be in their superiors not to deem this itself a far better thing than the contented, or more probably insolent and malignant, grossness of a stupid vulgarity?—as some little excess of self-complacenc in appearing in a handsome dress is accounted much less disgusting than a careless self-exposure in filth and rags.

As to their being rendered liable by more knowledge to be caught by declaimers, projectors, and agitators, we may confidently ask, whether it be the natural effect of more knowledge and understanding to be less suspicious of cajoling professions, less discerning of what is practicable and impracticable, and more credulous to extravagant doctrines, and wild theories and schemes. Is it the well-instructed and intelligent poor man that believes the demagogue who may assert or insinuate that, if things were ordered right, all men might live in the greatest plenty? Or if we advert to those of the lower order whom a diminutive freehold or other qualification may entitle to vote for a member of parliament, is it the well-instructed and intelligent man among them that is duped by the candidate's professions of kind solicitude for him and his family, accompanied with smiling equivocal hints that it may be of more advantage than he is aware for a man who has sons to provide for, to have a friend who has access and interest in a certain high quarter? Nor is it among the best instructed and most thinking part of the subordinate class, that we shall find persons capable of believing that a community might, if those who govern it so pleased, be rich and prosperous by other means than a general industry in ordinary employments.

If, again, it is apprehended that a great increase of intelligence among the people would destroy their deference and respectful deportment toward their superiors, the ground of this apprehension should be honestly assigned. If the claim to this respect be definable, and capable of being enforced upon good reasons, it is obvious that improved sense in the people will better appreciate them. Especially, if the claim is to owe any part of its validity to higher mental qualifications in the claimants, it will so far be incomparably better understood, and if it *be* valid, far more respected than it is now. By having a measure of knowledge, and of the power and practice of thinking, the people would be enabled to form some notion of what it must be, and what it is worth, to have a great deal more of these endowments. They would observe and understand the indications of this ampler possession in the minds of those above them, and so would be aware of the great disparity between themselves and these superiors. And since they would value *themselves* on their comparatively small share of these mental advantages, (for this is the very point of the objection against their attaining them,) they would be compelled to estimate by the same scale the persons dignified by so far surpassing a share of this admired wealth. Whereas an ignorant populace can understand nothing at all about the matter; they have no guess at the great disparity, nor impression of its importance; so that with them the cultivated superiors quite lose the weight of this grand difference, and can obtain none of the respect which they may deserve on account of it. The objection against enlightening the lower classes appears so remarkably absurd as viewed in this direction, that it might tempt us to suspect a motive not avowed. It is just the sort of caveat to be uttered by persons aware that themselves, or many of their class, might happen to betray to the sharpened inspection of a more intelligent people, that a higher ground in the allotments of fortune is no certain pledge for a superior rank of mind. It *were* strange, very strange indeed, if persons combining with superior station a great mental superiority, should be content, while claiming the deference of the subordinate part of the community around them, that this high distinction should go for nothing in that claim, and that the required respect should be paid only in reverence of the number of their acres, the size of their houses, the elegance of their equipage and domestic arrangements, and perhaps some official capacity, in which many a notorious blockhead has strutted and blustered.

We think such considerations as the above, opposed to the objection that any very material cultivation of the minds of the common people would destroy their industry in ordinary employments, their contentment with their station, and their respectful demeanour to their superiors; and would render them arrogant, disorderly, factious, liable to be caught by wild notions, misled by declaimers and impostors, and, in short, all the worse for being able to understand their duty and interest the better, ought to go far toward convicting that objection of great folly,—not to apply terms of stronger imputation.

But we need not have dwelt so long on such arguments, since fortunately there is matter of fact in answer to the objection. To the extent of the yet very limited experiment, it is proved that giving the people more knowledge and more sense does not tend to disorder and insubordination; does not excite them to impatience and extravagant claims; does not spoil them for the ordinary business of life, the tasks of duty and necessity; does not make them the dupes of knaves; nor teach them the most profitable use of their improved faculties is to turn knaves themselves. Employers can testify, from all sides, that there is a striking general difference between those bred up in ignorance and rude vulgarity, and those who have been trained through the well-ordered schools for the humble classes, especially when the habits at home have been subsidiary; a difference exceedingly in favour of the latter, who are found not only more apt at understanding and executing, but more decorous, more respectful, more attentive to orders, more ready to see and acknowledge the propriety of good regulations, and more disposed to a practical acquiescence in them; far less inclined to ebriety and low company; and more to be depended on in point of honesty. In almost any part of the country, where the experiment has been zealously prosecuted for a moderate number of years, a long resident observer can discern a modification in the character of the neighbourhood; a mitigation of the former brutality of manners, a less frequency of brawls and quarrels, and less tendency to draw together into rude riotous assemblages. There is especially a marked difference on the Sabbath, on which great numbers attend public worship, whose forefathers used on that day to congregate for boisterous sport on the common, or even within the inclosure vainly consecrated round the church;* and who would themselves in all probability have followed the same course, but for the tuition which has led them into a better. In not a few instances, the children have carried from the schools inestimable benefits home to their unhappy families; winning even their depraved thoughtless parents into consideration and concern about their most important interests,—a precious repayment of all the long toils and cares, endured to support them through the period of childhood, and an example of that rare class of phenomena, in which (as in the instance of the Grecian

* We know a church where, within the remembrance of an immediate ancestor, it was not unusual, or thought any thing amiss, for the foot-ball to be struck up within the "consecrated ground" at the close of the afternoon service of the Sunday.

Daughter) a superlative beauty arises from an inversion of the order of nature.

Even the frightful statements of the increase, in recent years, of active juvenile depravity, especially in the metropolis, include a gratifying testimony in favour of education—at least did so some years since. The result of special inquiries, of extensive compass, into the wretched history of juvenile reprobates, has fortified the promoters of schools with evidence that it was not from *these* seminaries that such noxious creatures were to go out, to exemplify that the improvement of intelligence may be but the greater aptitude for fraud and mischief. No, it was found to have been in very different places of resort, that these wretches had been, almost from their infancy, accomplished for crime; and that their training had not taken or needed any assistance from an exercise on literary rudiments, from Bibles, catechisms, or religious and moral poetry, or from an attendance on public worship. Indeed, as if Providence had designed that the substantial utility should be accompanied with a special circumstance to confound the cavillers, the children and youth of the schools were found to have been more generally preserved from falling into the class of premature delinquents, than a moral calculator, keeping in sight the quality of human nature and the immediate pressure of so much temptation, would have ventured to anticipate, upon the moderate estimate of the efficacy of instruction.

Experience equally falsifies the notion that knowledge, imparted to the lower orders, beyond what is necessary to the handling of their tools, tends to factious turbulence; to an impatience (from the instigation of certain wild theories,) under law and regular government in society. The maintainers of which notion should also affirm, that the people of Scotland have been to this day about the most disaffected, tumultuary, revolutionary rabble in Europe; and that the Cornish miners, now so worthily distinguished at once by exercised intellect and religion, are incessantly on the point of insurrection, against their employers or the state. And we shall be just as ready to believe them, if they also assert, that, in those popular irregularities which have too often disturbed, in particular places, the peace of our country, the clamorous bands or crowds, collected for purposes of intimidation or demolition, have consisted chiefly of the better instructed part of the poorer inhabitants;—yes, or that this class furnished one in twenty or fifty of the numbers forming such lawless bands; even though many of these more instructed of the people might be suffering, with their families, the extremity of want, the craving of hunger, which, no less than "oppression," may "make a wise man mad." Many of these, in their desolate abodes, with tears of parents and children mingled together, have been committing themselves to their Father in heaven, at the time that the ruder part of the population have been carrying alarm, and sometimes mischief, through the district, and so confirming the faith, we may suppose, of sundry magnates of the neighbourhood, who had vehemently asserted, a few years before, the pernicious tendency of educating the people.*

* What proportion were found to have been educated, in the very lowest sense of the term, of the burners of ricks and barns in the south-eastern counties, a few years since? What proportion of the ferocious, fanatical, and sanguinary rout who, the other day, near the centre of the metropolitan see of Canterbury, were brought into action by the madman Thom, *alias* Sir W. Courtenay; stout, well fed, proud Englishmen—Englishmen "the glory of all lands," who were capable of believing that madman a divine personage, Christ himself, invulnerable, till the fact happened otherwise, and then were confident he would come to life again? When will the

It would be less than what is due to suffering humanity, to leave this topic without observing, that if a numerous division of the community should be sinking under severe, protracted, unmitigated distress, distress on which there appears to them no dawn of hope from ordinary causes, it is not to be held a disparagement to the value of education, if some of those who have enjoyed a measure of that advantage, in common with a greater number who have not, should become feverishly agitated with imaginations of great sudden changes in the social system; and be led to entertain suggestions of irregular violent expedients for the removal of insupportable evils. It must, in all reason, be acknowledged the last lesson which education could be expected to teach with practical effect, that one part of the community should be willing to resign themselves to a premature mortality, that the others may live in sufficiency and tranquillity. Such heroic devotement might not be difficult in the sublime elation of Thermopylæ; but it is a very different matter in a melancholy cottage, and in the midst of famishing children.*

After thus referring to matter of fact, for contradiction of the notion, that the mental cultivation of the lower classes might render them less subject to the rules of good order, we have to say, in further reply, that we are not heard insisting on the advantages of increased knowledge and mental invigoration among the people, *unconnected with the inculcation of religion.*

Undoubtedly, the zealous friends of popular education

Government adopt some effectual means to avert from the nation the infamy of having such a populace in any part of the country, and especially *such* a part of it?

* This was almost the desperate condition of numberless families in this country at a period of which they, or the survivors of them, retain in memory an indelible record; and we think it right to retain *here* also that record. While thankful for all subsequent amendment, we say again, Look at Ireland.

account knowledge valuable absolutely, as being the apprehension of things as they are; a prevention of delusion; and so far a fitness for right volitions. But they consider religion, (besides being itself the primary and infinitely the most important part of knowledge,) as a principle indispensable for securing the full benefit of all the rest. It is desired, and endeavoured, that the understandings of these opening minds may be taken possession of by just and solemn ideas of their relation to the Eternal Almighty Being; that they may be taught to apprehend it as an awful reality, that they are perpetually under his inspection; and as a certainty, that they must at length appear before him in judgment, and find, in another life, the consequences of what they are in spirit and conduct here. It is to be impressed on them, that his will is the supreme law; that his declarations are the most momentous truth known on earth; and his favour and condemnation the greatest good and evil. Under an ascendency of this divine wisdom it is, that their discipline in any other knowledge is designed to be conducted; so that nothing in the mode of their instruction may have a tendency contrary to it, and everything be taught in a manner recognising the relation with it, as far as shall consist with a natural unforced way of keeping this relation in view. Thus it is sought to be secured that, as the pupil's mind grows stronger and multiplies its resources, and he therefore has necessarily more power and means for what is wrong, there may be luminously presented to him, as if celestial eyes visibly beamed upon him, the most solemn ideas that can enforce what is right.

Such is the discipline meditated, for preparing the subordinate classes to pursue their individual welfare, and act their part as members of the community.—

They are to be trained in early life to diligent employment of their faculties, tending to strengthen them, regulate them, and give their possessors the power of effectually using them. They are to be exercised to form clear, correct notions, instead of crude, vague, delusive ones. The subjects of these ideas will be, a very considerable number of the most important facts and principles; which are to be presented to their understandings with a patient repetition of efforts to fix them there as knowledge that cannot be forgotten. By this measure of actual acquirement, and by the habit formed in so acquiring, they will be qualified for making further attainment in future time, if disposed to improve their opportunities. During this progress, and in connexion with many of its exercises, their duty is to be inculcated on them in the various forms in which they will have to make a choice between right and wrong, in their conduct toward society. There will be reiteration of lessons on justice, prudence, inoffensiveness, love of peace, estrangement from the counsels and leagues of vain and bad men; hatred of disorder and violence, a sense of the necessity of authoritative public institutions to prevent these evils, and respect for them while honestly administered to this end. All this is to be taught, in many instances directly, in others by reference for confirmation, from the Holy Scriptures, from which authority will also be impressed, all the while, the principles of religion. And religion, while its grand concern is with the state of the soul towards God and eternal interests, yet takes every principle and rule of morals under its peremptory sanction; making the primary obligation and responsibility be towards God, of everything that is a duty with respect to men. So that, with the subjects of this education, the sense of *propriety* shall be *conscience;* the consideration of how they ought to be regulated in their conduct as a part of the community, shall be the recollection that their Master in heaven dictates the laws of that conduct, and will judicially hold them amenable for every part of it.

And is not a discipline thus addressed to the purpose of fixing religious principles in ascendency, as far as that difficult object is within the power of discipline, and of infusing a salutary tincture of them into whatever else is taught, the right way to bring up citizens faithful to all that deserves fidelity in the social compact?

But perhaps far less of sacred knowledge than all this pleading admits and assumes to be indispensable to them, will answer the end. For it is but a slender quantity of it that is, in effect, proposed to be imparted to them by those who would give them very little other knowledge. They will talk of giving the people an education specifically religious; a training to conduct them on through a close avenue, looking straight before them to descry distant spiritual objects, while shut out from all the scene right and left, by fences that tell them there is nothing that concerns them there. There may be rich and beautiful fields of knowledge, but they are not to be trampled by vulgar feet.

Now, may we presume that by knowledge, or information, is meant a clear understanding of a subject? If so, it is but little religious information that *can* be imparted while that of a more general nature is withheld. The case is so, partly because, in order to a clear conception of the principal things in the doctrine of religion, the mind wants facts, principles, associations of ideas, and modes of applying its thoughts, which are to be acquired from the consideration of various other subjects; and partly because, even though it did *not*, and though it *were* practicable to understand religious truths clearly without the subsidiary ideas, and the disciplined mental habit acquired in attention to other subjects, *it is flatly contrary to the radical disposition of human nature* that youthful spirits should yield themselves to a bare exclusively religious discipline. It were supposing a reversal of the natural taste and tendency, to expect them to apply their attention so patiently, so willingly, so long, and with such interest, to this one subject, as to be brought to an intelligent apprehension through the almost sole exercise of thinking on this. By thinking on this!—which is the subject on which they are by their very nature the least of all inclined to think; the subject on which it is the most difficult as well as the most important point in education to induce them to think; the subject which, while it is essential to give it the ascendency in the instruction of both the lower classes and all others, it requires so much care and address to present in an attractive light; and which it is so desirable to combine with other subjects naturally more engaging, in order to bring it oftener by such associations into the thoughts, in that secondary manner which causes somewhat less of recoil.

It is curious to see what some persons can believe, or affect to believe, when reduced to a dilemma. On the one hand, they cannot endure the idea of any considerable raising of the common people by mental improvement, in the general sense: that were ruin to social order. But then on the other, if it must not be plainly denied, that the said common people are of the very same rational nature as the most elevated divisions of the race; and that their essential worth must be in this spiritual thinking being, which worth is lost to them, if that being is sunk and degraded in gross ignorance, it follows that some kind of cultivation is required. Well then; we must give them some religious knowledge, unaccompanied by such other knowledge as would much more attractively invite them to exercise their minds, and *it will be practicable and easy enough* to engage their habitual attention to that very subject, almost exclusively, to which the natural taste of the species is peculiarly averse.

In exposing the absurdity of any scheme of education for the inferior classes, which should propose to make them intelligent about religion while intelligent about nothing else except their ordinary employments, we do not forget the instances now and then met with of pious poor men who, while very uncultivated in the general sense, evince a remarkable clearness of conception on religious topics, and in the application of these topics to their duties as men and citizens. But "remarkable" we involuntarily call these phenomena whenever adverting to them. We naturally use some expression importing a degree of wonder at such a fact. We think it a striking illustration of the power of *religion itself*, and not of the power of religious instruction. The extreme force with which the vital spirit has seized and actuated his faculties, has in a measure remedied the incapacity he had otherwise been under of forming clear ideas of the subject. Even, however, while acknowledging and admiring this effect of a special influence from heaven, we still find ourselves involuntarily surmising, in such an instance, that the man must also have been superior in natural capacity to the generality of ignorant persons ; so much out of the common course of things we account it for a man who knows so few things to know this one thing so well. We account it so from the settled conviction received through experience, that it is very unlikely a man ignorant of almost all other things *should* well understand *one* subject, of a nature quite foreign to that of his ordinary occupations.

It is superfluous to observe, that such instances of a very considerable comprehension of religious truth, obtained in spite of what naturally makes so much against its being attainable, cannot affect the calculation when we are devising schemes which can only work according to natural laws and with ordinary powers. They who devise and apply them will rejoice at these evidences that there is an Agent who can open men's minds to the light of religion independently and in the absence of other intellectual advantages. But the question being how to bring the people, by the ordinary means of education, to a competent knowledge of religious truth, we have to consider what way of attempting to impart that knowledge may be the best fitted, at once to obviate the natural indisposition to the subject, and to provide that when it does obtain a place in their understanding, it shall not be a meagre, diminutive, insulated occupant there, but in its proper dimensions and relations. And if, in attentively studying this, there be any who come to ascertain, that the right expedient is a bare inculcation of religious instruction, disconnected, on system, from the illustrative aid of other knowledge, divested of the modification and attraction of associated ideas derived from subjects less uncongenial with the natural feelings,—they really may take the satisfaction of having ascertained one thing more, namely, that human nature has become at last so mightily changed, that it may be left to work itself right very soon, as to the affair of religion, with little further trouble of theirs.

The special view in which we were pleading, on behalf of popular education, that religious instruction would form a material part of it, was, that this essential ingredient would be a security against its being injurious to the good order and subordination in society. It is the more necessary to be particular on this, as some of those who have professed to lay much stress on the *religious* instruction of the people have seemed to have little further notion of the necessity or use of religion to the lower classes, than as merely a preserver of good order. In this character it has been insisted on by persons who avowed their aversion to every idea of an education in a more enlarged sense. We have heard it so insisted on, no such long while past, by members of the most learned institutions, at the same moment that they expressed more than a doubt of the prudence of enabling the common people to read, literally to *read*, the Bible. But assuredly the good order of a populace left in the stupid general ignorance to which some of these good friends of theirs would have doomed them, cannot be preserved by any such feeble infusion of religious knowledge as these same good friends would instil into their mental grossness. As long as they are in this condition, there must be some far stronger power acting on them to preserve that good order. And if there actually *has* been such a power, hitherto competent to preserve it, with only such an impotent scantling of religious knowledge in the majority of the mass, and competent still to preserve it, a great deal of hypocritical canting might have been spared, on the part of those whose chief or only argument for teaching the people religion is the maintenance of that good order.

But all this while we are forgetting to inquire how much is to be understood as included in that good order, that deference and subordination, which the possession of more mind and knowledge by the people might disturb or destroy. May not the notion of it, as entertained by some persons, be rather an image of the polity of an age long past, or of that which remains unaltered as if it were a part of eternal nature in the dominions of the East, than a model for the conformation of society here in the present times? Is it required, that there should be a sentiment of obsequiousness in the people affecting them in a manner like the instinct by which a lower order of animals is in awe of a higher, by which the common tribe of beasts would cower at the sight of lions? Or, is the deference expected to be paid, not on any understanding of reciprocal advantage, but absolutely and unconditionally, as to a claim founded in abstract or divine right? Is it to be held a criminal presumption in the people, to think of examining their relations to the community any further than the obligation of being industrious in the employments to which it assigns them, and dutiful to its higher orders? Are they to entertain no question respecting the right adjustment of their condition in the arrangements of the great social body? Are they forbidden ever to admit a single doubt of its being quite a matter of course, that every thing which could be done for the interests of their class, consistently with the welfare of the whole, *is* done; or, therefore, to pretend to any such right as that of examining, representing, complaining, remonstrating, or an ultimate recourse, perhaps, in a severe necessity, to stronger expedients?

A subordination founded in such principles, and required to such a degree, it is true enough that the communication of knowledge is not the way to perpetuate. For the first use which men will infallibly make of an enlargement of their faculties and ideas, will be, to take a larger view of their interests; and they may happen, as soon as they do so, to think they discover that it was quite time; and the longer they do so, to retain still less and less of implicit faith that those interests will be done justice to, without their own vigilance and intervention. An educated people must be very slow indeed in the application of what they learn, if they do not soon grow out of all belief in the *necessary* wisdom and rectitude of any order of human creatures whatever. They will see how unreasonable it were to expect, that any sort of men will fail in fidelity to the great natural principle, of making their own advantage the first object; and therefore they will not be apt to listen, with the gravity which in other times and regions may have been shown in listening, to injunctions of gratitude for the willingness evinced by the higher orders to take on them the trouble of watching and guarding the people's welfare, by keeping them in due submission.

But neither will it necessarily be in the spirit of hostility, in the worst sense of the word, that a more instructed people will thus show a diminished credulity of reverence toward the predominant ranks in the social economy; and will keep in habitual exercise upon them a somewhat suspicious observation, and a judicial estimate; with an honest freedom in sometimes avowing disapprobation, and strongly asserting any right which is believed to be endangered or withheld. This will only be expressing that, since all classes naturally consult by preference their own interests, it is plainly unfit, that one portion of the community should be trusted with an unlimited discretion in ordering what affects the welfare of the others; and that, in all prudence, the people must refuse an entire affiance, and unconditional, unexamining acquiescence; "except the gods, whose dwelling is not with flesh," would come to harmonize, and then administer, interests which are so placed unappeasably at strife:—at strife; for, what is so often asserted of those interests being in reality the same, is true only on that comprehensive theory which neither party is prompt to understand, or willing to make sacrifices of a more immediate self-interest to realize; and it is evidently impossible for either, even if believing it true, to concede to the other the exclusive adjustment of the practical mode of identification.

But only let the utmost that is possible be done, to train the people, from their early years, to a sound use of their reason, under a discipline for imparting a valuable portion of knowledge, and assiduously inculcating the principles of social duty and of religion; and then something may be said, to good purpose, to their understanding and conscience, while they are maintaining the competition of claims with their superiors. They will then be capable of seeing put in a fair balance, many things which headlong ignorance would have taken all one way. They will be able to appreciate many explanations, alleged causes of delay, statements of difficulty between opposing reasons, which would be thrown away on an ignorant populace. And it would be an inducement to their making a real exertion of the understanding, that they thus found themselves so formally put upon their responsibility for its exercise; that they were summoned to a rational discussion, instead of being addressed in the style of Pharaoh to the Israelites. The strife of interests would thus come to be carried on with less fierceness and malice, in the spirit and manner, on the part of the people. And the ground itself of the contention, the substance of the matters in contest, would be gradually diminished, by the concessions of the higher classes to the claims of the lower: for there is no affecting to dissemble, that a great mental and moral improvement of the people would necessitate, though there were not a single movement of rude force in the case, important concessions to them, on the part of the superior orders. A people advanced to such a state, would make its moral power felt in a thousand ways, and every moment. This general augmentation of sense and right principle would send forth, against all arrangements and inveterate or more modern usages, of the nature of invidious exclusion, arbitrary repression, and the debasement of great public interests into a detestable private traffic, an energy, which could no more be resisted than the power of the sun, when he advances in the spring to annihilate the relics and vestiges of the winter. This plastic influence would modify the institutions of the national community, to a state better adapted to secure all the popular rights; and to convey the genuine, collective opinion, to bear directly on the counsel and transaction of national concerns. That opinion would be so unequivocally manifested, as to leave no pretence for a doubtful interpretation of its signs; and with such authority as to preclude any question whether to set it at defiance.

That such effects *would* be inseparable from a great general advancement of the people in knowledge and corrected character, must be freely acknowledged to its disapprovers. And is it *because* these would be the consequences, that they disapprove it? Then let them say, what it is that *they* would expect from an opposite system. *What* is it, that they could seriously promise themselves, from the conservative virtue of all the ignorance, that can henceforward be retained among the people of this part of the world? It is true, the remaining ignorance is so great that they cannot well overrate its *general* amount; but how can they fail to perceive the importance of those *particulars* in which its dominion has been broken up? There is indeed a hemisphere of "gross darkness over the people;" it may be possible to withhold from it long the illumination of the sun; but in the mean time it has been rent by portentous lights and flashes, which have excited a thought and agitation not to be stilled by the continuance of the gloom. There have come in on the popular mind some ideas, which the wisest of those who dread or hate their effect there, look around in vain for the means of expelling. And these glimpses of partial intelligence, these lights of dubious and possibly destructive direction amidst the night, will continue to prompt and lead that mind, with a hazard which can cease only with the opening upon it of the true daylight of knowledge. That knowledge should have been antecedent to the falling of these inflammatory ideas among the people; and if they have come before the proper time, that is to say, before the people were prepared to judge rationally of their rights, and to apprehend clearly the duties inseparable from them as a condition of their enjoyment, the calamitous consequences to the higher classes, as seen in the recent history of Europe, may be regarded as a righteous judgment of heaven upon them, for having suffered it to be *possible* for these new ideas of liberty and rights to come on the people in a state so unprepared. What were all their commanding authorities of government, their splendid ecclesiastical establishments, their great personal wealth and influence,—all their lofty powers and distinctions which even their basest sycophants, sacerdotal or poetical, told them, as one topic of adulation, that they were not entrusted with for their own sole gratification,—what were all these for, if the great body of the communities over which they presided were to be retained in a state in which they could not be touched by a few bold speculations in favour of popular rights, without exploding as with infernal fire? How appropriate a retribution of Sovereign Justice, that those who were wickedly the cause should be the victims of the effect.

Where such a consequence has not followed, but where, nevertheless, these notions of popular rights have come into the minds of the people very much in precedence and disproportion to the general cultivation of their intelligence and moral sense, it is most important that all diligence should be given to bring up these neglected improvements to stand in rank with those too forward speculations.

Whether this shall be done or not, these notions and feelings are not things come into life without an instinct of what they have to do. The disapprovers of schemes for throwing the greatest practicable measure of sound corrective knowledge into the minds of the multitude, may take instruction or may decline it from seeing that, both in this country and other states of Europe, there has gone forth among the mass of the people a spirit of revolt from the obligation, which would retain their reverence to institutions on the strength simply of their being established or being ancient; a spirit that re-acts, with deep and settled antipathy, against some of the arrangements and claims of the order into which the national community has been disposed by institutions and the course of events; a spirit which regards some of the appointments and requirements of that order, as little better than adaptations of the system to the will and gratification of the more fortunate divisions of the species. And it has shown itself in a very different character from that of a mere pining despondency, or the impotent resentment excited sometimes in timidity itself by severe grievance, but quelled by alarm at its own rashness. The element and the temperament of its nature, and the force of its action, have been displayed in the tremendous concussions attending its conflict with the power arrayed in behalf of the old order of things to crush it. And *is* this spirit crushed? Is it subdued? Is it in the least degree reduced?—reduced, we mean, in its internal power, as a combination of the most absolute opinion with the impulse of some of the strongest passions.

Is it, we repeat, repressed? There may have been persons who could not, "good easy men," conceive a possibility of its surviving the fiery storm of the whole resources of the world converted into the materials of war, to be poured on it, and followed by the mightiest leagues and the most systematic legislation, all aimed at its destruction; surviving to come forth with unabated vigour at the opportune junctures in the future progress of events; like some great serpent, coming out again to glare on the sight, with his appalling glance and length of volume, after a volley of missiles had sent him to his retreat. The old approved expedients against unreasonable discontents, and refractory tempers, and local movements of hostility excited by some worthless competitor for power, had been combined and applied on the grand scale; and henceforward all was to be still. It was not given to these spell-bound understandings to apprehend that the spirit to be repressed might be of a nature impassive to these expedients, possibly to be confirmed by their application. Repressed! What is it that is manifesting itself in the most remarkable events in the old, and what has been called the new world, at the present time? And what are the measures of several of the great state authorities of Europe, whether adopted in deliberate policy, or in a fitful mood between rashness and dismay; what are, especially, the meetings, conferences, and military preparations, of the mightiest despots of the globe, assembled at this very hour against a small and unoffending nation,*—what are these but a confession or proclamation, that the spirit which the most enormous exertions had been made to overwhelm, has preserved its life and energy; like those warring immortal powers whom Milton describes as having mountains thrown on them in vain? The progress of time renders it but more evident, that the principle in action is something far different from a superficial transient irritation; that it has gone the whole depth of the mind; has possessed itself of the very judgment and conscience of an innumerable legion, augmented by a continual and endless accession. No doubt is permitted to remain of the direction which has been taken by the current of the popular feeling,—to be recovered to its ancient obsequious course when some great river which has forced a new channel shall resume that which it has abandoned. For when once the great mass, of the lower and immensely larger division of the community, shall have become filled with an absolute, and almost unanimous conviction, that they, the grand physical agency of that community; that they, the operators, the producers, the preparers, of almost all it most essentially wants; that they, the part, therefore, of the social assemblage so obviously the most essential to its existence, and on which all the rest must depend; that they have their condition in the great social arrangement so disposed as not to acknowledge this their importance, as not to secure an adequate reward of these their services;—we say, when this shall have become the pervading intense conviction of the millions of Europe, we put it as a

* The meeting of imperial and royal personages at Troppau and Laybach, for the detestable purpose of crushing the newly acquired liberty of the kingdom of Naples.—January, 1821.

question to any rational thinker, whether and how this state of feeling can be reversed or neutralized, if the economy which has provoked it shall yield to no modification. But it *is* no question, he will confess. Then will he pretend not to foresee any material change in an order of things obnoxious to so vast a combination of wills and agents? This may indeed be seriously avowed by some, who are so walled up in old prejudice and presumption that they really have no look out; who, because a thing has been long established, mistake its artificial substruction of crumbling materials for the natural rock; and it will be pretended by others, who think the bravado of asserting the impossibility of the overthrow may be a good policy for deterring the attempt. There has not been one of the great alterations effected by the popular spirit within the last half century, that was not preceded by professions of contemptuous incredulity, on the part of the applauders of things as they were, toward those who calculated on the effects of that spirit. There were occasionally betrayed, under these shows of confidence and contempt, some signs of horror at the undeniable excitement and progress of popular feeling; but the scorn of all serious and monitory predictions of its ultimate result was at all events to be kept up,—in whatever proportions a time-serving interest and an honest fatuity might share in dictating this elated and contemptuous style. Should the latter of these ingredients at present predominate in the temper which throws off the fume of this high style, it will not leave much faculty in the defiers of all revolution, for explaining what it is they have to trust to as security against such consequences as we should anticipate from the progress of disapprobation and aversion in the people; unless indeed the security mainly relied on is just that plain simple expedient—force, for all nations on earth downright force. It is plainly this that is meant, when persons disinclined to speak out give us a circumlocution of delicate phrases, "the conservative energies of the public institutions," "the majesty of the Law," perhaps, and others of similar cast;—which fine phrases suggest to one's imagination the ornamented fashion of the handle and sheath of the scimitar, which is not the less keen, nor the less ready to be drawn, for all this finery that hides and garnishes so menacing a symbol of power.

The economy of states *shall* not be modified in favour of the great body of those who constitute them.—And are, then, the higher and privileged portions of the national communities to have, henceforward, just this one grand object of their existence, this chief employment for their knowledge, means, and power, namely, to keep down the lower orders of their fellow-citizens by stress of coercion? Are they resolved and prepared for a rancorous, interminable, hostility in prosecution of such a benign purpose; with a continual exhaustion upon it of the resources which might be applied to diminish that wretchedness of the people, which is the grand inflamer of those principles that have caused an earthquake under the foundations of the old social systems? But, "interminable" is no proper epithet to be applied to such a course. This policy of a bare uncompromising rigour, exerted to keep the people just where they are, in preference to adjustments formed on a calculation of a material change, and adapted to prepare them for it—how long could it be successful,—not to ask what would be the value or the glory of that success? With the light of recent history to aid the prognostication, by what superstitious mode of estimating the self-preserving, and self-avenging competence of any artificial form of social order, can we believe in its power to throw back the general opinions, determinations, and efforts, of the mass of mankind in endless recoil on themselves? That must be a very firm structure, must be of gigantic mass or most excellent basis and conformation, against which the ocean shall unremittingly wear and foam in vain. And it does not appear what there can be of such impregnable consistence in any particular construction of the social economy which is, by the supposition, resolved to be maintained in sovereign immutability, in permanent frustration of the persevering, ever-growing, aim and impulse of the great majority, pressing on to achieve important innovations in their favour; innovations in those systems of institution and usage, under which they will never cease to think they have had far less happiness, or means of happiness, than they ought to have had. We cannot see how this impulse can be so repelled or diverted that it shall not prevail at length, to the effect of either bearing down, or wearing away, a portion of the order of things which the ascendant classes in every part of Europe would have fondly wished to maintain in perpetuity, without one particle of surrender.

But though they cannot preserve its entireness, the manner in which it shall yield to modification is in a great measure at their command. And here is the important point on which all these observations are meant to bear. If a movement has really begun in the general popular mind of the nations, and if the principle of it is growing and insuppressible, so that it must in one manner or another ultimately prevail, what will the state be of any national community where it shall be an unenlightened, half-barbarous people that so prevails?—a people no better informed, perhaps, than to believe that all the hardship and distress endured by themselves and their forefathers were wrongs, which they suffered from the higher orders; than to ascribe to bad government, and the rapacity and selfishness of the rich, the very evils caused by inclement seasons; and than to assume it as beyond question, that the whole accumulation of their resentments, brought out into action at last, is only justice demanding and inflicting a retribution.

In such an event, what would not the superior orders be glad to give and forego, in compromise with principles, tempers, and demands, which they will know they should never have had to encounter, to the end of time, if, instead of spending their vast advantages on merely their own state and indulgence, they had applied them in a mode of operation and influence tending to improve, in every way, the situation and character of the people? It is true, that such a wild triumph of overpowering violence would necessarily be short. A blind turbulent monster of popular power never can for a long time maintain the domination of a political community. It would rage and riot itself out of breath and strength, succumb under some strong coercion of its own creating, and lie subject and stupified, till its spirit should be recovered and incensed for new commotion. But this impossibility of a very prolonged reign of confusion, would be little consolation for the classes against whose privileged condition the first tremendous eruption should have driven. It would not much cheer a man who should see his abode carried away, and his fields and plantations devastated, to tell him that the agent of this ruin was only a transient mountain torrent. A short prevalence of the overturning force would have sufficed for the subversion of the proudest, longest established state of privilege; and most improbable would it be, that those who lost it in the tumult, would find the new authority, of whatever shape or name it were, that would arise as that tumult subsided, either able or disposed to restore it. They might perhaps, (on a favourable supposition,) survive in personal safety, but in humiliated fortunes, to ruminate on their manner of occupying their former elevated situation, and of employing its ample means of power, a due share of which, exerted for the improvement of the general condition, both intellectual and civil, with an accompanying liberal yet gradual concession of privileges to the people, would have prevented the catastrophe.

Let us urge then, that a zealous endeavour to render it absolutely impossible that, in any change whatever, the destinies of a nation should fall under the power of an ignorant infuriated multitude, may take place of the presumption that there *is* no great change to be ever effected by the progressive and conscious importance of the people; a presumption than which nothing can appear more like infatuation, when we look at the recent scenes and present temperament of the moral world. Lay hold on the myriads of juvenile spirits, before they have time to grow up through ignorance into a reckless hostility to social order; train them to sense and good morals; inculcate the principles of religion, simply and solemnly *as* religion, as a thing directly of divine dictation, and not as if its authority were chiefly in virtue of human institutions; let the higher orders generally make it evident to the multitude that they are desirous to raise them in value, and promote their happiness; and then *whatever* the demands of the people as a body, thus improving in understanding and the sense of justice, shall come to be, and *whatever* modification their preponderance may ultimately enforce on the great social arrangements, it will be infallibly certain that there never *can* be a love of disorder, an insolent anarchy, a prevailing spirit of revenge and devastation.

Such a conduct of the ascendant ranks would, in this nation at least, secure that, as long as the world lasts, there never would be any formidable commotion, or violent sudden changes. All those modifications of the national economy to which an improving people would aspire and would deserve to obtain, would be gradually accomplished, in a manner by which no party would be wronged, and all would be the happier.*

* The considerations in the latter part of this section (so plainly on the surface of the subject that they would occur to any thoughtful and observant man) have been verified in part by the course of events in our country, since the time they were written. At that time the superior, and till then irresistibly and invariably predominant, portion of the community, felt themselves in perfect security against any comprehensive and radical change within the ensuing twelve or fourteen years. There might indeed be one or two subordinate matters in the established national system in which they might deem it not unlikely that the advocates and labourers for innovation would be successful; but such an amount of innovation did not come within the view of even a feverish dream. Any man who should have predicted, especially, the recent greatest achievement against the inveterate system,* would have been laughed at as an incorrigible visionary; so proudly confident were they that the structure would be kept compact and impregnable in all its essential parts, by the cement of ancient institution, national veneration, opulence, and the inherence of actual power, possessed from generation to generation.

In the next place, they were obstinately resolute against all material concessions. When at intervals the complaints, claims, and remonstrances of the people sought to be heard, they treated them as unreasonable, absurd, factious; and asserted that none of the good sense and right feeling of the nation went that way. They declared that the existing order of things was on the whole so superlatively excellent that, if there were, perhaps, any trifling defects, it were far better to let them alone than to presume to touch with an innovating hand the integrity of so noble a system, the admiration and envy of all the world. As it was, it had "worked well" for our happiness and glory; and who could say, if a tampering of alteration were once suffered to begin, where it might end? Order the people to be quiet; let their factious demands and seditious movements be promptly and firmly repressed by authority; and they would sink into insignificance and silence. To think of such a thing as condescending to conciliate by moderate concessions

* The Reform Bill.

would be weakness, and might eventually bring a hazard which otherwise could have no existence.

And now for the consequence: the popular spirit, thus set at nought in present account and in calculation for the future, was discouraged from active outward manifestation, by the inveterate, perfectly organized, and, for the present, resistless domination. But under the pressure of wide-spread and unabating grievance, which quickened and envenomed every sentiment previously entertained regarding the rights and wrongs of the people, it was gradually acquiring, throughout the country, a more determinate sense of being absolved from all submissive respect toward the ascendant party, a more entire conviction of its right to vindicate its claims in any manner that should become practicable, and a hostility, but the more deep and intense for its being kept under by despondency of present success, against those who were rejecting and contemptuously defying those claims. It wanted, then, only some occurrence that should present a possibility and a hope of success to burst out in sudden ardour. It was thus in collective power and readiness for action, when several events of prodigious excitement came close together; and then, like a stream in one of the Swiss valleys, dammed up by a mound of earth or ice fallen across, to a lake, deepening without noise till its vast weight breaks away the obstruction with a tremendous tumult, the popular will bore down the aristocratic embankment, consolidated through so many years or ages. The overpowered party found the consequence of their obstinate and *entire* resistance; and had to reflect with unmixed mortification how much less than they had lost, and without mitigating by the loss the hostile feeling of those who had taken it from them, would have been received with gratitude if yielded in the way of gradual voluntary concession. Happily the change was not left to be accomplished by physical force, as all such changes must be in purely despotic states; but the people fully believe that they chiefly owe the forced surrender to the alarm which their demonstrations excited lest they should bring the question ere long to that arbitrement.

But in the last place, there is a deplorable circumstance, attending this sudden rising of the popular spirit into power, and which throws a strong light on the criminal infatuation of a State that suffers the commonalty of its citizens to remain grossly uncultivated and uncivilized—perhaps even fancies it sees in that ignorance a main security for its own stability. The fact is, that the people have acquired their power and privileges, before they are (speaking as to many of them) qualified for a wise and useful exercise of them. A large proportion of those who are now brought into what may be called political existence have grown up so destitute of all means and habits for a right use of their minds, that their notions, wishes, expectations, and determinations, respecting public interests, will exemplify any thing rather than a competent judgment. And the proportion so raised is but perhaps a minor part of the multitude in which the popular spirit is embodied and vehemently excited. Great numbers on a lower level, and having no formal political capacity to act in, are nevertheless pervaded by a spirit which will bring the rude impulse of mass and combination into the movement of the popular will.

If alarmed at such a view, will not they who have so long held the sovereign control over the national economy feel the bitterest regret that it had not been given them to obviate the possible dangers of such a crisis and such a change, or rather to prevent such a crisis and a change so abrupt, by exertions in every way, and on the widest scale, to rescue the people from their ignorance and barbarism, instead of trusting to it for an uncontested undisturbed continuance of their own domination? But they scorned the idea, if it ever occurred, that the many-headed, many-handed "monster," (so named in the dialect of some of them,) after lying prône, and inert, and submissive, from time immemorial, should at last become instinct with spirit, and rise up roaring in defiance of their power.

It is now for them to consider whether, by maintaining a temper and attitude of sullen, vindictive, pugnacious alienation from the people, they shall wilfully aggravate whatever injurious consequences may be threatened by so sudden a revolution; or endeavour to intercept them by giving their best assistance to every plan and expedient for rescuing the lower orders from the curse and calamity of ignorance and debasement. Other remedial measures, besides that of education, are imperiously demanded by the miserable and formidable condition of the populace, but no other, nor all others together, can avail without it.

Since the date of the above note, the spirit and policy of the ascendant class have been just that which a philanthropist would have deprecated, and a cynic predicted.

Their mortal chagrin at the acquisition by the people of a new political rank, an event by which they, (the ascendant class) had for a while appeared amazed and stunned, has soon recovered to a prodigious activity of device and exertion to nullify that rightful acquisition. For this purpose have been brought into play, on the widest scale, that of the whole kingdom, all the means and resources of wealth, station, and power; with the utmost recklessness of equity, honour, and even humanity; deluding the ignorant, corrupting the venal, and intimidating and punishing the conscientious: insomuch that the nominally conceded right or privilege is practically reduced to an inconsiderable proportion of its pre-estimated worth; while aristocratic tyranny has rendered it to many of the most deserving to possess it no better than an inflicted grievance. One important measure for the improvement of the condition of the lower orders has been effected, because the anti-popular party saw it advantageous also to their own interests. But for the general course of their policy, we have witnessed a systematic determination to frustrate measures framed in recognition of the rights and wants of the people. As to their education, it continues abandoned to the efforts and totally inadequate means of private individuals and societies; except a comparative trifle from the state, not so much for the whole nation for the whole year as the cost of some useless, gaudy, barbaric pageant of one day.—It is evident the predominant portion of the higher classes trouble themselves very little about the mental condition of the populace. It is even understood that a chief obstacle in the way of any comprehensive legislation on the subject is found or apprehended in the repugnance of those classes to any liberal scheme: any scheme that, aiming simply at the general good, should boldly set aside invidious restrictions and a jealous parsimonious limitation; a scheme that should not work in subjection to the mean self-interest of this party or that, but for the one grand purpose of raising millions from degradation into rationa existence.

SECTION V.

The most serious form of the evil caused by a want of mental improvement, is that which is exposed to us in its consequences with respect to the most important concern of all, Religion. This has been briefly adverted to in a former part of these descriptive observations. But the subject seems to merit a more amplified illustration, and may be of sufficient interest to excuse some appearance of repetition. The special view in which we wish to place it, is that of *the inaptitude of uncultivated minds for receiving religious instruction.*—But first, a slight estimate may be attempted of the actual state of religious notions among our uneducated population.

Some notion of such a concern, something different in their consciousness from the absolute negation of the idea, something that faintly responds to the terms which would be used by a person conversing with them, in the way of questioning them on the subject, may be presumed to exist in the minds of all who are advanced a considerable way into youth, or come to mature age, in a country where all are familiar with several of the principal terms of theology, and have the monitory spectacle of edifices for religious use, on spots appointed also for the interment of the dead. If this sort of measured caution in the assumption seem bordering on the ridiculous, we would recommend those who would smile at it to make some little experiments. Let them insinuate themselves into the company of some of the innumerable rustics who have grown up destitute of every thing worth calling education; or of the equally ill-fated beings in the alleys, precincts, and lower employments of towns. With due management to avoid the abruptness and judicial formality, which would preclude a communicative disposition, they might take occasion to introduce remarks tending, without the express form of questions in the first instance, to draw out the thoughts of some of these persons respecting God, Jesus Christ, the human soul, the invisible world. And the answers would often put them to a stand to conceive, under what suspension of the laws of rational existence the utterers could have been passing so many years in the world. These answers might dispel as by a sudden shock the easy and contented assurance, if so unknowing a notion had been entertained, that almost all the people *must*, in one way or another, have become decently apprised of a few first principles of religion; that this *could* not have failed to be the case in what was expressly constituted a great christian community, with an obligation upon it, that none of its members should be left destitute of the most essential requisite to their well-being. This agreeable assurance would vanish, like a dream interrupted, at the spectacle thus presented, of persons only not quite as devoid of those first principles, after living eighteen, thirty, forty, or twice forty years, under the superintendence of that community, as if they had been the aboriginal rovers of the American forests, or natives of unvisited coral-built spots in the ocean.

If these examiners were to prosecute the investigation widely, and with an effect on their sentiments correspondent to the enlarging disclosure of facts, they would find themselves fallen into a very altered estimate of this our christian tract of the earth. A fancied sunshine, spread over it before, would have faded away. From appearing to them, according to an accustomed notion, peculiarly auspicious, as if almost by some virtue of its climate, to the growth of religious intelligence in the minds of the people, it might come to be regarded as favourable to the development of *all things rather than that.* Plants and trees, the diversity of animal forms and powers, the human frame, the features enlarging or enlarged to manhood in the younger persons looked at by the supposed examiner while answering his questions, with their passions also, and prevailing dispositions,—see how all things can unfold themselves in our territory, and grow and enlarge to their completeness,—except the ideas of the human soul relating to the Almighty, and to the grand purpose of its own existence!

The supposed answers would in many instances betray, that any thought of God at all was of very rare occurrence, the idea having never become strongly associated with any thing beheld in the whole creation. We should think it probable, as we have said before, that with many, while in health, weeks or months often pass away without this idea being once so presented as to fix the mind in attention to it for one moment of time. If they could be set to any such task as that of retracing, at the end of the days or the weeks, the course of their thoughts, to recollect what particulars in the series had struck the most forcibly and staid the longest, it may be suspected that *this* idea, thus impressively apprehended, would be as rare a recollection as that of having seen a splendid meteor. Yet during that space of time, their thoughts, such as they were, shall have run through thousands of changes; and even the name of God may have been pronounced by them a multitude of times, in jocularity or imprecation. Thus there is a broad easy way to atheism through thoughtless ignorance, as well as a narrow and difficult one through subtle speculation.

But that idea of God which has, by some means, found its way into their understandings, to abide there so nearly in silence and oblivion,—what is it, when some direct call does really evoke it? It is generally a gross approximation of the conception of the Infinite Being to the likeness of man. If what they have heard of his being a Spirit, has indeed some little effect in prevention of the total debasement of the idea, it prevents it rather by confusion than by magnificence. It may somewhat restrain and baffle the tendency of the imagination to a direct degrading definition; but it does so by a dissolution of the idea as into an attenuated cloud. And ever and anon, this cloudy diffusion is again drawing in, and shaping itself toward an image, vast perhaps, and spectral, portentous across the firmament, but in some near analogy to the human mode of personality.

The divine attribute which is apprehended by them with most of an impression of reality, is a certain vastness of power. But, through the grossness of their intellectual atmosphere, this appears to them in the character of something prodigiously huge, rather than sublimely glorious.—As considered in his quality of moral judicial Governor, God is regarded by some of them as more disposed, than there is any reasonable cause, to be displeased with what is done in this world. But the far greater number have no prevailing sentiment that he takes any very vigilant account or concern.* And even those who entertain the more

* Some have no very distinct impression the one way or the other. Not very long since, a friend of the writer, in one of the

ungracious apprehension, have it not in sufficient force to make them, once in whole months, deliberately think it worth while to care what he may disapprove.

The notions that should answer to the doctrine of a Providence, are a confusion of some crude idea of a divine superintendence, with stronger fancies and impressions of luck and chance; a confusion of them not unaptly exemplified in a grave and well-meaning sentiment heard from a man in a temporal condition to be envied by many of his neighbours, "Providence must take its chance." And these are still further, and most uncouthly, confounded by the admixture of the ancient heathen notion of fate, reduced from its philosophy to its dregs. In many instances, however, this last obtains such a predominance, as to lessen the confusion, and withal to preclude, in a great measure, the sense of accountableness. In neither of these rude states of the understanding, (that which confounds Providence and chance, and that which sinks in dull

midland counties, fell into talk, on a Sunday, with a man who had been in some very plain violation of the consecrated character of the day. He seriously animadverted on this, adding, Don't you think God will be displeased at and punish such conduct? or words to that effect. The man, after a moment's consideration, answered, with unaffected cool simplicity, exactly thus: "That's according as how a takes it."

Numerous anecdotes of the same cast have been more recently heard; and among them that of a conversation with a thoughtless man, of worthless character, not in the lowest condition in society, and then consciously near death. The religious visitor represented to him the serious and alarming situation of a man on the point of going from a sinful life into the presence of God as a Judge. The man, with a sort of general acknowledgment that it was so, yet hoped that God would not be severe with him. But the visitor anxiously pressed upon him the consideration that God is a just Being, and judges by a holy law: to which at last the answer was, with little emotion, "Then God and I must fight it out as well as we can." The phrase, in his use of it, did not mean any thing of the nature of a hostile contest, but simply the *settling of an affair*, which he thought might be done without any great danger or trouble.

acquiescence to something obscurely imagined like fate,) is there any serious admission, at least during the enjoyment of health, of the duty or advantage of prayer.

The supposed examiner may endeavour to possess himself of the notions concerning the Redeemer of the world. They would be found, in numerous instances, amounting literally to no more than, that Jesus Christ was a worthy kind of person, (the word has actually been "gentleman," in more than one instance that we have heard from unquestionable testimony,) who once, somewhere, (these national Christians had never in their lives, thought of inquiring when or where,) did a great deal of good, and was very ill used by bad people. The people now, they think, bad as they may be, would not do so in the like case. Some of these persons may occasionally have been at church; and are just aware that his name often recurs in its services; they never considered why; but they have a vague impression of its repetition having some kind of virtue, perhaps rather in the nature of a spell.—The names of the four evangelists are by some held literally and technically available for such an use.

A few steps withdrawn from this thickest of the mental fog, there are many who are not entirely uninformed of something having been usually affirmed, by religious formularies and teachers, of Jesus Christ's being more than a man, and of his having done something of great importance toward preventing our being punished for our sins. This combination of a majestic superiority to the human nature, with a subsistence yet confessedly human, just passes their minds like a shape formed of a shadow, as one of the unaccountable things that may be as it is said, for what they know, but which they need not trouble themselves to think about.

As to the great things said to be done by him, to save men from being punished, they see indeed no necessity for such an expedient, but if it is so, very right, and so much the better; for between that circumstance in our favour, and God's being too good, after all that is said of his holiness and wrath, to be severe on such poor creatures, we must have a good chance of coming off safely at last. But multitudes of the miserably poor, however wicked, have a settled assurance of this coming off well at last, independently of anything effected for men by the Mediator: they shall be exempted, they believe, from any future suffering in consideration of their having suffered so much here. There is nothing, in the scanty creed of great numbers, more firmly held than this.

It is true, they believe that the most atrociously wicked must go to a state of punishment after death. They consider murderers, especially, as under this doom. But the offences so adjudged, according to any settled estimate they have of the demerit of bad actions, are comprised in a very short catalogue. At least it is short if we could take it exclusively of the additions made to it by the resentments of individuals. For each one is apt to make his own particular addition to it, of some offence which he would never have accounted so heinous, but that it has happened to be committed against *him*. We can recollect the exultation of sincere faith, seen mingling with the anger, of an offended man, while *predicting*, as well as imprecating, this retribution of some injury he had suffered; a real injury, indeed, yet of a kind which he would have held in small account had he only seen it done to another person.—As to the nature of that future punishment, the ideas of these neglected minds go scarcely at all beyond the images of corporal anguish, conveyed by the well-known metaphors. They have no impressive idea of the pain of remorse, and scarcely the faintest conception of an infelicity inflicted by the conscious loss of the Divine favour.

It is most striking to observe how almost wholly negative are their conceptions of that future happiness which must be *something*—but what?—as the necessary alternative of the evil they so easily assure themselves of escaping. The abstracted, contemplative, and elevated ideas of the celestial happiness are far above their apprehension; and indeed, though they were not, would be little attractive. And the more ordinary modes of representing it in religious discourse, (if they should ever have heard enough of such discourse to be acquainted with them,) are too uncongenial with their notions of pleasure to have a welcome, or abiding place, in their imagination or affections. Thus the soul, as to this great subject, is vacant and cold. And here the reflection again returns, what an inexpressible poverty of the mind there is, when the people have no longer a mythology, and yet have not obtained in its place any knowledge of the true religion. The martial vagrants of Scandinavia glowed with the vivid anticipations of Valhalla; the savages of the western continent had their animating visions of the "land of souls;" the modern Christian barbarians of England, who also expect to live after death, do not know what they mean by their phrase of "going to heaven."

Most of this class of persons think very little in any way whatever of the invisible spiritual economy. And some of them would be pleased with a still more complete exemption from such thought. For there are among them those who are liable to be occasionally affected with certain ghostly recognitions of something out of the common world. But it is remarkable how little these may contribute to enforce the salutary impressions of religion. For instance, a man subject to the terror of apparitions shall not therefore be in the smallest degree the less profane, except just at the time that this terror is upon him. A number of persons, not one of whom durst walk, alone, at midnight, round a lonely church, encompassed with graves, to which has perhaps lately been added that of a notoriously wicked man, will nevertheless, on a fine Sunday morning, form a row of rude idlers, standing in the road to this very church, to vent their jokes on the persons going thither to attend the offices of religion, and on the performers of those offices.

Such, as regarding religion, is the state out of which it is desired to redeem a multitude of the people of this land. Or rather we should say, it is sought to save a multitude from being consigned to it. For consider, in the next place, (what we wished especially to point at, in this most important article in the enumeration of the evils of ignorance,) consider what a fatal inaptitude for receiving the truths of religion is created by the neglect of training minds to the exercise of their faculties, and the possession of the elements of knowledge.

How inevitably it must be so, from the nature of the case!—There is a sublime economy of invisible realities. There is the Supreme Existence, an infinite and eternal Spirit. There are spiritual existences, that have kindled into brightness and power, from nothing, at his creating will. There is an universal government, omnipotent, all-wise, and righteous, of that Supreme Being over the creation. There is the immense tribe of human spirits, in a most peculiar and alarming predicament, held under eternal obligation of conformity to a law proceeding from the holiness of that Being, but perverted to a state of disconformity to it, and opposition to him. Next, there is a signal anomaly of moral government, the constitution of a new state of relation between the Supreme Governor and this alienated race, through a Mediator, who makes an atonement for human iniquity, and stands representative before Almighty Justice, for those who in grateful accordance to the mysterious appointment consign themselves to this charge. There are the several doctrines declaratory of this new constitution through all its parts. There is the view of religion in its operative character, or the doctrine of the application of its truths and precepts by a divine agency to transform the mind and rectify the life. And this solemn array of all the sublimest reality, and most important intelligence, is extending infinitely away beyond the sensible horizon of our present state to an invisible world, to which the spirits of men proceed at death for judgment and retribution, and with the prospect of living for ever.

Look at this scene of faith, so distinct, and stretching to such remoteness, from the field of ordinary things; of a subsistence which it is for intellect alone to apprehend; presenting objects with which intellect alone can hold converse. Look at this scene; and then consider, what manner of beings you are calling upon to enter into it by contemplation. Beings who have never learned to think at all. Beings who have hardly ever once, in their whole lives, made a real effort to direct and concentrate the action of their faculties on anything abstracted from the objects palpable to the senses; whose entire attention has been engrossed, from their infancy, with the common business, the low amusements and gratifications, the idle talk, the local occurrences, which formed the whole compass of the occupation, and practically acknowledged interests, of their progenitors. Beings who have never been made in the least familiar with even the matters of fact, those especially of the scripture history, by which religious truths have been expressed and illustrated in the substantial form of events, and personal characters. Beings who, in natural consequence of this unexercised and unfurnished condition of their understandings, will combine the utmost aversion to any effort of purely intellectual labour, with the especial dislike which it is in the human disposition to feel toward this class of subjects. What kind of ideas should you imagine to be raised in their minds, by all the words you might employ, to place within their intellectual vision some portion of this spiritual order of things,—even should you be able, which you often would not, to engage any effort of attention to the subject?—And yet we have heard this disqualification for receiving religious knowledge, in consequence of the want of early mental culture, made very light of by men whose pretensions to judgment had no less a foundation than an academical course and a consecrated profession. They would maintain, with every appearance of thinking so, that a very little, that the barest trifle, of regulated exercise of the mind in youth, would be enough for the common people as a preparation for gaining as much knowledge of religion as they could ever want; that any such thing as a practice of reading, (a practice of hazardous tendency), would be needless for the purpose, since they might gain a competence of that knowledge by attendance on the public ministration in the church. And there must have been a very recent acquiescence in a new fashion of opinion, if numbers of the same class of men would not, in honestly avowing their thoughts, say something not far different at this hour.

But the pretended facility of gaining a competence of religious knowledge by such persons on such terms, can only mean, that the smallest conceivable portion of it may suffice. For we may appeal to those pious and benevolent persons who have made the most numerous trials, for testimony to the inaptitude of uneducated people to receive that kind of instruction. You have visited, perhaps, some numerous family, or Sunday assemblage of several related families; to which you had access without awkward intrusion, in consequence of the acquaintance arising from near neighbourhood, or of little services you had rendered, or of the circumstance of any of their younger children coming to your charity schools. It was to you soon made sensible what a sterile blighted spot of rational nature you were in, by indications unequivocal to your perception, though, it may be, not easily reducible to exact description. And those indications were perhaps almost equally apparent in the young persons, in those advanced to the middle of life, and in those who were evidently destined not long to remain in it, the patriarch, perhaps, and the eldest matron, of the kindred company. You attempted by degrees, with all managements of art, as if you had been seeking to gain a favour for yourselves, to train into the talk some topic bearing toward religion; and which could be followed up into a more explicit reference to that great subject, without the abruptness which causes instant silence and recoil. We will suppose that the gloom of such a moral scene was not augmented to you, by the mortification of observing impatience of this suspension of their usual and favourite tenour of discourse, betrayed in marks of suppressed irritation, or rather by the withdrawing of one, and another, from the company. But it was quite enough to render the moments and feelings some of the most disconsolate you had ever experienced, to have thus immediately before you a number of rational beings as in a dark prison-house, and to feel the impotence of your friendly efforts to bring them out. Their darkness of ignorance infused into your spirit the darkness of melancholy, when you perceived that the fittest words you could think of, in every change and combination in which you could dispose them, failed to impart to their understanding, in the meaning you wanted to convey, the most elementary and essential ideas of the most momentous subject.

You thought again, perhaps, and again, Surely *this* mode of expression, or *this*, as it is in words not out of common usage, will define the thing to their apprehension. But you were forced to perceive that the common phraseology of the language, those words which make the substance of ordinary discourse on ordinary subjects, had not, for the understandings of these persons, a general applicableness. It seemed as if the mere elemental vehicle, (if we may so name it,) available indifferently for conveying all sorts of sense, except science, had become in its meaning special and exclusive for their own sort of topics. Their narrow associations had rendered it incapable of conveying sense to them on matters foreign to their habits. When used on a subject to which they were quite unaccustomed, it became like a stream which, though one and the same current, flows clear on the one side, and muddy (as we sometimes see for a space) on the other; and to them it was clear only at their own edge. And if thus even the plain popular language turned dark on their understandings when employed in explanation of religion, it is easy to imagine what had been the success of a more peculiarly theological phraseology, though it were limited to such terms as are of frequent use in the Bible.

You continued, however, the effort for a while. As

desirous to show you due civility, some of the persons, perhaps the oldest, would give assent to what you said, with some sign of acknowledgment of the importance of the concern. The assent would perhaps be expressed in a form meant and believed to be equivalent to what you had said. And when it gave an intelligible idea, it might probably betray the grossest possible misconception of the first principles of Christianity. It might be a crude formation from the very same substance of which some of the worst errors of popery are constituted; and might strongly suggest to you, in a glance of thought, how easily popery might have become the religion of ignorance; how naturally ignorance and corrupt feeling mixing with a slight vague notion of Christianity, would turn it into just such a thing as popery. You tried, perhaps, with repeated modifications of your expression, and attempts at illustration, to loosen the false notion, and to place the true one contrasted with it in such a near obviousness to the apprehension, that at least the difference should be seen, and (perhaps you hoped) a little movement excited to think on the subject, and make a serious question of it. But all in vain. The hoary subject of your too late instruction, (a spectacle reminding you painfully of the words which denominate the sign of old age "a crown of glory,") either would still take it that it came all to the same thing, or, if compelled to perceive that you really were trying to make him *unthink* his poor old notions, and learn something new and contrary, would probably retreat, in a little while, into a half sullen, half despondent silence, after observing, that he was too old, "the worse was the luck," to be able to learn about such things, which he never had, like you, the "scholarship" and the time for.

In several of the party you perceived the signs of

almost a total blank. They seemed but to be waiting for any trifling incident to take their attention, and keep their minds alive. Some one with a little more of listening curiosity, but without caring about the subject, might have to observe, that it seemed to him the same kind of thing that the methodist parson, (the term most likely to be used if any very serious and earnest christian instructor had appeared in the neighbourhood,) was lately saying in such a one's funeral sermon. It is too possible that one or two of the visages of the company, of the younger people especially, might wear, during a good part of the time, somewhat of a derisive smile, meaning, "What odd kind of stuff all this is;" as if they could not help thinking it ludicrously strange that any one should be talking of God, of the Saviour of mankind, the facts of the Bible, the welfare of the soul, the shortness and value of life, and a future account, when he might be talking of the neighbouring fair, past or expected, or the local quarrels, or the last laughable incident or adventure of the hamlet. It is particularly observable, that grossly ignorant persons are very apt to take a ludicrous impression from high and solemn subjects; at least when introduced in any other time or way than in the ceremonial of public religious service; when brought forward as a personal concern, demanding consideration every where, and which may be urged by individual on individual. You have commonly enough seen this provoke the grin of stupidity and folly. And if you asked yourselves, (for it were in vain to ask *them*,) why it produced this so perverse effect, you had only to consider that, to minds abandoned through ignorance to be totally engrossed by the immediate objects of sense, the grave assumption, and emphatic enforcement, of the transcendent importance of a wholly unseen and spiritual economy, has much the appearance and effect of a great lie attempted to be passed on them. You might indeed recollect also, that the most which some of them are likely to have learnt about religion, is the circumstance, that the persons professing to make it an earnest concern are actually regarded as fit objects of derision by multitudes, not of the vulgar order only, but including many of the wealthy, the genteel, the magisterial, and the dignified in point of rank.

Individuals of the most ignorant class may stroll into a place of worship, bearing their character so conspicuously in their appearance and manner as to draw the particular notice of the preacher, while addressing the congregation. It may be, that having taken their stare round the place, they go out, just, it may happen, when he is in the midst of a marked, prominent, and even picturesque illustration, perhaps from some of the striking facts or characters of the scripture history, which had not made the slightest ingress on their thoughts or imagination. Or they are pleased to stay through the service; during which his eye is frequently led to where several of them may be seated together. Without an appearance of addressing them personally, he shall be excited to direct a special effort toward what he surmises to be the state of their minds. He may in this effort acquire an additional force, emphasis, and pointedness of delivery; but especially his utmost mental force shall be brought into action to strike upon their faculties with vivid rousing ideas, plainly and briefly expressed. And he fancies, perhaps, that he has at least arrested their attention; that what is going from his mind is in some manner or other taking a place in theirs; when some inexpressibly trivial occurring circumstance shows him, that the hold he has on them is not of the strength of a spider's web. Those thoughts, those intellects, those souls, are instantly and wholly gone—from a representation of one of the awful visitations of divine judgment in the ancient world—a description of sublime angelic agency, as in some recorded fact in the Bible—an illustration of the discourse, miracles, or expiatory sorrows of the Redeemer of the world—a strong appeal to conscience on past sin—a statement, perhaps in the form of example, of an important duty in given circumstances—a cogent enforcement of some specific point as of most essential moment in respect to eternal safety;—from the attempted grasp, or supposed seizure, of any such subject, these rational spirits started away, with infinite facility, to the movements occasioned by the falling of a hat from a peg.

By the time that any semblance of attention returns, the preacher's address may have taken the form of pointed interrogation, with very defined supposed facts, or even real ones, to give the question and its principle as it were a tangible substance. Well; just at the moment when his questions converged to a point, which was to have been a dart of conviction striking the understanding, and compelling the common sense and conscience of the auditors to answer for themselves,—at that moment, he perceives two or three of the persons he had particularly in view begin an active whispering, prolonged with the accompaniment of the appropriate vulgar smiles. They may possibly relapse at length, through sheer dulness, into tolerable decorum; and the instructor not quite losing sight of them, tries yet again to impel some serious ideas through the obtuseness of their mental being. But he can clearly perceive, after the animal spirits have thus been a little quieted by the necessity of sitting still awhile, the signs of a stupid vacancy, which is hardly sensible that any thing is actually saying, and probably makes, in the case of some of the individuals, what is mentally but a slight transition to yawning and sleep.

Utter ignorance is a most effectual fortification to a bad state of the mind. Prejudice may perhaps be removed; unbelief may be reasoned with; even demoniacs have been compelled to bear witness to the truth; but the stupidity of confirmed ignorance not only defeats the ultimate efficacy of the means for making men wiser and better, but stands in preliminary defiance to the very act of their application. It reminds us of an account, in one of the relations of the French Egyptian campaigns, of the attempt to reduce a garrison posted in a bulky fort of mud. Had the defences been of timber, the besiegers might have set fire to and burnt them; had they been of stone, they might have shaken and ultimately breached them by the battery of their cannon; or they might have undermined and blown them up. But the huge mound of mud had nothing susceptible of fire or any other force; the missiles from the artillery were discharged but to be buried in the dull mass; and all the means of demolition were baffled.

The most melancholy of the exemplifications of the effect of ignorance, as constituting an incapacity for receiving religious instruction, have been presented to those who have visited persons thus devoid of knowledge in sickness and the approach to death. Supposing them to manifest alarm and solicitude, it is deplorable to see how powerless their understandings are, for any distinct conception of what, or why, it is that they fear, or regret, or desire. The objects of their apprehension come round them as vague forms of darkness, instead of distinctly exhibited dangers and foes, which they might steadily contemplate, and think how to escape or encounter. And how little does the benevolent instructor find it possible for him to do, when he applies his mind to the painful task of reducing this gloomy confused vision to the plain defined truth of their unhappy situation, set in order before their eyes.

He deems it necessary to speak of the most elementary principles—the perfect holiness and justice of God—the corresponding holiness and the all-comprehending extent of his law, appointed to his creatures—the absolute duty of conformity to it in every act, word, and thought—the necessary condemnation consequent on failure—the dreadful evil, therefore, of sin, both in its principle and consequences. God—perfect holiness—justice—law—universal conformity—sin—condemnation! Alas! the hapless auditor has no such sense of the force of terms, and no such analogical ideas, as to furnish the medium for conveying these representations to his understanding. He never had, at any time; and now there may be in his mind all the additional confusion, and incapacity of fixed attention, arising from pain, debility, and sleeplessness. All this therefore passes before him with a tenebrious glimmer; like lightning faintly penetrating to a man behind a thick black curtain.

The instructor attempts a personal application, endeavouring to give the disturbed conscience a rational direction, and a distinct cognizance. But he finds, as he might expect to find, that a conscience without knowledge has never taken but a very small portion of the man's habits of life under its jurisdiction; and that it is a most hopeless thing to attempt to send it back reinforced, to reclaim and conquer, through all the past, the whole extent of its rightful but never assumed dominion. So feeble and confined in the function of judgment through which it must see and act, it is especially incapable of admitting the monitor's estimate of the measure of guilt involved in omission, and in an irreligious state of the mind, as an exceedingly grave addition to the account of criminal action. The man is totally and honestly unable to conceive of the substantial guilt of any thing of which he can ask, what injury it has done to any body. This single point—whether positive harm has been done to any one—comprehends the whole essence and sum of the conscious accountableness of very ignorant people. Material wrong, *very* material wrong, to their fellow mortals, they have a conscience that they should not do; a conscience, however, which they would deem it hard to be obliged to maintain entire even to this confined extent; and which therefore admits some compromise and gives some license, with respect especially to any kind of wrong which has the extenuation, as they deem it, of being commonly practised in their class; and against which there is a sort of understanding that each one must take the best care he can of himself. At this confine, so undecidedly marked, of practical tangible wrong, these very ignorant persons lose the sense of obligation, and feel absolved from any further jurisdiction. So coarse and narrow a conscience as to what they *do*, is not likely to be refined and extended into a cognizance of what they *are*. As for a duty absolute in the nature of things, or as owing to themselves, in respect to their own nature, or as imposed by the Almighty—*that their minds should be in a certain prescribed state*—there does really require a perfectly new manner of the action of intellect to enable them to apprehend its existence. And this habitual insensibility to any jurisdiction over their internal state, now meets, in its consequences, the supposed instructor. In consideration of the vast importance of this part of a rational creature's accountableness, and partly, too, from a desire to avoid the invidiousness of appearing as a judicial censor of the sick man's practical conduct, he insists in an especial manner on this subject of the state within, endeavouring to expose that dark world by the light of religion to the sick man's conscience. But to give in an hour the *understanding* which it requires the discipline of many years to render competent! How vain the attempt! The man's sense of guilt fixes almost exclusively on something that has been improper in his practical courses. He professes to acknowledge the evil of this; and perhaps with a certain stress of expression; intended, by an apparent respondence to the serious emphasis which the monitor is laying on another part of the accountableness and guilt, to take him off from thus endeavouring, as it appears to the ignorant sufferer, to make him more of a sinner than there is any reason, so little can he conceive that it should much signify what his thoughts, tempers, affections, motives, and so forth, may have been. By continuing to press the subject, the instructor may find himself in danger of being regarded as having taken upon him the unkind office of inquisitor and accuser in his own name, and of his own will and authority.

When inculcating the necessity of repentance, he will perceive the indistinctness of apprehension of the difference between the horror of sin merely from dread of impending consequences, and an antipathy to its essential nature. And even if this distinction, which admits of easy forms of exemplification, should thus be rendered in a degree intelligible, the man cannot make the application. The instructor observes, as one of the most striking results of a want of disciplined mental exercise, an utter inability for self-inspection. There is before his eyes, looking at him, but a stranger to himself, a man on whose mind no other mind, except One, can shed a light of self-manifestation, to save him from the most fatal mistakes.

If the monitor would turn, (rather from an impulse to relieve the gloom of the scene, than from anything he sees of a hopeful approach toward a right apprehension of the austerer truths of religion), if he would turn his efforts, to the effect of directing on this dark spirit the benign rays of the Christian redemption, what is he to do for terms,—yes, for very terms? Mediator, sacrifice, atonement, satisfaction, faith; even the expression believing in Christ; merit of the death of Christ, acquittal, acceptance, justification:—he knows, or soon will find, that he is talking the language of an occult science. And he is forced down to such expedients of grovelling paraphrase, and humiliating analogy, that he becomes conscious that his method of endeavouring to make a divine subject comprehensible, is to divest it of its dignity, and reduce it, in order that it may not confound, to the rank of things which have not majesty enough to impress with awe. And after this has been done, to the utmost of his ability, and to the unavoidable weariness of his suffering auditor, he is distressed to think of the proportion between the insignificance of any ideas which this man's mind now possesses of the economy of redemption, and the magnitude of the interest in which he stands dependent on it. A symptom or assurance which should impart to the sick man a confidence of his recovery, would appear to him a far greater good than all that he can comprehend as offered to him from the Physician of the soul. Some crude sentiment, as, that he, "hopes Jesus Christ will stand his friend;" that it was very good of the Saviour to think of us; that he wishes he knew what to do to get his help: that Jesus Christ has done him good in other things, and he hopes he will now again at the last;*—such expressions will afford little to alleviate the gloomy feelings, with which the serious visiter descends from the chamber in which, perhaps, he may hear, a few days after, that the man he conversed with lies a dead body.

But such benevolent visiters have to tell of still more melancholy exemplifications of the effects of ignorance in the close of life. They have seen the neglect of early cultivation, and the subsequent estrangement from all knowledge and thinking, except about business and folly, result in such a stupefaction of mind, that irreligious and immoral persons, expecting no more than a few days of life, and not in a state of physical lethargy, were absolutely incapable of being alarmed at the near approach of death. They might not deny, nor in the infidel sense disbelieve, what was said to them of the awfulness of that event and its consequences; but they had actually never thought enough of death to have any solemn associations with the idea. And their faculties were become so rigidly shrunk up, that they could not now admit them; no, not while the portentous spectre was unveiling his visage to them, in near and still nearer approach; not when the element of another world was beginning to penetrate through the rents of their mortal tabernacle. It appeared that literally their thoughts *could not* go out from what they had been through life immersed in, to contemplate, with any realizing feeling, a grand change of being, expected so soon to come on them. They could not go to the fearful

* Such an expression as this would hardly have occurred but from recollection of fact, in the instance of an aged farmer, (the owner of the farm,) in his last illness. In the way of reassuring his somewhat doubtful hope that Christ would not fail him when now had recourse to, at his extreme need, he said, (to the writer,) "Jesus Christ has sent me a deal of good crops."

brink to look off. It was a stupor of the soul not to be awaked but by the actual plunge into the realities of eternity. In such a case the instinctive repugnance to death might be visible and acknowledged. But the feeling was, If it must be so, there is no help for it; and as to what may come after, we must take our chance. In this temper and manner, we recollect a sick man, of this untaught class, answering the inquiry how he felt himself, "Getting worse; I suppose I shall make a die of it." And some pious neighbours, earnestly exhorting him to solemn concern and preparation, could not make him understand, we repeat with emphasis, *understand* why there was occasion for any extraordinary disturbance of mind. Yet this man was not inferior to those around him in sense for the common business of life.

After a tedious length of suffering, and when death is plainly inevitable, it is not very uncommon for persons under this infatuation to express a wish for its arrival, simply as a deliverance from what they are enduring, without disturbing themselves with a thought of what may follow. "I know it will please God soon to release me," was the expresion to his religious medical attendant, of such an ignorant and insensible mortal, within an hour of his death, which was evidently and directly brought on by his vices. And he uttered it without a word, or the smallest indicated emotion, of penitence or solicitude; though he had passed his life in a neighbourhood abounding with the public means of religious instruction and warning.

When earnest, persisting, and seriously menacing admonitions, of pious visiters or friends, almost literally compel such unhappy persons to some precise recognition of the subject, their answers will often be faithfully representative, and a consistent completion, of their course through mental darkness, from childhood to the mortal hour. We recollect the instance of a wicked old man, who, within that very hour replied to the urgent admonitions by which a religious neighbour felt it a painful duty to make a last effort to alarm him, "What! do you believe that God can think of damning me because I may have been as bad as other folk; I am sure he will do no such thing: he is far too good for that."

We cannot close this detailed illustration of so gloomy a subject, without again adverting to a phenomenon as admirable as, unhappily, it is rare; and for which the observers who cannot endure mystery in religion, or religion itself, may go, if they choose, round the whole circle of their philosophy, and begin again, to find any adequate cause, other than the most immediate agency of the Almighty Spirit. Here and there an instance occurs, to the delight of the christian philanthropist, of a person brought up in utter ignorance and barbarian rudeness, and so continuing till late in life; and then at last, after such a length of time and habit has completed its petrifying effect, suddenly seized upon by a mysterious power, and taken, with an alarming and irresistible force, out of the dark hold in which the spirit has lain imprisoned and torpid, into the sphere of thought and feeling.

Occasion is taken this once more of adverting to such facts, not so much for the purpose of magnifying the nature, as of simply exhibiting the effect, of an influence that can breathe with such power on the obtuse intellectual faculties; which it appears, in the most signal of these instances, almost to create anew. It is exceedingly striking to observe how the contracted rigid soul seems to soften, and grow warm, and expand, and quiver with life. With the new energy infused, it painfully struggles to work itself into freedom, from the wretched contortion in which it has so long been fixed as by the impressed spell of some infernal magic. It is seen filled with a distressed and indignant emotion at its own ignorance; actuated with a restless earnestness to be informed; acquiring an unwonted pliancy of its faculties to thought; attaining a perception, combined of intelligence and moral sensibility, to which numerous things are becoming discernible and affecting, that were as non-existent before. It is not in the very extreme strength of their import that we employ such terms of description; the malice of irreligion may easily parody them into poetical excess; but we have known instances in which the change, the intellectual change, has been so conspicuous, within a brief space of time, that even an infidel observer must have forfeited all claim to be esteemed a man of sense, if he would not acknowledge,—This that you call divine grace, whatever it may really be, is the strangest awakener of faculties after all. And to a devout man, it is a spectacle of most enchanting beauty, thus to see the immortal plant, which has been under a malignant blast while sixty or seventy years have passed over it, coming out at length in the bloom of life.

We cannot hesitate to draw the inference, that if religion is so auspicious to the intellectual faculties, the cultivation and exercise of those faculties must be of great advantage to religion.

These observations on ignorance, considered as an incapacitation for receiving religious instruction, are pointed chiefly at that portion of the people, unhappily the largest, who are little disposed to attend to that kind of instruction. But we should notice its prejudicial effect on those of them to whom religion has become a matter of serious and inquisitive concern.

The preceding assertions of the efficacy of a strong religious interest to excite and enlarge the intellectual faculty will not be contradicted by observing, nevertheless, that in a dark and crude state of that faculty those well-disposed persons, especially if of a warm temperament withal, are unfortunately liable to receive delusive impressions and absurd notions, blended with religious doctrine and sentiment. It would be no less than plain miracle or inspiration, a more entire and specific superseding of ordinary laws than that which we have just been denominating "an immediate agency of the Almighty Spirit," if a mind left uncultivated all up through the earlier age, and perhaps far on in life, should not come to its new employment on a most important subject with a sadly defective capacity for judgment and discrimination. The situation reminds us of an old story of a tribe of Indians denominated "moon-eyed," who, not being able to look at things by the light of the sun, were reduced to look at them under the glimmering of the moon, by which light it is an inevitable circumstance of human vision to receive the images of things in perverted and deceptive forms.

Even in such an extremely rare instance as that above described, an example of the superlative degree of the animating and invigorating influence of religion on the uncultivated faculties, there would be visible some of the unfortunate consequences of the inveterate rudeness; a tendency, perhaps, to magnify some one thing beyond its proportionate importance; to adopt hasty conclusions; to entertain some questionable or erroneous principle because it appears to solve a difficulty, or perhaps falls in with an old prepossession; to make too much account of variable and transitory feelings; or to carry zeal beyond the limits of discretion. In examples of a lower order of the correction or reversal of the effects of ignorance by the influence of religion, the remains will be still more palpable. So that, while it is an unquestionable and gratifying fact, that among the uneducated subjects of genuine religion many are remarkably improved in the power and exercise of their reason; and while we may assume that *some* share of this improvement reaches to all who are really under this most beneficent influence in the creation,* it still is to be acknowledged of too many, who are in a measure, we may candidly believe, under the genuine efficacy of religion, that they have attained, through its influence, but so inferior a proportion of the improvement of intellect, that they can be well pleased with a great deal of absurdity of religious notions and language. But while we confess and regret that it is so, we should not overlook the causes and excuses that may be found for it, in unfortunate superaddition to their lack of education; partly in the natural turn of the mind, partly in extraneous circumstances. Many whose attention is in honest earnestness drawn to religion, are endowed by nature with so scanty an allotment of the thinking power, strictly so denominated, that it would have required high cultivation to raise them to the level of moderate understanding. There are some who appear to have constitutionally an invincible tendency to an uncouth fantastic mode of forming their notions. It is in the nature of others, that what-

* *Really* under this influence, we repeat, pointedly; for we justly put all others out of the account. It is nothing (as against this asserted influence on the intelligent faculty) that great numbers who may contribute to swell a public bustle about religion; who may run together at the call of whim, imposture, or insanity, assuming that name; who may acquire, instead of any other folly, a turn for talking, disputing, or ranting, about that subject; it is nothing, in short, that *any* who are not in real, conscientious seriousness the disciples of religion, can be shown to be no better for it, in point of improved understanding.

ever cultivation they might have received, it would still have been by their passions, rather than, in any due proportion, by their reason, that an important concern would have taken and retained hold of them. It may have happened to not a few, that circumstances unfavourable to the understanding were connected with the causes or occasions of their first effectual religious impressions. Some quaint cast in the exposition of the Christian faith, not essentially vitiating, but very much distorting and cramping it, or some peculiarity or narrow-mindedness of the teachers, may have conveyed their effect, to enter, as it were, at the door at the same moment that it was opened by the force of a solemn conviction, and to be retained and cherished ever after on the strength of this association. This may have tended to give an obliquity to the disciple's understanding, or to arrest and dwarf its growth; to fix it in prejudices instead of training it to judgments; or to dispense with its exercise by merging it in a kind of quietism; so that the proper tendency of religion to excite intellectual activity was partly overruled and frustrated. It is most unfortunate that thus there may be, from things casually or constitutionally associated with a man's piety, an influence operating to disable his understanding; as if there had been mixed with the incense of a devout service in the temple, a soporific ingredient which had the effect of closing the worshipper's eyes in slumber.

Now suppose all these worthy persons, with so many things of a special kind against them, to be also under the one great calamity of a neglected education, and is it any wonder that they can admit religious truths in shapes very strange and faintly enlightened; that they have an uncertain and capricious test of what is genuine, and not much vigilance to challenge plausible semblances; that they should be caught by some fanciful exhibition of a truth which would be of too intellectual a substance as presented in its pure simplicity; and should be ready to receive with approbation not a little of what is a heavy disgrace to the name of religious doctrine and ministration? Where is the wonder that crudeness, incoherence, and inconsistency of notions, should not disappoint and offend minds that have not, ten times since they came into the world, been compelled to form two ideas with precision and then compare them discriminately or combine them strictly, on any subject beyond the narrow scope of their ordinary pursuits? Where is the wonder, if many such persons take noise and fustian for a glowing zeal and a lofty elevation; if they mistake a wheedling cant for affectionate solicitude; if they defer to pompous egotism and dogmatical assertion, when it is so convenient a foundation for all their other faith to believe their teacher is an oracle? No marvel if they are delighted with whimsical conceits as strokes of discovery and surprise, and yet at the same time are pleased with common-place, and endless repetition, as an exemption from mental effort; and if they are gratified by vulgarity of diction and illustration, as bringing religion to the level where they are at home? Nay, if an artful pretender, or half-lunatic visionary, or some poor set of dupes of their own inflated self-importance, should give out that they are come into the world for the manifestation, at last, of true Christianity, which the divine revelation has failed, till their advent, to explain to any of the numberless devout and sagacious examiners of it,—what is there in the minds of the most ignorant class of persons desirous to secure the benefits of religion, that can be securely relied on to certify them, that they shall not forego the greatest blessing ever offered to them by setting at nought these pretensions?

It is grievous to think there should be an active extensive currency of a language conveying crudities, extravagances, arrogant dictates of ignorance, pompous nothings, vulgarities, catches of idle fantasy, and impertinences of the speaker's vanity, as religious instruction, to assemblages of ignorant people. But then for the means of depreciating that currency, so as to drive it at last out of circulation? The thing to be wished is, that it were possible to put some strong coercion on the *minds* (we deprecate all other restraint) of the teachers; a compulsion to feel the necessity of information, sound sense, disciplined thinking, the correct use of words, and an honest careful purpose to make the people wiser. There are signs of amendment, certainly; but while the passion of human beings for notoriety lasts, (which will be yet some time,) there will not fail to be men, in any number required, ready to exhibit in religion, in any manner in which the people are willing to be pleased with them. Let us, then, try the inverted order, and endeavour to secure that those who assemble to be taught, shall already have learnt so much, *by other means*, that no professed teacher shall feel at liberty to treat them as an unknowing herd. But by what other means, except the discipline of the best education possible to be given to them, and the subsequent voluntary self-improvement to which it may be hoped that such an education would often lead?

We cannot dismiss this topic, of the unhappy effect of extreme ignorance on persons religiously disposed, in rendering them both liable and inclined to receive their ideas of the highest subject in a disorderly, perverted, and debased form, mixed largely with other men's folly and their own, without noticing with pleasure an additional testimony to the connexion between genuine religion and intelligence. It arises from the fact, apparent to any discriminating observer, that as a *general* rule the most truly pious of the illiterate disciples of religion, those who have the most of its devotional feeling and its humility, do certainly manifest more of the operation of judgment in their religion than is evinced by those of less solemn and devout sentiment. The former will unquestionably be found, when on the same level as to the measure of natural faculty and the want of previous cultivation, to show more discernment, to be less captivated by noise and extravagance, and more intent on obtaining a clear comprehension of that faith, which they feel it is but a reasonable obligation that they should endeavour to understand, if they are to repose on it their most important hopes.

SECTION VI.

THUS it has been attempted, we fear with too much prolixity and repetition, to describe the evils attendant on a neglected state of the minds of the people. The representation does not comprehend all those even of magnitude and prominence; but it displays that portion of them which is the most serious and calamitous, as being the effect which the people's ignorance has on their moral and religious interests. And we think no one who has attentively surveyed the state and character of the lower orders of the community, in this country, will impute exaggeration to the picture. It is rather to be feared that the reality is of still darker shade; and that a more strikingly gloomy exhibition might be formed, by such a process as the following:—That a certain number of the most observant of the philanthropic persons, who have had most intercourse with the classes in question, for the purposes of instruction, charitable aid, or perhaps of furnishing employment, should relate the most characteristic circumstances and anecdotes within their own experience, illustrative of this mental and moral condition; and that these should be arranged, without any comment, under the respective heads of the preceding sketch, or of a more comprehensive enumeration. Each of them might repeat, in so many words, the most notable things he has heard uttered as disclosing the notions entertained of the Deity, or any part of religion; or those which have been formed of the ground and extent of duty and accountableness; or the imaginations respecting the termination of life, and a future retribution. They might relate the judgments they have heard pronounced on characters and particular modes of conduct; on important events in the world; on any thing, in short, which may afford a test of the quality and compass of uncultivated thought. Let the recital include both the expressions of individual conception, and those of the most current maxims and common places; and let them be the sayings of persons in health, and of those languishing and dying. Then let there be produced a numerous assortment of characteristic samples of practical conduct; conduct not simply proceeding, in a general way, from wrong disposition, but bearing the special marks of the cast and direction which that disposition takes through extreme ignorance: samples of action that is wrong because the actor cannot think right, or does not think at all. The assemblage of things thus recounted, when the actual circumstances were also added of the wretchedness corresponding and inseparable, would constitute such an exhibition of fact, as any description of those evils in general terms would incur the charge of rhetorical excesses in attempting to rival. We can well imagine that some of these persons, of large experience, may have accompanied us through the foregoing series of illustrations, with a feeling that they could have displayed the subject with a far more striking prominence.

And now again the mortifying reflection comes on us, that all this is the description of too probably the major part of the people of our own nation. Of this nation, the theme of so many lofty strains of panegyric; of this nation, stretching forth its powers in ambitious enterprise, with infinite pride and cost, to all parts of the globe;—just as if a family were seen eagerly intent on making some new appropriation, or going out to maintain some competition or feud with its neighbours, or mixing perhaps in the strife of athletic games, or drunken frays, at the very time that several of its members are lying dead in the house. So that the fame of the nation resounded, and its power made itself felt, in every clime, it was not worth a consideration that a vast proportion of its people were systematically consigned, through ignorance and the irreligion and depravity inseparable from it, to a wretchedness on which that fame was the bitterest satire. It is matter for never-ending amazement, that during one generation after another, the presiding wisdom in this chief of Christian and Protestant States, should have thrown out the living strength of that state into almost every mode of agency under heaven, rather than that of promoting the state itself to the condition of a happy community of cultivated beings. What stupendous infatuation, what disastrous ascendency of the Power of Darkness, that this energy should have been sent forth to pervade all parts of the world in quest of objects, to inspirit and accomplish innumerable projects, political and military, and to lavish itself, even to exhaustion and fainting at its vital source, on every alien interest; while here at home, so large a part of the social body was in a moral and intellectual sense dying and putrefying over the land. And it was thus perishing for want of the vivifying principle of knowledge, which one-fifth part of this mighty amount of exertion would have been sufficient to diffuse into every corner and cottage in the island. Within its circuit, a countless multitude were seen passing away their mortal existence little better, in any view, than mere sentient shapes of matter, and by their depravity immeasurably worse; and yet this hideous fact had not the weight of the very dust of the balance, in the deliberation whether a grand exertion of the national vigour and resource could have any object so worthy, (with God for the Judge,) as some scheme of foreign aggrandizement, some interference in remote quarrels, an avengement by anticipation of wrongs pretended to be foreseen, or the obstinate prosecution of some fatal career, begun in the very levity of pride, by a decision in which some perverse individual or party in ascendency had the influence to obtain a corrupt, deluded, or forced concurrence.

The national *honour*, perhaps, would be alleged, in a certain matter of punctilio, for the necessity of undertakings of incalculable consumption, by men who could see no national *disgrace* in the circumstance that several millions of the persons composing the nation could not read the ten commandments. Or the national *safety* has been pleaded to a similar purpose, with a rant or a gravity of patriotic phrases, upon the appearance of some slight threatening symptoms; and the wise men so pleading, would have scouted as the very madness of fanaticism any dissuasion that should have advised,—"Do you, instead, apply your best efforts, and the nation's means, to raise the barbarous population from their ignorance and debasement, and you really may venture some little trust in Divine Providence for the nation's safety meanwhile."

If a contemplative and religious man, looking back through little more than a century, were enabled to take, with an adequate comprehension of intellect, the sum and value of so much of the astonishing course of the national exertions of this country, as the Supreme Judge has put to the criminal account of pride and ambition; and if he could then place in contrast to the transactions on which that mighty amount has been expended, a sober estimate of what so much exerted vigour *might* have accomplished for the intellectual and moral exaltation of the people, it could not be without an emotion of horror that he would say, Who is to be accountable, who *has been* accountable, for this difference? He would no longer wonder at any plagues and judgments which may have been inflicted on such a state. And he would solemnly adjure all those, especially, who profess in a peculiar manner to feel the power of the Christian Religion, to beware how they implicate themselves, by avowed or even implied approbation, in what must be a matter of fearful account before the highest tribunal. If some such persons, of great merit and influence, honoured performers of valuable public services in certain departments, have habitually given, in a public capacity, this approbation, he would urge it on their consciences, in the evening of life, to consider whether, in the prospect of that tribunal, they have not one duty yet to perform,—to throw off from their minds the servility to party associations, to estimate as Christians, about to retire from the scene, the actual effects on this nation of a policy which might have been nearly the same if Christianity had been extinct; and then to record a solemn, recanting, final protest against a system to which they have concurred in the profane policy of degrading that religion itself into a party.

Any reference made to such a prospect implies, that there is attributed to those who can feel its seriousness a state of mind perfectly unknown to the generality of what are called public men. For it is notorious that, to the mere working politician, there is nothing on earth that sounds so idly or so ludicrously as a reference to a judgment elsewhere and hereafter, to which the policy and transactions of statesmen are to be carried. If the Divine jurisdiction would yield to contract its comprehension, and retire from all the ground over which a practical infidelity heedlessly disregards or deliberately rejects it, how large a province it would leave free! If it be assumed that the province of national affairs *is* so left free, on the pretence that they *cannot* be transacted in faithful conformity to the christian standard, that plea is reserved to be tried in the great account, when the responsibility for them shall be charged. For assuredly there will be persons found, to be summoned forth as accountable for that conduct of states which we are contemplating. Such a moral agency could not throw off its responsibility into the air, to be dissipated and lost, like the black smoke of forges or volcanoes. This one grand thing (the improvement of the people) left undone, while a thousand arduous things have been done or strenuously endeavoured, cannot be less than an awful charge *somewhere.* And where?—but on all who have voluntarily concurred and cooperated in systems and schemes, which could deliberately put *such* a thing last? Last! nay, not even that; for they have, till recently, as we have seen, thrown it almost wholly out of consideration. A long succession of men invested with ample power are gone to this audit. How many ot those who come after them will choose to proceed on the same principles, and meet the same award?

We were supposing a thoughtful man to draw out to his view a parallel and contrast, exhibiting, on the one side, the series of objects on which, during several ages, an enormous exertion of the national energy has been directed; and on the other, those improvements of the people which might have been effected by so much of that exertion as he deems to have been worse than wasted. In this process, he might often be inclined to single out particular parts in the actual series, to be put in special contrast over against the possibilities on the opposite line. For example; there may occur to his view some inconsiderable island, the haunt of fatal diseases, and rendered productive by means involving the most flagrant iniquity; an iniquity which it avenges by opening a premature grave for many of his countrymen, and by being a moral corrupter of the rest. Such an infested spot, nevertheless, may have been one of the most material objects of a widely destructive war, which has in effect sunk incalculable treasure in the sea, and in the sands, ditches, and fields of plague-infested shores; with a dreadful sacrifice of blood, life, and all the best moral feelings and habits. Its possession, perhaps, was the chief prize and triumph of all the grand exertion, the equivalent for all the cost, misery, and crime.

Or there may occur to him the name of some fortress, in a less remote region, where the Christian nations seem to have vied with one another which of them should deposit the greatest number of victims, securely kept in the charge of death, to rise and testify for them, at the last day, how much they have been governed by the peaceful spirit of their professed religion. He reads that his countrymen, conjoined with others, have battled round this fortress, wasting the vicinity, but richly manuring the soil with blood. They have cooperated in hurling upon the abodes of thousands of inhabitants within its walls, a thunder and lightning incomparably more destructive than those of nature; and have put fire and earthquake under the fortifications; shouting, "to make the welkin ring," at sight of the consequent ruin and chasm, which have opened an entrance for hostile rage, or compelled an immediate submission, if, indeed, it would then be accepted to disappoint that rage of its horrible consummation. They have taken the place,—and they have surrendered it. The next year perhaps they have taken it again; to be again at last given up, on compulsion or in compromise, to the very same party to which it had belonged previously to all this destructive commotion. The operations in this local and very narrow portion of the grand affray of monarchies, he may calculate to have cost his country as much as the amount earned by the toils of half the life of all the inhabitants of one of its populous towns; setting aside from his view the more portentous part of the account, —the carnage, the crimes, and the devastation perpetrated on the foreign tract, the place of abode of people who had little interest in the contest, and no power to prevent it. And why was all this? He may not be able to divest himself of the principles that should rule the judgment of a moralist and a Christian, in order to think like a statesman; and therefore may find no better reason than that, when despots would quarrel, Britain must fancy itself called upon to take the occasion to prove itself a great power, by bearing a high hand amidst their rivalries; or must seize the opportunity of revenging some trivial offence of one of them; though this should be at the expense of having the scene at home chequered between children learning little more than how to curse, and old persons dying without knowing how to put words together to pray.

The question may have been, in one part of the world or another, which of two wicked individuals of the same family, competitors for sovereign authority, should be actually invested with it, they being equal in the qualifications and dispositions to make the worst use of it. And the decision of such a question was worthy that England should expend what remained of her depressed strength from previous exertions of it in some equally meritorious cause.

Or the supposed reviewer of our national history may find, somewhere in his retrospect, that a certain brook or swamp in a wilderness, or a stripe of waste, or the settlement of boundaries in respect to some insignificant traffic, was difficult of adjustment between jealous, irritated, and mutually incursive neighbours; and therefore, national honour and interest equally required that war should be lighted up by land and sea, through several quarters of the globe. Or a dissension may have arisen upon the matter of some petty tax on an article of commerce: an absolute will had been rashly signified on the claim; pride had committed itself, and was peremptory for persisting; and the resolution was to be prosecuted through a wide tempest of destruction, protracted perhaps many years; and only ending in the forced abandonment by the leading power concerned, of infinitely more than war had been made in the determination not to forego; and after an absolutely fathomless amount of every kind of cost, financial and moral, in this progress to final frustration.—But there would be no end of recounting facts of this order.

Now the comparative estimator has to set against the extended rank of such enormities the forms of imagined good, which might, during the ages of this retrospect, have been realized by an incomparably less exhausting series of exertion, an exertion, indeed, continually renovating its own resources. Imagined good, we said;—alas! the evil stands in long and awful display on the ground of history; the hypothetical good presents itself as a dream; with this circumstance only of difference from a dream, that there is resting on the conscience of beings somewhere still existing, a fearful accountableness for its not having been a reality.

For such an *island*, as we have supposed our comparer to read of, he can look, in imagination, on a space of proportional extent in any part of his native country, taking a district as a detached section of a general national picture. And he can figure to himself the result, resplendent upon this tract, of so much energy, there beneficently expended, as that island had cost: an energy, we mean *equivalent in measure*, while put forth in the infinitely different *mode* of an exertion, by all appropriate means, to improve the reason, manners, morals, and with them the physical condition of the people. What a prevalence of intelligence, what a delightful civility of deportment, what represssion of the more gross and obtrusive forms of vice, what domestic decorum, attentive education of the children, appropriateness of manner and readiness of apprehension in attendance on public offices of religion, sense and good order in assemblages for the assertion and exercise of civil and political rights! All this he can imagine as the possible result.

We were supposing his attention fixed awhile on the recorded operations against some strongly fortified place, in a region marked through every part with the traces and memorials of the often renewed conflicts of the Christian states. And we suppose him to make a collective estimate of all kinds of human ability exerted around and against that particular devoted place; an estimate which divides this off as a portion of the whole immense quantity of exertion, expended by his country in all that region in the campaigns of a war, or of a century's wars. He may then again endeavour, by a rule of equivalence, to conceive the same amount of exertion in quite another way; to imagine human forces equal in *quantity* to all that putting forth of strength, physical, mental, and financial, for annoyance and destruction, expended instead, in the operation of effecting the utmost improvement which they *could* effect, in the mental cultivation and the morals of the inhabitants of one large town in his own country.

In figuring to himself the channels and instrumentality, through which this great stream of energy might have passed into this operation, on a detached spot of his country, he will soon have many specific means presented to his view: schools of the most perfect appointment, in every section and corner of the town; a system of friendly but cogent dealing with all the people of inferior condition, relatively to the necessity of their practical accordance to the plans of education;* an exceedingly copious supply, for individual possession, of the best books of elementary knowledge; accompanied, as we need not say, by the sacred volume; a number of assortments of useful and pleasing books for circulation, established under strict order, and with appointments of honorary and other rewards to those who gave evidence of having made the best use of them; a number of places of resort where various branches of the most generally useful and attainable knowledge and arts should be explained and applied, by every expedient of familiar, practical, and entertaining illustration, admitting a degree of co-operation by those who attended to see and hear; and an abundance of commodious places for religious instruction on the sabbath, where there should be wise

* It is here confidently presumed, that any man who looks, in a right state of his senses, at the manner in which the children are still brought up, in many parts of the land, will hear with contempt any hypocritical protest against so much interference with the discretion, the liberty of parents;—the discretion, the liberty, forsooth, of bringing up their children a nuisance on the face of the earth.

and zealous men to impart it. Our speculator has a right to suppose a high degree of these qualifications in his public teachers of religion, when he is to imagine a parallel in this department to the skill and ardour displayed in the supposed military operations. He may add as subsidiary to such an apparatus, every thing of magistracy and municipal regulation; a police, vigilant and peremptory against every cognizable neglect and transgression of good order; a resolute breaking up of all haunts and rendezvous of intemperance, dishonesty and other vice; and the best devised and administered institutions for correcting and reclaiming those whom education had failed to preserve from such depravity; and besides all this, there would be a great variety of undefinable and optional activity of benevolent and intelligent men of local influence.

Under so auspicious a combination of discipline, he will not indeed fancy, in his transient vision, that he beholds Athens revived, with its bright intelligence all converted to minister to morality, religion, and happiness; but he will, in sober consistency, we think, with what is known of the relation of cause and effect, imagine a place far surpassing any actual town or city on earth. And let it be distinctly kept in view, that to reduce the ideal exhibition to reality, he is not dreaming of means and resources out of all human reach, of preternatural powers, discovered gold-mines, grand feats of genius. He is just supposing to have been expended, on the population of the town, a measure of exertion and means equal, (as far as agencies in so different a form and direction can be brought to any rule of comparative estimate) to what has been expended by his country in investing, battering, undermining, burning, taking, and perhaps retaking, one particular foreign town, in one or several campaigns.

If he should perchance be sarcastically questioned, how he can allow himself in so strange a conceit as that of supposing such a quantity of forces concentrated to act in one exclusive spot, while the rest of the country remained under the old course of things; or in such an absurdity as that of fancying that *any* quantity of those forces could effectually raise one local section of the people eminently aloft, while continuing surrounded and unavoidably in constant intercourse with the general mass, remaining still sunk in degradation—he has to reply, that he is fancying no such thing. For while he is thus converting, in imagination, the military exertions against one foreign town, into intellectual and moral operations on one town at home, why may he not, in similar imagination, make a whole country correspond to a whole country? He may conceive the incalculable amount of exertion made by his country, in martial operations over all that wide foreign territory of which he has selected a particular spot, to have been, on the contrary, expended in the supposed beneficent process on the great scale of this whole nation. Then would the hypothetical improvement in the one particular town, so far from being a strange insulated phenomenon, absurd to be conceived as existing in exception and total contrast to the general state of the people, be but a specimen of that state.

He may proceed along the series of such confronted spectacles as far as bitter mortification will let him. But he will soon be sick of this process of comparison. And how sick will he thenceforward be, to perpetual loathing, of the vain raptures with which an immoral and anti-christian patriotism can review a long history of what it will call national glory, acquired by national energy ambitiously consuming itself in a continual succession and unlimited extent of extraneous operations, cf that kind which has been the grand curse of the human race ever since the time of Cain; while the one thing needful of national welfare, the very *summum bonum* of a state, has been regarded with contemptuous indifference.

These observations are not made on an assumption, that England could in all cases have kept clear of implication in foreign interests, and remote and sanguinary contests. But they are made on the assumption of what is admitted and deplored by every thoughtful religious man, whose understanding and moral sense are not wretchedly prostrated in homage to a prevailing system, and chained down by a superstition that dares not question the wisdom and probity of high national authorities and counsels. What is so admitted and deplored by the true and christian patriots is, that this nation has gone to an awfully criminal extent beyond the line of necessity; that it has been extremely prompt to find or make occasions for appearing again, and still again, in array for the old work of waste and death; and that the advantage possessed by the preponderating classes in this protestant country, for being instructed (if they had cared for such instruction) to look at these transactions in the light of religion, has reflected a peculiar aggravation on the guilt of a policy persevered in from age to age, in disregard of the laws of Christianity, and the warning of accountableness to the Sovereign Judge.

These observations assume, also, that there *cannot* be such a thing as a nation so doomed to a necessity and duty of expending its vigour and means in foreign enterprise, as to be habitually absolved from the duty of raising its people from brutish ignorance. *This* concern is a duty at all events and to an entire certainty; is a duty imperative and absolute; and any pretended necessity for such a direction of the national exertion as would be, through a long succession of time, incompatible with a paramount attention to this, would be a virtual denial of the superintendence of Providence. It would be the same thing as to assert of an individual, that his duties of other kinds are so many and great, as to render it impossible for him to give a competent attention to his highest interests, and that therefore he stands exempted from the obligations of religion.

Such as we have described has been, for ages, the degraded state of the multitude. And such has been the indifference to it, manifested by the superior, the refined, the ascendant portion of the community; who, generally speaking, could see these sharers with them of the dishonoured human nature, in endless numbers around them, in the city and the field, without its ever flashing on conscience that on them was lying a solemn responsibility, destined to press one day with all its weight, for that ill arrangement of the social order which abandoned these beings to an exclusion from the sphere of rational existence. It never occurred to many of them as a question of the smallest moment, in what manner the mind might be living in all these bodies, if only it were there in competence to make them efficient as machines and implements. Contented to be gazed at, to be envied, or to be regarded as too high even for envy, and to have the rough business of the world performed by these inhalers of the vital air, they perhaps thought, if they reflected at all on the subject, that the best and most privileged state of such creatures was to be in the least possible degree morally accountable: and that therefore it would be but doing them an injury to enlarge their knowledge. And might not the thought be suggested at some moment, (see how many things may be envied in their turns!) how happy *they* should be, if, with the vast superiority of their advantages, they could still be just as little accountable? But if even in this way, of envy, they received an unwelcome admonition of their own high responsibility, not even then was it suggested to them, that they should ever be arraigned on a charge to which they would vainly wish to be permitted to plead, "Were we our brothers' keepers?" And if an office designated in those terms had been named to them, as a part of their duty, by some unearthly voice of imperious accent, their thoughts might have traversed hither and thither, in various conjectures and protracted perplexity, before the objects of that office had been presented explicitly to their apprehension as no other than the reason, principles, consciences, and the whole moral condition of the vulgar mass. They would understand that its condition was, *in some way or other*, a concern lying at their door, but probably not in this.—We speak generally, and not universally.

But we would believe there are signs of a revolution beginning; a more important one, by its higher principle and its expansive impulse toward a wide and remote beneficence, than the ordinary events of that name. What have commonly been the matter and circumstance of revolutions? The last deciding blow in a deadly competition of equally selfish parties; actions and reactions of ambition and revenge; the fiat of a conqueror; a burst of blind fury, suddenly sweeping away an old order of things, but overwhelming too all attempts to substitute a better institution; plots, massacres, battles, dethronements, restorations: all actuated by a fermentation of the ordinary or the basest elements of humanity. How little of the sublime of moral agency has there been, with one or two partial exceptions, in these mighty commotions; how little wisdom or virtue, or reference to the Supreme Patron of national interests; how little nobleness or even distinctness of purpose, or consolidated advantage of success! But here is, as we trust, the approach of a revolution with different phenomena. It displays the nature of its principle and its ambition in a conviction, far more serious and extensive than heretofore, of the necessity of education to the mass of the population, with earnest discussions of its scope and methods by both speculative and practical men; in schemes, more speedily animated into operation than good designs were wont to be, for spreading useful knowledge over tracts of the dead waste where there was none; in exciting tens of thousands of young persons to a benevolent and patient activity in the instruction of the children of the poor; in an extended and extending system of means and exertions for the universal diffusion of the sacred scriptures; in multiplying endeavours, in all regular and all uncanonical ways, to render it next to impossible for the people to avoid hearing some sounds at least of the voice of religion; in the formation of useful local institutions too various to come under one denomination; in enterprises to attempt an opening of the vast prison-houses of human spirits in dark distant regions; in bringing to the test of principles many notions and practices which have stood on the authority of prejudice, custom, and prescription: and all this taking advantage of the new and powerful spirit which has come on the world to drive its affairs into commotion and acceleration; as bold adventurers have sometimes availed themselves of a formidable torrent to be conveyed whither the stream in its ordinary state would never have carried them; or as we have heard of heroic assailants seizing the moment of a tempest to break through the enemy's lines.—Such are some of the insignia by which it stands distinguished out and far off from the rank of ordinary revolutions.

We are not unaware that, with certain speculators on this same subject of meliorating the state and character of the people, some of the things here specified will be of small account, either as signs of a great change, or as means of promoting it. The widely spreading activity of a humble class of labourers, who seek no fame for their toils and sacrifices, is but a creeping process, almost invisible in the survey. The multiplied, voluntary, and extraordinary efforts to diffuse some religious knowledge and sentiment among the vulgar, appear to them, if not even of doubtful tendency, at least of such impotence for corrective operation, that any confidence founded on them is simple fanaticism; that the calculation is, to use a commercial term, mere moonshine. We remember when a publication of great note and influence flung contempt on the sanguine expectations entertained from the rapid circulation of Bibles among the inferior population. At the hopeful mention of expedients of the religious kind especially, the class of speculators in question might perhaps be reminded of Glendower's grave and believing talk of calling up spirits to perform his will; or (should they ever have happened to read the Bible), of the people who seized, in honest credulous delight, the mockery of a proposal of pulling a city, to the last stone, into the river with ropes, as a prime stroke of generalship.

When we see such expedients rated so low in the process for raising the populace from their degradation, we ask what means these speculators themselves would reckon on for the purpose. And it would appear that their scheme would calculate mainly on some supposed dispositions of a political and economical nature. Let the people be put in possession of all their rights as citizens, and thus advanced in the scale of society. Let all invidious distinctions which are artificial, arbitrary, and not inevitable, be abolished; together with all laws and regulations injuriously affecting their temporal well-being. Give them thus a sense of being *something* in the great social order, a direct palpable interest in the honour and prosperity of the community. There will then be a dignified sense of independence; the generous, liberalizing, ennobling, sentiments of freedom; the self-respect and conscious responsibility of men in the full exercise of their rights; the manly disdain of what is base; the innate perception of what is worthy and honourable, developing itself spontaneously on the removal of the ungenial circumstances in the constitution of society, which have been as a long winter on the intellectual and moral nature of its inferior portions. All this will conduce to the practicability and efficacy of education. It will be an education *to fit them for an education* to be introduced with the progress of that fitness; intellectual culture finding a felicitous adaptation of the soil. We may then adopt with some confidence a public system, or stimulate and assist all independent local exertions for the instruction of the people in the rudiments of literature and general knowledge; and religion too, if you will.

But, to say nothing of the vain fancies of the virtues ready to disclose themselves in a corrupt mass, under the auspices of improved political institutions, it is unfortunate for any such speculation that what it insists on as the primary condition cannot as yet, but very imperfectly, be had. The higher and commanding portion of the community have, very naturally, the utmost aversion to concede to the people what are claimed as theoretically their rights. They have, indeed, latterly been constrained to make considerable concessions in name and semblance. But their great and various power will be strenuously exerted, for probably a long while yet, to render the acquisitions made by the people as nearly as possible profitless in their hands. And unhappily these predominant classes have to allege the mental and moral rudeness of the lower, in vindication of this determined policy of repression and frustration; thus turning the consequences of their own criminal neglect into a defence of their injustice. They will say, If the subordinate millions had grown up into a rational existence; if they had been rendered capable of thinking, judging, distinguishing; if they were in possession of a moderate share of useful information, and withal a strong sense of duty; then might this and the other privilege, or call it right, in the social constitution be yielded to them. But as long as they continue in their present mental grossness they are unfit for the possession, because unqualified for the exercise, of any such privileges as would take them from under our authoritative control.

Since they can and will, for the present, maintain this controlling power, to the extent of nearly invalidating any political advancement attained, or likely to be soon attained, by the lower grades, a speculation that should place on that advancement, as a pre-requisite, our hope of a great change in the mental condition of the people, would be, to adopt a humble figure, setting us to climb to an upper platform without a ladder, or rather telling us not to climb at all. And while this supposed pre-requisite will be refused, on the allegation that the uncultivated condition of the people renders them unfit for a liberal political arrangement, the parties so refusing will be little desirous to have the obstacle removed; foreseeing, as the inevitable consequence of a highly improved cultivation, a more resolute demand of the advantages withheld, a constantly augmenting force of popular opinion, and therefore a diminution of their own predominant power. They will deem it much more commodious for themselves, that the people should not be so enlightened and raised as to come into any such competition. And since they, with these dispositions, have the preponderance in what we denominate the State, we fear we are not to look with much hope to the State for a liberal and effective system of national education.

What then is to be done?—We earnestly wish it might please the Sovereign Ruler to do one more new thing in the earth, compelling the dominant powers in the nations to an order of institutions and administrations that *would* apply the energy of the state to so noble a purpose. Nor can we imagine any test of their merits so fair as the question whether, and in what degree, they do this; nor any test by which they may more naturally decline to have those merits tried. But since, to the shame of our nature, there is no use to which we are so prone to turn our condemnation of evil in one form, as that of purchasing a license for it in another, the persons who are justly arraigning the powers at the head of nations should be warned that they do not take from the guilty omissions of states a sanction for individuals to do nothing. Let them not suffer an imposition on their minds in the notion entertained of a state, as a thing to be no otherwise accounted of than in a collective capacity, acting by a government; as if the collective power and agency of a nation became, in being exerted through that political organ, an affair altogether foreign to the will, the action, the duty, the responsibility, of the persons of whom the nation is composed. Let them not put out of sight that whatever is the duty of the national body in that collective capacity, acting through its government, is such only because it is the duty of the individuals composing that body, as far as it is in the power of each; and that it would be their duty individually not the less, though the government, as the depositary of the national power, neglect it. But more than this; to speak generally, and with certain degrees of possible exception, we may affirm that a government *cannot* be lastingly neglectful of a great duty but because the individuals constituting the community are so. An assertion, that a government has been utterly and criminally neglectful of the moral condition of the inferior population, age after age, and through every change of its administrators; but that, nevertheless, the generality of the individuals of intelligence, wealth, and influence, have all the while been of a quite opposite spirit, zealously intent on remedying the flagrant evil, would be instantly rejected as a contradiction. Such an enlightened and philanthropic spirit prevailing widely among the individuals of the nation would carry its impulse into the government in one manner or another. It would either constrain the administrators of the state to act in conformity, or ultimately displace them in favour of better men. Even if, short of such a *general* activity of the respectable and locally influential members of society, a large proportion of them had vigorously prosecuted such a purpose, it would have compelled the administrators of the state to consider, even for their own sake, whether they should be content to see so important a process going on independently of them, and in contrast with their own disgraceful neglect.

But at the worst, and on the supposition that they were obstinately inaccessible to all moral and philanthropic considerations, still a grand improvement would have been accomplished, if many thousands of the responsible members of the community had attempted it with zealous and persevering exertion. The neglect, therefore, of the improvement of the people, so glaring in the review of our conduct as a nation, has been, to a very great extent, the insensibility of individuals to obligations lying on them as such, independently of the institutions and administration of the state.

And are individuals *now* absolved from all such responsibility; and the more so, that the conviction of the importance of the object is come upon them with such a new and cogent force? When they say, reproachfully, that the nation, as a body politic, concentrating its powers in its government, disowns or neglects a most important duty, is it to be understood that this accusatory testimony is *their* share, or something equivalent in substitution for their share, of that very duty? Does a collective duty of such very solid substance, vanish into nothing under any attempted process of resolving it into fractions and portions for individuals? And do they themselves, as some of the individuals to whom this duty might thus be distributively assigned,—do they themselves, in spite of self-love, self-estimation, and all the sentiments which they will at other times indulge in homage of their own importance,—do they, when this assignment is attempted to be made to them, instantly and willingly surrender to a feeling of crumbling down from this proud individuality into an undistinguishable existence in the mass; and, profaning the language of religion, say to the State, "In thee we live, move, and have a being?" Or, will they, (in assimilation to eastern pagans, who hold that a divinity so pervades them as to be their wills and do their actions, leaving the mere human vehicle without power, duty, or accountableness,) will they account themselves but as passive matter, moved or fixed, and in all things necessitated, by a sovereign mythological something denominated the state?

No, not in all things. It is not so that they feel with respect to those other interests and projects, which they are really in earnest to promote, though those concerns may lie in no greater proportion than the one in question does within the scope of their individual ability. The incubus has then vanished; and they find themselves in possession of a free agency, and a degree of power which they will not patiently hear estimated in any such contemptuous terms. What is there then that should reduce them, as individual agents, to such utter and willing insignificance in the affair of which we are speaking? Besides, they may form themselves, in indefinite number, into combination. And is there no power in any collective form in which they can be associated, save just that one in which the aggregation is constituted under the political shape and authority denominated a state? Or is it at last that some alarm of superstitious loyalty comes over them; that they grow uneasy in conscience at the high-toned censure they have been stimulated and betrayed to pronounce on the state; that they relapse into the obsequiousness of hesitating, whether they should presume to do good of a kind which the "Power ordained of God" has not seen fit to do; that they must wait for the sanction of its great example; that till the "shout of kings is among them" it were better not to march against the vandalism and the paganism which are, the while, quite at their ease, destroying the people?

But if such had always been the way in which private individuals, single or associated, had accounted of themselves and their possible exertions, in regard to great general improvements, but very few would ever have been accomplished. For the case has commonly been, that the schemes of such improvements have originated with persons not invested with political power; have been urged on by the accession and cooperation of such individuals; and at length slowly and reluctantly acceded to by the holders of dominion over the community, always, through some malignant fatality, the last to admit what had long appeared to the majority of thinking men no less than demonstrative evidence of the propriety and advantage of the reformation.

In all probability, the improvement of mankind is destined, under Providence, to advance nearly in proportion as good men feel the responsibility for it resting on themselves as individuals, and are actuated by a bold sentiment of independence, (humble at the same time, in reference to the necessity of Divine intervention,) in the prosecution of it. Each person who is standing still to look, with grief or indignation, at the evils which are overrunning the world, would do well to recollect what he may have read of some gallant partizan, who, perceiving where a prompt movement, with the comparatively slender force at his own command, would make an impression infallibly tending to the success of the warfare, could not endure to lose the time till some great sultan should find it convenient to come in slow march, and the pomp of state, to take on him the direction of the campaign.

In laying this emphasis of incitement and hope on the exertions of good men as individuals, we cannot be understood to mean that the government of states, if ever they did come to be intent on rendering the condition of society better and happier, could not contribute beyond all calculation to the force and efficacy of *every* project and measure for that grand purpose. How far from it! it is melancholy to consider what they might do and do not. But it is because their history, thus far, affords such feeble prognostics of their becoming, till some better age, actuated by such a spirit,—it is because the Divine Governor has hitherto put upon them so little of the honour of being the instruments of his beneficence,—that the anticipations of good, and the exhortations to attempt it, are so peculiarly directed to its promoters in an individual capacity.

Happily, the accusatory part of such exhortations is becoming, we trust we may say fast becoming, less extensively applicable; and we return with pleasure to the animating idea of that revolution of which we were noting the introductory signs. It is a revolution in the manner of estimating the souls of the people, and consequently in the judgment of what should be done for both their present and future welfare. Through many ages, that immense multitude had been but obscurely presented to view in any such character as that of rational improvable creatures. They were recognised no otherwise than as one large mass of rude moral substance, but faintly distinguishable into individuals; existing, and to be left to exist, in their own manner; and that manner hardly worth concern or inquiry. Little consideration could there be of how much spiritual immortal essence must be going to waste, absorbed in the very earth, all over the wide field where the inferior portion of humanity was seen only through the gross medium of an economical estimate, by the more favoured part of the race. But now it is as if a mist were rising and dispersing from that field, and leaving the multitude of possessors of uncultivated and degraded mind exhibited in a light in which they were never seen before, except by the faithful promoters of Christianity, and a few philanthropists of a less special order

It is true, this manifestation forms so tragic a vision, that if we had only to behold it *as a spectacle*, we might well desire that the misty obscurity should descend on it again, to shroud it from sight; while we should be left to indulge and elate our imaginations by dwelling on the pomps and splendours of the terrestrial scene,—the mighty empires, the heroes, the victories, the triumphs; the refinements and enjoyments of the most highly cultivated of the race; the brilliant performances of genius, and the astonishing reach of science. So the tempter would have beguiled our Lord into a complacent contemplation of the kingdoms and glories of the world. But he was come to look on a different aspect of it! Nor could he be withdrawn from the gloomy view of its degradation and misery. And a good reason why. For the sole object for which he had appeared in the only world where temptation could even in form approach him was to begin in operation, and finish in virtue, a design for changing that state of degradation and misery. In the prosecution of such a design, and in the spirit of that divine benevolence in which it sprung, he could endure to fix on the melancholy and odious character of the scene, the contemplation which was vainly attempted to be diverted to any other of its aspects. What, indeed, could sublunary pomps and glories be to him in any case; but emphatically what, when his object was to redeem the people from darkness and destruction?

Those who, actuated by a spirit in some humble resemblance to his, have entered deeply into the state of the people, such as it is found in our own nation, have often been appalled at the spectacle disclosed to them. They have been astonished to think, what *can* have been the direction, while successive ages have passed away, of so many thousands of acute and vigilant mental eyes, that so dreadful a sight should scarcely have been descried. They have been aware that in describing it as they actually saw it, they would be regarded by some as gloomy fanatics, tinctured with insanity by the influence of some austere creed; and that others, of kinder nature, but whose sensibility has more of self-indulging refinement than tendency to active benevolence, would almost wish that so revolting an exhibition had never been made, though the fact be actually so. There may have been moments when they themselves have experienced a temporary recoil of their benevolent zeal, under the impression at once of the immensity of the evil, so defying the feebleness of their remedial means and efforts, and of its noisome quality. At times, the rudeness of the subjects, and perhaps the ungracious reception and thankless requital of their disinterested labours, aggravating the general feeling of the miserableness, (so to express it) of seeing so much misery, have lent seduction to the temptations to ease and self-indulgence. Why should they, just *they* of all men, condemn themselves to dwell so much in the most dreary climate of the moral world, when they could perhaps have taken their almost constant abode in a little elysium of elegant knowledge, taste, and refined society? Then was the time to revert to the example of Him "who, though he was rich, for our sakes became poor."

Or, again, they may have been betrayed to indulge too long in the bitter mood of thinking, how entirely the higher and more amply furnished powers leave such generous designs to proceed as they can, in the mere strength of private individual exertion. And they may have yielded to depressive feelings after the fervour of indignant ones; for such indignation, unless qualified by the purest principle—unless it be the "anger that sins not"—is very apt, when it cools, to settle into misanthropic despondency. It is as if (they have said) armies and giants would stand aloof to amuse themselves, while we are to be committed and abandoned in the ceaseless unavailable toil of a conflict, which these armies and giants have no business even to exist as such but for the very purpose of waging. We are, if we will, —and if we will we may let it alone—to try to effect in diminutive pieces, and detached local efforts, a little share of that, to the accomplishment of which the greatest human force on earth might be applied on system, and to the widest compass. So they have said, perhaps, and been tempted to leave their object to its destiny.

But really it is now too late for this resentful and desponding abandonment. They cannot now retire in the tragic dignity of despair. It must be some more forlorn predicament that would allow them any grace of rhetoric in saying, as in parody of Cato, "Witness heaven and earth, that we have done our duty, but the stars and fate are against us; and here it becomes us to terminate a strife, which would degenerate into the ridiculous if prosecuted against impossibilities." On the contrary, the zeal which could begin so onerous a work, and prosecute it thus far, could not now remit without convicting its past ardour of cowardice lurking under its temporary semblance of bravery. Is it for the projectors of a noble edifice for public utility, to abandon the undertaking when it has risen from its foundation to be seen above the ground; or is just come to be level with the surface of the waters, in defiance of which it has been commenced, and the violence of which it was designed to control, or the unfordable depths and streams of which it was to bear people over? Let the promoters of education and Christian knowledge among the inferior classes, reflect what has already been accomplished; though regarding it as quite the incipient stage. It is most truly as yet "the day of small things;" and shall they despise it, from an idea of what it might have been if the great powers had been directed to its advancement? They have found that in the good cause thus unaided they have not wholly laboured in vain; that it *can* be brought in contact with a considerable portion of what would otherwise be so much human existence abandoned; and that already, as from the garments of the Divine Healer of diseases, a sanative virtue goes out of it. Let them recount the individuals they have seen, and not despond as to many more, rescued from what had all the signs of a destination to the lowest debasement, and utter ruin; some of whom are returning animated thanks, and will do so in the hour of death, for what these, their best human friends, have been the means of imparting to them. Let them recollect of how many families they have seen the domestic condition pleasingly, and in some instances eminently and delightfully amended. And let them reflect how they have trampled down prejudices, nearly silenced a heathenish clamour, and provoked the imitative and rival efforts of many who would, but for them, have been willing enough for all such schemes to lie in abeyance to the end of time. Let them think of all this, and faithfully persist in the trial what it may please God that they shall accomplish, whether the possessors of national power will acknowledge his demand for such an application of it or not; whether, when the infinite importance of the concern is represented to them, they will hear, or whether they will forbear.

But let them not doubt that the time will come, when the rulers and the ascendant classes in states will comprehend it to be their best policy to promote all possible improvement of the people. It will be given to them to understand, that the highest glory of those at the head of great communities, must consist in the eminence attained by those communities generally, in whatever it is that constitutes the worth, the honour, the happiness, of individuals; a glory with which would be combined the advantage that the office of presiding over such a nation could be administered in a liberal spirit. They will one day have learned to esteem it a far nobler form of power to lead and direct an immense society of intelligent minds, than to delude, coerce, and drive a vast semibarbarous herd. Providence surely will one day, in the progress of society, confer on it such wise and virtuous rulers as can feel, that it is better for them to have a people who can understand and rationally approve, when deserving of approbation, their system and measures, than one bent in stupid submission, even if ignorance could henceforward suffice (which it cannot) to retain the people in that posture: better, therefore, by a still stronger reason, than to have a people fermenting in ignorant disaffection, constantly believing the governors to be in the wrong, and without the sense to comprehend any arguments in justification, excepting such as might be addressed in the shape of bribes to corruption. And a time will come when it will not be left to the philanthropic or censorial speculatists alone, to make the comparative estimate between what has been effected by the enormously expensive apparatus of coercive and penal administration—the prisons, prosecutions, transportations, and a large military police, (things quite necessary in our past and present national condition,)—and what *might* have been effected by one half of that expenditure devoted to popular reformation, to be accomplished by means of schools, and every practicable variety of methods for placing men's judgment and conscience as the "lion in the way," when they are inclined and tempted to go wrong.—All this will come to pass at length. And if the promoters of the best designs see cause to fear that the time is remote, this should but enforce upon them the more strongly the admonition that no time is *theirs*, but the present.

It was not possible to pursue the long course of these observations so nearly to the conclusion, without being reminded still again of what we have adverted to before, that there will be persons ready to impute sanguine extravagance to our expectations of the result of such an order of means and exertions, for the improvement of the education and mental condition of the people, as we see already beginning to work. When the means are of so little splendid a quality, it will be said, by what inflation of fancy is their power admeasured to such effects?

And what *is* it, then, and how much, that is expected as the result, by the zealous advocates of schools, and the whole order of expedients, for the instruction of that part of the rising generation till lately so neglected. Are they heard maintaining that the communication of knowledge, or true notions of things, to youthful minds, will *infallibly* ensure their virtue and happiness? They are not quite so new to the world, to experimental labour in the business of tuition, or to self-observation. Their vigilance would hardly overlook such a circumstance as the very different degree of assurance with which the effects may be predicted, of ignorance on the one hand, and of knowledge on the other. There is very nearly an absolute certainty of success in the method for making clowns, sots, vagabonds, and ruffians. You may safely leave it to themselves to carry on the process for becoming complete. Let human creatures grow up without discipline, destitute therefore of salutary information, sound judgment, or any conscience but what will shape itself to whatever they like, serving in the manner of some vile friar pander in the old plays, —and no one takes any credit for foresight in saying they will be a noxious burden on the earth; except indeed in those tracts of it where they seem to have their appropriate place and business, in being matched against the wolves and bears of the wilderness. When they infest what should be a civilized and christianized part of the world, the philanthropist is sometimes put in doubt whether to repress, or indulge, the sentiment which tempts him to complacency in the operation of an epidemic which is thinning their numbers.

The consequences of ignorance are certain, unless almost a miracle interpose; but unhappily those of knowledge are of diffident and restricted calculation; unless we could make a trifle of the testimony of all ages, and suppress the evidence of present experience, that men may see and approve the better, and yet follow the worse. It is the hapless predicament of our nature, that the noblest of its powers, the understanding, has but most imperfectly and precariously that commanding hold on the others, which is essential to the good order of the soul. Our constitution is like a machine in which there is a constant liability of the secondary wheels to be thrown out of the catch and grapple of the master one. And worse than so, these powers which ought to be subordinate and obedient to the understanding, are not left to stand still when detached from its control. They have a strong activity of their own, from the impulse of other principles: indeed, it is this impulse that *causes* the detachment. It is frightful to look at the evidence from facts, that these active powers *may* grow strong in the perversity which will set the judgment at defiance, during the very time that it is successfully training to a competence for dictating to them what is right. The assertions of those who are determined to find the chief or only cause of the wrong direction of the passions and will in misapprehension of the understanding, are a gross assumption, in a question of fact, against an infinite crowd of facts pressing round with their evidence. This evidence is offered by men without number distinctly and deliberately acknowledging their conviction of the evil quality and fatal consequences, of courses which they are soon afterwards seen pursuing, and without the smallest pretence of a change of opinion; by the same men in more advanced stages still owning the same conviction, and sometimes in strong terms of self-reproach, in the checks and pauses of their career; and by men in the near prospect of death and judgment expressing, in bitter regret, the acknowledgment that they had persisted in acting wrong when they knew better. And this assumption, made against such evidence, is to be maintained for no better reason, that appears, than a wilful determination that human nature cannot, must not, shall not, be so absurd and depraved as to be capable of such madness: as if human nature were taking the smallest trouble to put on any disguise before them, to beguile them into a good opinion; as if it could be cajoled by their flattery to assume even a semblance of deserving it; as if it had the complaisance to check one bad propensity, to save them from standing contradicted and exposed to ridicule for speaking of it with indulgence or respect; as if it staid or cared to thank them for their pains in attempting to make out a plausible extenuation. It has, and keeps, and shows its character, in perfect indifference to the puzzled efforts of its apologists to reduce its moral turpitude to just so much error of the understanding. But, as for understanding—it should be time to look to their own, when they find themselves asserting, in other words, that there is actually as much virtue in the world as there is knowledge of its principles and laws. We should rather have surmised that, deplorably deficient as that knowledge is, the reduction of a fifth or tenth part of it to practice would make a glorious change in England and Europe.

The persons, therefore, whose zeal is combined with knowledge in the prosecution of plans for the extension of education, proceed on a calculation of an effect more limited, in apparent proportion to the means, and with less certainty of even that more limited measure in any single instance, than they would have been justified in anticipating in many other departments of operation. They would, for example, predict more positively the results of an undertaking to cultivate any tract of waste land, to reclaim a bog, or to render mechanical forces available in an untried mode of application; or, in many cases, the decided success of the healing art as applied to a diseased body. They must needs be moderate in their confidence of calculation for good, on a moral nature whose corruption would yield an enemy of mankind a gratifying probability in calculating for evil. In comparing these opposite calculations, they would be glad if they might make an exchange of the respective probabilities. That is to say, let a man, if such there be, who could be pleased with the depravity and misery of the race, a sagacious judge too, of their moral constitution, and a veteran observer of their conduct,—let him survey with the look of an evil spirit a hundred children in one of the benevolent schools, and indulge himself in prognosticating, on the strength of what he knows of human nature, the proportion, in numbers and degree, in which these children will, in subsequent life, exemplifying the *failure* of what is done for their wisdom and welfare;—let him make his calculation, and, we say, there may be times when the friends of these institutions would be glad to transfer the quantity of probability from his side to theirs; would feel they should be happy if the proportion in which they fear he may be right in calculating on evil from the nature of the beings under discipline, were, instead, the proportion in which it is rational to reckon on good from the efficacy of that discipline. "Evil, be thou my good," might be their involuntary apostrophe, in the sense of wishing to possess the stronger power, transmuted to the better quality.

But we shall know where to stop in the course of observations of this darkening colour; and shall take off the point of the derider's taunt, just forthcoming, that we are here unsaying, in effect, all that we have been so laboriously urging about the vast benefit of knowledge to the people. It was proper to show, that the prosecutors of these designs are not suffering themselves to be duped out of a perception of what there is, in the nature of the youthful subjects, to counteract the intention of the discipline, and with too certain a power to limit its efficacy to a very partial measure of the effect desired. These projectors might fairly be required to prove they are not unknowing enthusiasts; but then, in keeping clear of the vain extravagances of expectation, they are not to surrender their confidence that something great and important can be done: it should be possible for a man to be sober, short of being dead. They are not to gravitate into a state of feeling as if they thought the understanding and the moral powers are but casually associated in the mind; as if an important communication to the one, might, so to speak, never be heard of by the others; as if these subordinates had just one sole principle of action—that of disobeying their chief, so that it could be of no use to appeal to the master of the house respecting the conduct of his inmates; as if, therefore, *all* presumption of a relation between means and ends, as a ground of confidence in the efficacy of popular instruction, must be illusory. It might not indeed be amiss for them to be *told* that the case is so, by those who would desire, from whatever motive, to repress their efforts and defeat their designs. For so downright a blow at the vital principle of their favourite object would but serve to provoke them to ascertain more definitely what there really is for them to found their schemes and hopes upon, and therefore to verify to themselves the reasons they have for persisting, in assurance that the labour will be far from wholly lost. And for this assurance it is, at the very lowest, self-evident, that there is at any rate such an efficacy in cultivation, as to give a certainty that a well-cultivated people *cannot* remain on the same degraded moral level as a neglected ignorant one—or any where near it. None of those even that value such designs the least, ever pretend to foresee, in the event of their being carried into effect, an undiminished prevalence of rudeness and brutality of manners, of delight in spectacles and amusements of cruelty, of noisy revelry, of sottish intemperance, or of disregard of character. It is not pretended to be foreseen, that the poorer classes will then continue to display so much of that almost desperate improvidence respecting their temporal means and prospects, which has aggravated the calamities of the present times. It is not predicted that an universal school-discipline will bring up several millions to the neglect, and many of them in an impudent contempt, of attendance on the ministrations of religion. The result will at all hazards, by every one's acknowledgment, be *the contrary of this.*

But more specifically:—The promoters of the plans of popular education see a most important advantage gained in the very outset, in the obvious fact, that in their schools a very large portion of time is employed well, that otherwise would infallibly be employed ill. Let any one introduce himself into one of these places of concourse, where there has been time to mature the arrangements. He should not enter as an important personage, in patronizing and judicial state, as if to demand the respectful looks of the whole tribe from their attention to their printed rudiments and their slates; but glide in as a quiet observer, just to survey at his leisure the character and operations of the scene. Undoubtedly he may descry here and there the signs of inattention, weariness or vacancy, not to say of perverseness. Even these individuals, however, are out of the way of practical harm; and at the same time he will see a multitude of youthful spirits acknowledging the duty of directing their best attention to something altogether foreign to their wild amusements; of making a rather protracted effort in one mode or another of the strange business of *thinking.* He will perceive in many the unequivocal indications of a serious and earnest effort made to acquire, with the aid of visible signs and implements, a command of what is invisible and immaterial. They are thus rising from the mere animal state to tread in the precincts of an intellectual economy; the economy of thought and truth, in which they are to live for ever; and never, in all futurity, will they have to regret, for itself,* *this*

* *For itself*—a phrase of qualification inserted to meet the captious remark, that there have been instances of bad men, under the reproach of conscience and the dread of consequences, expressing

period and part of their employments. He will be delighted to think how many regulated actions of the mind, how many just ideas distinctly admitted, that were unknown or unimpressed at the beginning of the day's exercise, (and among these ideas, some to remind them of God and their highest interest,) there will have been by the time the busy and well ordered company breaks up in the evening, and leaves silence within these walls. He will not indeed grow romantic in hope; he knows the nature of which these beings partake; knows therefore that the desired results of this process will but partially follow; but still rejoices to think those partial results which will most certainly follow, will be worth incomparably more than all they will have cost to the learners, or the teachers, or the patrons.

Now let him, when he has contemplated this scene, consider how the greatest part of this numerous company would have been employed during the same hours, whether of the sabbath or other days, but for such a provision of means for their instruction. And, for the contrast, he has only to leave the school, and walk a mile round the neighbourhood, in which it will be very wonderful, (we may say this of most parts of England,) if he shall not, in a populous district, especially near a great town, and on a fine day, meet with a great number of wretched disgusting imps, straggling or in knots, in the activity of mischief and nuisance, or at least the full cry of vile and profane language; with here and there, as a lord among them, an elder larger one growing fast into an insolent adult blackguard. He may make the comparison, quite sure that such as they are, and so employed, would many now under the salutary

a regret that they had ever been well instructed, since this was an aggravation of their guilt, and perhaps had subserved their evil propensities with the more effectual means and ability.

discipline of yonder school have been, but for its institution. But the two classes so beheld in contrast, might they not seem to belong to two different nations? Do they not seem growing into two extremely different orders of character? Do they not even seem preparing for different worlds in the final distribution?

The friends of these designs for a general and highly improved education, may proceed further in this course of verifying to themselves the grounds of their assurance of happy consequences. A number of ideas, the most important that were ever formed in human thought, or imparted to men from the Supreme Mind, will be so communicated and impressed in these institutions, that it is absolutely certain they will be fixed irrevocably in the minds of the pupils. And in the case of many, if not the majority of these destined adventurers into the temptations of life, these important ideas, thus inserted deep in their souls, will distinctly present themselves to judgment and conscience an incalculable number of times. What a number, if the sum of all these reminiscences, in all the minds now assembled in a numerous school, could be conjectured! But if one in a hundred of these recollections, if one in a thousand, shall be efficacious, who can compute the amount of the good resulting from the instruction which shall have so enforced and fixed these ideas that they shall inevitably be thus recollected? And is it altogether out of reason to hope that the desired efficacy will, far oftener than once in a thousand times, attend the luminous rising again of a solemn idea to the view of the mind! Is still less than *this* to be predicted for our unhappy nature, while, however fallen, it is not abandoned by the care of its Creator!

The institutions themselves will gradually improve,

in both the method and the compass of their discipline. They will acquire a more vigorous mechanism, and a more decidedly intellectual character. In this latter respect, it is but comparatively of late years that schools for the inferior classes have ventured any thing beyond the humblest pretensions. Mental cultivation —enlarged knowledge—elements of science—habit of thinking—exercise of judgment—free and enlightened opinion—higher grade in society—were terms which they were to be reverently cautious of taking in vain. There would have been an offensive sound in such phrases, as seeming to betray somewhat of the impertinence of a *disposition*, (for the idea of the *practicability* of any such invasion would have been scorned,) to encroach on a ground exclusively appropriate to the superior orders. Schools for the poor were to be as little as possible scholastic. They were to be kept down to the lowest level of the workshop, excepting perhaps in one particular—that of working hard: for the scholars were to throw time away rather than be occupied with any thing beyond the merest rudiments. The advocates and the petitioners for aid of such schools, were to avow and plead how little it was that they pretended or presumed to teach. The argument in their behalf was either to begin or end with saying, that they taught *only* reading and writing; or if it could not be denied that there was to be some meddling with arithmetic and grammar,—we may safely appeal to some of the veterans of these pleaders, whether they did not, thirty or forty years since, bring out this addition with the management and hesitation of a confession and apology. It is a prominent characteristic of that happy revolution we have spoken of as in commencement, that this aristocratic notion of education is breaking up. The theory of the subject is loosening into enlargement, and will cease by degrees to impose a niggardly restriction on the extent of the cultivation, proper to be attempted in schools for the inferiors of the community.

As these institutions go on, augmenting in number and improving in organization, their pupils will bring their quality and efficacy to the proof, as they grow to maturity, and go forth to act their part in society. And there can be no doubt, that while too many of them may be mournful exemplifications of the power with which the evil genius of the corrupt nature, combined with the infection of a bad world, resists the better influences of instruction, and may, after the advantage of such an introductory stage, be carried down towards the old debasement, a very considerable proportion will take and permanently maintain a far higher ground. They will have become imbued with an element, which must put them in strong repulsion to that coarse vulgar that will be sure to continue in existence, in this country, long enough to be a trial of the moral taste of this better cultivated race. It will be seen that they cannot associate with it by choice, and in the spirit of companionship. And while they are thus withheld on their part, from approximating, it may be hoped that in certain better disposed parts of that vulgar, there may be a conversion of the repelling principle into an impulse to approach and join them on their own ground. There will be numbers among it who cannot be so entirely insensate or perverse, as to look with carelessness at the advantages obtained through the sole medium of personal improvement, by those who had otherwise been exactly on the same level of low resources and estimation as themselves. The effect of this view on pride, in some, and on better propensities, it may be hoped, in others, will be to excite them to make their way upward to a community which, they will clearly see, could commit no greater folly than to come downward to them. And we will presume a friendly disposition in most of those who shall have been raised to this higher standing, to meet such aspirers and help them to ascend.

And while they will thus draw upward the less immovable and hopeless part of the mass below them, they will themselves, on the other hand, be placed, by the respectability of their understanding and manners, within the influence of the higher cultivation of the classes above them; a great advantage, as we have taken a former occasion to notice:—a great advantage, that is to say, if the cultivation among those classes *be* generally of such a quality and measure, that the people could not be brought a few degrees nearer to them without becoming, through the effect of their example, more in love with sense, knowledge, and propriety of conduct. For it were somewhat too much of simplicity, perhaps, to take it for quite a thing of course that the people would always perceive such intellectual accomplishments as would keep them modest or humble in their estimate of their own, and such liberal spirit and manners as would at once command their respect and conduce to their refinement, when they made any approach to a communication with the classes superior in possessions and station. If this *might* have been assumed as a thing of course, and if therefore it might have been confidently reckoned on, that the more improving of the people would receive from the ranks above them a salutary influence, similar to that which we have been supposing they will themselves exert on a part of the vulgar mass below them, there had been a happy omen for the community; and if it may not be so assumed, are we to have the disgraceful deficiencies of the upper classes pleaded as an argument against raising the lower from their degradation? Must the multitude flounder along the mud at the bottom of the upward slope, because their betters will not be at the cost of making for themselves a higher terraced road across it than that they are now walking on?

But it would be an admirable turn to make the lower orders act beneficially on the higher. And it is an important advantage likely to accrue from the better education of the common people, that their rising attainments would compel not a few of their superiors to look to the state of their own mental pretensions, on perceiving that *this*, at last, was becoming a ground on which, in no small part, their precedence was to be measured. Surely it would be a most excellent thing, that they should find themselves thus incommodiously pressed upon by the only circumstance, perhaps, that could make them sensible there are more kinds of poverty than that single one to which alone they had hitherto attached ideas of disgrace; and should be forced to preserve that ascendency for which wealth and station would formerly suffice, at the cost, now, of a good deal more reading, thinking, and general self discipline. And would it be a worthy sacrifice, that to spare some substantial agriculturalists, idle gentlemen, and sporting or promenading ecclesiastics, such an afflictive necessity, the actual tillers of the ground, and the workers in manufacture and mechanics, should continue to be kept in stupid ignorance?

It is very possible this may excite a smile, as the threatening of a necessity or a danger to these privileged persons, which it is thought they may be comfortably assured is very remote. This danger (namely, that a good many of them, or rather of those who are coming in the course of nature to succeed them in the same rank, will find that its relative consequence cannot be sustained but at a very considerably higher pitch of mental qualification) is threatened upon no stronger presages than the following:—Allow us first to take it for granted, that it is not a very protracted length of time that is to pass away before the case comes to be, that a large proportion of the children of the lower classes are trained, through a course of assiduous instruction and exercise in the most valuable knowledge, during a series of years, in schools which every thing possible is done to render efficient. Then, if we includ in one computation all the time they will have spent in real mental effort and acquirement there, and all those pieces and intervals of time which we may reasonably hope that many of them will improve to the same purpose in the subsequent years, a very great number of them will have employed, by the time they reach middle age, many thousands of hours more than people in their condition have heretofore done, in a way the most directly tending to place them greatly further on in whatever of importance for repute and authority intelligence is to bear in society. And how must we be estimating the natural capacities of these inferior classes, or the perceptions of the higher, not to foresee as a consequence, that these latter will find their relative situation greatly altered, with respect to the measure of knowledge and mental power requisite as one most essential constituent of their superiority, in order to command the unfeigned deference of their inferiors?

Our strenuous promoters of the schemes for cultivating the minds of all the people, are not afraid of professing to foresee, that when schools, of that completely disciplinarian organization which they are, we hope, gradually to attain, shall have become general, and shall be vigorously seconded by all those auxiliary expedients for popular instruction which are also in progress, a very pleasing modification will become apparent in the character, the moral colour, if we might so express it, of the people's ordinary employment. The young persons so instructed, being appointed, for the most part, to the same occupations to which they would have been destined had they grown up in utter ignorance and vulgarity, are expected to give evidence that the meanness, the debasement almost, which had characterised many of those occupations in the view of the more refined classes, was in truth the debasement of the men more than of the callings; which will come to be in more honourable estimation as associated with the sense, decorum, and self-respect of the performers, than they were while blended and polluted with all the low habits, manners, and language, of ignorance and vulgar grossness. And besides, there is the consideration of the different degrees of merit in the performance itself; and who will be the persons most likely to excel, in the many branches of workmanship and business which admit of being better done in proportion to the degree of intelligence directed upon them? And again, who will be most in requisition for those offices of management and superintendence, where something must be confided to judgment and discretion, and where the value is felt, (often vexatiously felt from the want,) of some capacity of combination and foresight?

Such as these are among the subordinate benefits reasonably, we might say infallibly, calculated upon. Our philanthropists are confident in foreseeing also, that very many of these better educated young persons will be valuable cooperators with all who may be more formally employed in instruction, against that ignorance from which themselves have been so happily saved; will exert an influence, by their example and the steady avowal of their principles, against vice and folly in their vicinity; and will be useful advisers of their neighbours in their perplexities, and sometimes moderators in their discords. It is predicted, with a confidence so much resting on general grounds of probability, as hardly to need the instances already afforded in various parts of the country to confirm it, that here and there one of the well-instructed humbler class will become a competent and useful public teacher of the most important truth. It is, in short, anticipated with delightful assurance, that great numbers of those who shall go forth from under the friendly guardianship which will take the charge of their youthful minds, will be examples through life and at its conclusion, of the power and felicity of religion.

Here we can suppose it not improbable that some one may, in pointed terms, put the question,—Do you then, at last, mean to affirm that you can, by the proposed course, by any cause, of discipline, absolutely secure that effectual operation and ascendency of religion in the mind, which shall place it in the right condition toward God, and in a state of fitness for passing, without fear or danger, into the scenes of its future endless existence?

We think the cautious limitation of language, hitherto observed in setting forth our expectations, might preclude such a question. But let it be asked, since there can be no difficulty to reply. We do *not* affirm that any form of discipline, the wisest and best in the power of the wisest and best men to apply, is competent of itself thus to subject the mind decidedly and permanently to the power of religion. On the contrary, we believe that grand effect can be accomplished only by a special influence of the Divine Being, operating by the means applied in a well-judged system of instruction, or, if he pleases, independently of them. But next, it is perfectly certain, notwithstanding, that the application of these human means will, in a multitude of instances, be efficacious to that most happy end.

This certainty arises from a few very plain general considerations. The first is, that the whole system of means appointed by the Almighty to be employed as a human process for presenting religion solemnly in view before men's minds, and enforcing it on them, is an appointment *expressly intended* for working that great effect which secures their final felicity; though to what extent in point of number is altogether unknown to the subordinate agents. They are perfectly certain, in employing the appointed expedients in prosecution of the work, that they must be proceeding on the strength of a positive relation subsisting between those means and the results to be realized, in what instances, in what measure, at what time, it shall please the sovereign Power. The appointment cannot be one of mere exercise for the faculties and submissive obedience of those who are summoned to be active in its execution.

Accordingly, there are in the divine revelation very many explicit and animating assurances, that their exertions shall certainly be in a measure effectual to the proposed end. And if these assurances are made in favour of the exertions for inculcating religion generally, that is, on men of all conditions and ages, they may be assumed as giving special encouragement to those for impressing it on young minds, before they can be preoccupied and hardened by the depravities of the world. There is plainly the more hope for the efficacy of those exertions the less there is to frustrate them. But besides, the authority itself, which has assured a measure of success to religious instruction as administered generally, has marked with peculiar strength the promise of its success as applied to the young; thus affording rays of hope which have in ten thousand instances animated the diligence of pious parents, and the other benevolent instructors of children.

There is also palpable matter of fact to the point, that an education which combines the discipline of the conscience and the intellectual faculty will be rendered, in many instances, efficacious to the formation of a religious character. This obvious fact is, that a much greater proportion of the persons so educated do actually become the subjects of religion, than of a similar number of those brought up in ignorance and profligacy. Take collectively any number of families in which such an education prevails, and the same number in which it does not, and follow the young persons respectively into subsequent life. But any one who hears the suggestion, feels there is no need to wait the lapse of time and follow their actual course. As instructed by what he has already seen in society, he can go forward with them prophetically, with perfect certainty that many more of the one tribe than that of the other, will become persons not only of moral respectability but decided piety. Any one that should assert respecting them that the probabilities are equal and indifferent, would be considered as sporting a wilful absurdity, or betraying that he is one of those who did not come into the world for any thing they can learn in it. And the experience which thus authorizes a perfect confidence of prediction, is evidence that, though discipline must wholly disclaim an absolute power to effect the great object in question, there is, nevertheless, such a constitution of things that it most certainly will, as an instrumental cause, in many instances effect it.

The state of the matter, then, is very simple. The Supreme Cause of men's being "made wise to salvation," in appointing a system of means, to be put by human activity in operation toward this effect, has also appointed that in this operation they shall infallibly be attended with a measure of success in accomplishing that highest good,—a measure which was not to be accomplished otherwise than by such means. So much he has signified to men as an absolute certainty: but then, he has connected this certainty in an arbitrary, and as to our knowledge, indefinite manner with the system. It is a certainty connected with the system *as taken generally and comprehensively;* and which it is not given to us to affix to the particular instances in which the success will take place. It is a Divine Volition suspended over the whole scene of cultivation; like a cloud from which we cannot tell where precisely the shower to fertilize it will fall, certain, however, that there are spots whose verdure and flowers will tell after awhile. The agents under the Sovereign Dispenser are to proceed on this positive assurance that the success *shall be somewhere,* though they cannot know that it will be in this one instance, or in the other: "In the morning sow thy seed, and in the evening withhold not thy hand; for thou knowest not whether shall prosper, this, or that." If they rate the value of their agency so high, as to hold it derogatory to their dignity that any part of their labours should be performed under the condition of possibly being unsuccessful, they may be assured that such is not exactly the estimate of Him to whom they look for the acceptance of their services, and for the reward.

But it may be added, that the great majority of those who are intent on the schemes for enlightening and reforming mankind, are entertaining a confident hope of the approach of a period, when the success will be far greater in proportion to the measure of exertion in every department of the system of instrumentality for that grand object. We cherish this confidence, not on the strength of any pretension to be able to resolve prophetic emblems and numbers, into precise dates and events of the present and approaching times. It rests on a more general mode of apprehending a relation between the extraordinary indications of the period we live in, and the substantial purport of the divine predictions. There unquestionably gleams forth, through the plainer lines, and through the mystical imagery of prophecy, the vision of a better age, in which the application of the truths of religion to men's minds will be irresistible. And what should more naturally be interpreted as one of the dawning signs of its approach, than a new spirit come into action with insuppressible impulse, at once to dispel the fog from their intellects and bring the heavenly light to shine close upon them; accompanied by a prodigious convulsion in the old system of the world, which hardly recognised in the inferior millions the very existence of souls to need or be worth such an illumination? It is true that an eruptive activity of evil, beyond what was witnessed by our forefathers, has attended and followed that convulsion; as mephitic exhalations are emitted through the rents of an earthquake. Viewed in itself, this outbreak of the bad principles and passions might seem to portend any thing rather than a grand improvement in the state of a nation or of mankind. It appears like an actual augmentation of the evil previously existing. But it should rather be regarded as the setting loose of the noxious elements accumulated and rankling under the old system; a phenomenon inevitably attendant on its breaking up, by a catastrophe absolutely necessary to open and clear the field for operations on the great scale against those evils themselves, and to give scope and means for the advancement toward a better condition of humanity.

The labourers in the institutions for instructing the young descendants of an ill-fated generation, may often regret to perceive how little the process is as yet informed with the energy which is ultimately to pervade the world. But let them regard as one great undivided economy and train of operation, these initiatory efforts and all that is to follow, till that time "when all shall know the Lord;" and take by anticipation, as in fraternity with the happier future labourers, their just share of that ultimate triumph. Those active spirits, in the happier periods, will look back with this sentiment of kindred and complacency to those who sustained the earlier toils of the good cause, and did not suffer their zeal to languish under the comparative smallness of their success.

We shall conclude with a few sentences in the way of reply to another question, which we can surmise there may be persons ready to ask, after this long iteration of the assertion of the necessity of knowledge to the common people. The question would be to this effect: What do you, all this while, mean to assign as the *measure* of knowledge proper for the people to be put in possession of?—for you do not specify the kinds, or limit the extent: you talk in vague general terms of mental improvement; you leave the whole matter indefinite; and for all that appears, the people are never to know when they know enough.

It is answered, that we *do* leave the extent undefined, and should request to be informed where, and why, the line of circumscription and exclusion should be drawn.

Is it, we could really wish to know, a point at all yet decided, wherein consist the value and importance of the human nature? Any liberal scheme for its universal cultivation is met by such a jealous parsimony toward the common people, such a ready imputation of wild theory, such protesting declamations against the mischief of practically applying abstract principles, such an undisguised or betrayed precedence given to mere interests of state, and those perhaps very sordid ones, before all others, and such whimsical prescriptions for making a salutary compound of a little knowledge and much ignorance,—that it might seem to be doubtful, after all, whether the human nature, in the mass of mankind at least, be of any such consistence, or for any such purpose, as is affirmed in our common-places on the subject. It is uniformly assumed in the language of divines, and of the philosophers in most repute, that the worth, the dignity, the importance of man, are in his rational immortal nature; and that therefore the best condition of *that* is his true felicity and glory, and the object chiefly to be aimed at in all that is done by him, and for him, on earth. But whether this should be regarded as any thing more than the elated faith of ascetics, a fine dogma of academics, or a theme for show in the pomp of moral rhetoric? For we often see, and it is very striking to see, how principles which are suffered to pass for infallible truth while content to stay within the province of speculation, and to be pronounced as mere doctrine, may be disowned and repelled when they come demanding to have their appropriate place and influence in the practical sphere. Even many pretended advocates of Christianity, who in naming certain principles would seem to make them of the very essence of the moral part of that religion, and, in discoursing merely *as religionists*, will insist on their vital importance, will yet shuffle and equivocate about these principles, and in effect set them aside, when they are attempted to be applied to some of their most legitimate uses. If, for example, these religionists are among the servile adherents of corrupted institutions and iniquity invested with power, they will easily find accommedating interpretations, or pleas of exemption from the direct authority, of some of the most sacred maxime of their professed religion. Serve the true God when we happen to be in the right place; but at all events we must attend our master to pay homage in the temple of Rimmon, or, should he please to require it, that of Moloch,—with this signal difference from the ancient instance of peccant servility, that whereas in that case pardon for it was implored, in the present case a merit is made of the sycophancy and the idolatry. Unless the principles of Christianity will acknowledge the supremacy of *something else* than Christianity, in the mode of their application to estimate the importance of the popular mind, they may take their repose in bodies of divinity, sermons, catechisms, systems of ethics, or wherever they can find a place.

But *is* it really admitted, as a great principle for practical application, that the mind, the intelligent imperishable existence, is the supremely valuable thing in man? It is then admitted, inevitably, that the discipline, the correction, the improvement, the maturation of this spiritual being to the highest attainable degree, is the great object to be desired by men, for themselves and one another. That is to say, that knowledge, cultivation, salutary exercise, wisdom, all that can conduce to the perfection of the mind, form the state in which it is due to man's nature that he should be endeavoured to be placed. But then, this is due to his nature by an absolutely *general* law. He cannot be so circumstanced in the order of society that this shall *not* be due to it. No situation in which the arrangements of the world, or say of Providence, may place him, can constitute him a specific kind of creature, to which is no longer fit and necessary that which is necessary to the well-being of man considered generally, as a spiritual, immortal nature. The essential law of this nature cannot be abrogated by men's being placed in humble and narrow circumstances, in which a very large portion of their time and exertions are required for mere subsistence. This accident of a confined situation is no more a reason why their minds should not require the best attainable cultivation, than would be the circumstance that the body in which a man's mind is lodged happens to be of smaller dimensions than those of other men.

That under the disadvantages of this humble situation they *cannot* acquire all the mental improvement desirable for the perfection of their intelligent nature, that the situation renders it impracticable, is quite another matter. So far as this inhibition is real and absolute, that is, so far as it must remain after the best exertion of human wisdom and means in their favour, it must be submitted to as one of the infelicities of their allotment by Providence. What we are insisting on is, that since by the law of their nature there is to them the same general necessity as to any other human beings, of that which is essential to the well-being of the mind, they should be advanced in this improvement *as far as they can;* that is, as far as a wise and benevolent disposition of the community can make it practicable for them to be advanced.

It is an odious hypocrisy to talk of the narrow limits to this advancement as an ordination of Providence, when a well-ordered constitution and management of the community might enlarge those limits. At least it is so in the *justifiers* of that social system: those who deplore and condemn it *may* properly speak of the appointment of Providence, but in another sense; as they would speak of the dispensations of Providence in consolation to a man iniquitously imprisoned or impoverished.

Let the people then be advanced in the improvement of their rational nature as far as they can. A greater degree of this progress will be more for their welfare than a less. This might be shown in forms of illustration easily conceived, and as easily vindicated from the imputation of extravagance, by instances which every observer may have met with in real life. A poor man, cultivated in a small degree, has acquired a few just ideas of an important subject, which lies out of the scope of his daily employments for subsistence. Be that subject what it may, if those ideas are of any use to him, by what principle would one idea more, or two, or twenty, be of *no* use to him? Of no use!—when all the thinking world knows, that every additional clear idea of a subject is valuable by a ratio of progress greater than that of the mere numerical increase, and that by a large addition of ideas a man triples the value of those with which he began. He has read a small meagre tract on the subject, or perhaps only an article in a magazine, or an essay in the literary column of a provincial newspaper. Where would be the harm, on supposition he can fairly afford the time, in consequence of husbanding it for this very purpose, of his reading a well-written concise book, which would give him a clear comprehensive view of the subject?

But perhaps another branch of the tree of knowledge bends its fruit temptingly to his hand. And if he should indulge, and gain a tolerably clear notion of one more interesting subject, (still punctually regardful of the duties of his ordinary vocation) where, we say again, is the harm? Converse with him; observe his conduct; compare him with the wretched clown in a neighbouring dwelling; and say that he is the worse for having thus much of the provision for a mental subsistence. But if thus much has contributed greatly to his advantage, why should he be interdicted still further attainments? Are you alarmed for him, if he will needs go the length of acquiring some knowledge of geography, the solar system, and the history of his own country and of the ancient world?* Let him proceed; supply him gratuitously with some of the best books on these subjects; and if you shall converse with him again, after another year or two of his progress, and compare him once more with the ignorant, stunted, cankered beings in his vicinity, you will see whether there be any thing essentially at variance between his narrow circumstances in life and his mental enlargement.

You are willing, perhaps, that he *should* know a few facts of ancient times, and can, though with hesitation, trust him with some such slight stories as Goldsmith's Histories of Greece and Rome. But if he should then by some means find his way into such a work as that of Rollin (of moral and instructive tendency, however defective otherwise,) or betray that he covets an acquaintance with those of Gillies, or even Thirlwall,—it is all over with him for being an useful member of society in his humble situation. You would consent (may we suppose?) to his reading a slender abridgment

* These denominations of knowledge, so strange as they will to some persons appear, in such a connexion, we have ventured to write from observing that they stand in the schemes of elementary instruction in the Missionary schools for the children of the natives of Bengal. But of course we are to acknowledge, that the vigorous, high-toned spirits of those Asiatic idolaters are adapted to receive a much superior style of cultivation to any of which the feeble progeny of England can be supposed to be capable.

of voyages and travels; but what *is* to become of him if nothing less will content him than the whole-length story of Captain Cook? He will direct, it is to be hoped, some of his best attention to the supreme subject of religion. And you would quite approve of his perusing some useful tracts, some manuals of piety, some commentary on a catechism, some volume of serious plain discourses; but he is absolutely undone if his ambition should rise at length to Barrow, or Howe, or Jeremy Taylor.* He is by all means, you say, to be kept out of all such pernicious company, in which it is impossible he can learn any lesson but one,— an aversion to good morals, just laws, virtuous kings, a polished and benevolent gentry, and learned and pious teachers. Well; *let* him be kept as far as possible from the mischief of all such books and knowledge; let him hardly know that there *was* an ancient world, or that there *are* on the globe such regions and wonders as travellers have described; or that a reason and eloquence above the pitch of some plain homily ever illustrated and enforced religion. *Let him* keep clear of all such evil communications; and then, (since we were expressly making it a condition, that he can fairly

* It should be unnecessary to observe, that the object in citing *any* names in this paragraph was, to give a somewhat definite cast to the description of the supposed progress of the plebeian self-instructor. The principal of them are mentioned simply as being of such note in their departments, that he would be likely to hear of them among the first of the authors to be sought, if he were aspiring to something beyond his previously humble and abridged reading. The reader may substitute for these names any others, of the superior order, that he may think more proper to stand in their place. It would therefore be animadversion or ridicule mispent, to make the charge of extravagance on this imagined course of a plain man's reading, with a specific reference to the authors here named, as if it had been meant that precisely these, by a peculiar selection, were to be the authors he may be supposed to peruse, and in perusing, to waste his time and destroy his sense of duty.

spare the time for such reading from his common employment) and then,—he will have just so much the more time for needless sleep, for discussing the trifles and characters of the neighbourhood, or, (supposing him still of a religious habit,) for tiring his friends and family with the well-meant but very unattractive iteration of a few serious phrases and remarks, of which they will have long since learnt to anticipate the last word from hearing the first. Advantages like these he certainly may enjoy in consequence of his preclusion from the higher and wider field of ideas. But however valuable these may be in themselves, they will not ensure his being better qualified for the common business and proprieties of his station, than another man in the same sphere of life whose mind has acquired that larger reach which we are describing. It is no more than what we have repeatedly seen exemplified, when we represent this transgressor into the prohibited field as probably acquitting himself with exemplary regularity and industry in his allotted labours, and even in this very capacity preferred by the men of business to the illiterate tools in his neighbourhood; nay, most likely preferred, in the more technical sense of the word, to the honourable, but often sufficiently vexatious office, of directing and superintending the operations of those tools.

And where, now, is the evil he is incurring or causing, during this progress of violating, step after step, the circumscription by which the aristocratic compasses were again and again, with small reluctant extensions to successive greater distances, defining the scope of the knowledge proper for a man of his condition? It is a bad thing, is it, that he has a multiplicity of ideas to relieve the tædium incident to the sameness of his course of life; that, with many things which had else been but mere insignificant facts, or plain ,ry notions and principles, he has a variety of interesting associations; like woodbines and roses wreathing round the otherwise bare ungraceful forms of erect stones or withered trees; that the world is an interpreted and intelligible volume before his eyes; that he has a power of applying himself to *think* of what it becomes at any time necessary for him to understand? Is it a judgment upon him for his temerity, in "seeking and intermeddling with wisdom" with which he had no business, that he has so much to impart to his children as they are growing up, and that if some of them are already come to maturity, they know not where to find a man to respect more than their father? Or if he takes a part in the converse and devotional exercises of religious society, is no one there the better for the clearness and the plenitude of his thoughts and the propriety of his expression?—But there would be no end of the preposterous suppositions fairly attachable to the notion, that the mental improvement of the common people has some proper limit of arbitrary prescription, on the ground simply of their *being* the common people, and quite distinct from the restriction which their circumstances may invincibly impose on their ability.

Taken in this latter view, we acknowledge that their condition would be a subject for most melancholy contemplation,—if we did not hope for better times. The benevolent reflector, when sometimes led to survey in thought the endless myriads of beings with minds within the circuit of a country like this, will have a momentary vision of them as they would be if all improved to the highest mental condition to which it is *naturally possible* for them to be exalted: a magnificent spectacle; but it instantly fades and vanishes. And the sense is so powerfully upon him of the unchangeable economy of the world, which, even if the fairest visions of the millennium itself were realized, would still render such a thing *actually* impossible, that he hardly regrets the bright scene was but a beautiful *mirage*, and melts away. His imagination then descends to view this immense tribe of rational beings in another, and comparatively moderate state of the cultivation of their faculties, a state not one-third part so lofty as that in which he had beheld all the individuals improved to the utmost of their natural capacity; and he thinks, that the condition of man's abode on earth *might* admit of their being raised to *this* elevation. But he soon sees that, till a mighty change shall come on the management of the affairs of nations, this too is impossible; and with regret he sees even this inferior ideal spectacle pass away, to rest on an age in distant prospect. At last he takes his imaginary stand on what he feels to be a very low level of the supposed improvement of the general popular mind; and he says, Thus much, at the least, should be a possibility allowed by the circumstances of the people under *any* tolerable disposition of national interests;—and then he turns to look down on an actual condition in which care, and toil, and distress, render it impossible for a great proportion of the people to reach, or even approach, this his last and lowest conception of what the state of their minds ought to be.

In spite of all the optimists, it *is* a grievous reflection, after the race has had on earth so many thousands of years for attaining its most advantageous condition there, that all the experience, the philosophy, the science, the art, the power acquired by mind over matter,—that all the contributions of all departed and all present spirits and bodies, yes, and all religion too, should have come but to this;—to this, that in what is self-adulated as the most favoured and improved nation of all terrestrial space and time, a vast proportion of the people are found in a condition which confines them, with all the rigour of necessity, to a mere childhood of intelligent existence, without its innocence.

But at the very same time, and while the compassion rises, at such a view, there comes in on the other hand the reflection, that even in the actual state of things, there are a considerable number of the people who *might* acquire a valuable share of improvement which they do not. Great numbers of them, grown up, waste by choice, and multitudes of children waste through utter neglect, a large quantity of precious time which their narrow circumstances still leave free from the iron dominion of necessity. And they will waste it, it is certain that they will, till education shall have become general, and much more vigorous in discipline. If through a miracle there were to come down on this country, with a sudden delightful affluence of temporal melioration, resembling the vernal transformation from the dreariness of winter, an universal prosperity, so that all should be placed in comparative ease and plenty, it would require another miracle to prevent this benignity of heaven from turning to a dreadful mischief. What would the great tribe of the uneducated people do with the half of their time, which we will suppose that such a state would give to their voluntary disposal? Every one can answer infallibly, that the far greater number of them would consume it in idleness, vanity, or every sort of intemperance. Educate them, then, bring them under a grand process of intellectual and moral reformation;—or, in all circumstances and events, calamitous or prosperous, they are still a race made in vain!

In taking leave of the subject, we wish to express, in strong terms, the applause and felicitations due to those excellent individuals, found here and there, who in very humble circumstances, and perhaps with very little advantage of education in their youth, have been excited to a strenuous, continued exertion for the improvement of their minds; and thus have made (the unfavourable situation considered,) admirable attainments, which are verifying to them that "knowledge is power," over rich resources for their own enjoyment, and are in many instances passing with inestimable worth into the instruction of their families, and a variety of usefulness within their sphere. They have nobly struggled with their threatened destiny, and have overcome it. When they think, with regret, how confined, after all, is their portion of knowledge, as compared with the possessions of those who have had from their infancy all facilities and the amplest time for its acquirement, let them be consoled by reflecting, that the value of mental progress is not to be measured solely by the quantity of knowledge possessed, but partly, and indeed still more, by the corrective, invigorating effect produced on the mental powers by the resolute exertions made in attaining it. And therefore, since under their great disadvantages, it has required a much greater degree of this resolute exertion in them to force their way victoriously out of ignorance, than it has required in those who have had every thing in their favour to make a long free career over the field of knowledge, they may be assured they possess one greater benefit in *proportion* to the measure of their acquirements. This persistence of a determined will to do what has been so difficult to be done, has infused a peculiar energy into the exercise of their powers; a valuable compensation, in part, for their more limited share of the advantage that one part of knowledge becomes more valuable in itself by the accession of many others. Let them persevere in this worthy self-discipline, appropriate to the introductory period of an endless mental life. Let them go on to complete the proof how much a mind incited to a high purpose may triumph over a depression of its external condition;—but solemnly taking care, that all their improvements may tend to such a result, that at length the rigour of their lot and the confinement of mortality itself bursting at once from around them, may give them to those intellectual revelations, that everlasting sunlight of the soul. in which the truly wise will expand all their faculties in a happier economy.

A DISCOURSE

ON THE

PROPAGATION OF CHRISTIANITY IN INDIA;

THE SUBSTANCE OF WHICH WAS DELIVERED

AT THE ANNUAL MEETING

OF

A MISSIONARY SOCIETY,

IN 1818.

ADVERTISEMENT.

It is very true, as several friends have suggested, that the following Discourse might, on some accounts, have been more properly denominated an Essay. But, as the series of thoughts of which it consists was actually addressed, in the order in which they here occur, though with much less amplification, to a public assembly, and as somewhat of the manner of expression proper to such an address is retained in the composition, the author thinks there might be an appearance of literary affectation in giving it any other title than one describing it in that character.

ON THE

PROPAGATION OF CHRISTIANITY IN INDIA.

They came not to the help of the Lord, to the help of the Lord against the mighty."—JUDGES v. 23.

THE practice may be too frequent, of accommodating objects and effects in the world of nature, the relations and transactions in that of human society, and the merely secular facts of the Scripture history, to the purpose of representing, in the way of formal and protracted similitude, the truths and interests of religion. We may observe, however, that it seems to the honour of religion that so many things *can* be accommodated to its illustration, without any recourse to that perverted ingenuity which fancifully descries or invents resemblances. It is an evident and remarkable fact, that there is a certain principle of correspondence to religion throughout the economy of the world. Things bearing an apparent analogy to its truths, obviously or more remotely, present themselves on all sides to a thoughtful mind. He that made all things for Himself appears to have willed that they should be a great system of emblems, reflecting or shadowing that system of principles which is the true theory concerning Him, and our relations to Him. So that religion, standing up in grand parallel to an infinity of things, receives their testimony and homage, and speaks with a voice which is echoed by the creation.

It may therefore be permitted us to fix upon a circumstance in the secular conduct of an ancient people, as adapted to suggest more than it essentially contains, and to carry our thoughts, by analogy, to a kind of duty and of delinquency more directly related to religion. Under this licence our subject is introduced by a sentence pronounced, we may presume at the divine dictation, in reproach of a refusal to co-operate in a different kind of service from that which we have to recommend on the present occasion.

The negative form of the charge,—They came *not* to the help of the Lord,—may remind us of the grievous fact, that by far the greater number of the judicial negative statements in the Bible, respecting the conduct of men, are accusations. The mention that they did *not* do the thing in question is very generally the implied assertion that they ought to have done it. And the consideration becomes still more impressive, on recollection that we are told, that the last negative statement to be uttered on earth, and uttered by the greatest voice, will be with an emphasis of condemnation ; "Inasmuch as ye did it *not*—."

Observe how much guilt there may be in mere omission, and that, even though we should suppose the persons, who decline the one specific duty, to be occupied, while neglecting it, in employments in themselves innocent and laudable. It is very possible that the people of whose absence from the appointed scene of action we have just read the accusing record, might have brought a plea on this ground, against the justice of the consequent malediction. They might perhaps have had to say, that they were diligently prosecuting the labours of their rural economy, which there might be, at the time, particular reasons why they should not suspend ; or that they were intent on certain plans for rectifying disorders in their society; or that they were employing the time in some religious solemnity, perhaps imploring the intervention of Heaven in the alarming crisis, under a persuasion of the sufficiency of the Divine Power independently of human means. But no such pleas would have availed, to avert the vindictive sentence which the prophetess was instructed to pronounce on their refusal to do *that one thing* which the summons of unquestionable authority had signified to be, in that juncture, their precise duty. Such allegations might indeed have been dishonestly made, as an attempt to veil selfishness and cowardice, the real causes probably for withholding the required service; and then the hypocrisy would have incurred a prompt exposure and a severity of rebuke; but even had they been made sincerely, and proved to be true, they would not have arrested or revoked the condemnation. The appeal of the defaulters would have been silenced by the decision, that it is of the essence of disobedience and rebellion to assume to make commutations and substitutions of duty, to transfer obligation to where it would be less inconvenient that it should be enforced, and to affect to render, in the form of preferred and easier services, an equivalent for the obedience which the righteous and supreme authority has distinctly required to be rendered in that harder service which is evaded.

Supposing these people to have really been of a quiet and harmless disposition, and assiduous in the useful vocations of ordinary life, there may appear, notwithstanding the urgency of the occasion, something hard in the alternative they were placed in, of suddenly abandoning their homes to rush into the perils of battle, or suffering all that was denounced in so heavy an execration. And, in the survey of the many forms into which human duty has been diversified by occasions, as displayed in the Bible and other records, we see many situations of exceeding hardship —no reflection implied on that Authority which prescribed their arduous exercises. The great contest against Evil, in all its modes of invasion of this world, (but our reference is chiefly to those requiring men's resistance in the religious capacity,) has been a service assigned in every possible difference of circumstance and proportion; and some men's shares have involved a vehemence of exertion, or weight of suffering, which we look upon with wonder and almost with terror. We shudder to think of mortals like ourselves having been brought into such fearful dilemmas between obedience and guilt. We shrink from placing ourselves but in imagination under such tests of fidelity to God and a good cause. The painful retrospective sympathy with those agents and sufferers terminates in self-congratulation, that their allotment of duty has not been ours. The tacit sentiment is, I am very glad I can be a good man on less severe conditions.

And the sentiment is justified by the laws of our nature. It may become an emotion of piety, and rise in gratitude to God for having appointed us to a less formidable service. But it may also be indulged in such a manner as to betray us into dangerous delusion. In pleasing ourselves with the thought of our exemption from an order of duties involving the sacrifice of everything gratifying in mortal existence but a good conscience,—duties to be performed at the cost of suffering oppressive and unmitigated toil, pain, want, reproach, loss of liberty and even of life itself,—duties imposing such a trial of fidelity as confessors and martyrs have sustained,—we may be led into a wrong estimate of the difference between their situation and ours, as if our obligations were constituted under an *essentially* different economy. With an unthinking self-assurance that the satisfaction we feel is gratitude to God for a less rigorous appointment, we may be making exemptions for ourselves which he has never made. Delighted that, at the easy price of only being thankful to him, we are allowed to take so much indulgence, we may with a deluded confidence widen out the sphere of privilege beyond one point, and beyond another, where he has marked the boundary; with always the strongest propensity to this enlargement on that side where the hardest duties are placed; till the mind at length reposes in a scheme of duty adjusted, on its own authority, to its own convenience, and far from coincident with that which has been dictated by the divine will.

There *is* delusion in our self-congratulation at the contrast between what is enjoined on us and the severer duties imposed on some of our great Master's subjects, if we do not perceive that, nevertheless, the matter of our required service is of the very same substance, (with only a favourable difference of mode and proportion,) as that which appears to us of such rigour in theirs. There *is* delusion, if we are permitted to escape from the habitual sense of being placed, in character of the servants of God, under the duty and necessity of an intense moral warfare, against powers of evil as real and palpable as ever were encountered in the field of battle. Not to feel ourselves pressed upon by resistless evidence and admonition of this, is an utter ignorance or oblivion of our commission on earth. And the natural consequence is a fate like that of strangers thoughtlessly straying and surrendering themselves to sleep, in a place where it is a law of the barbarian inhabitants to sacrifice all strangers to their infernal gods.

Yet there is in general so faint an impression of the

fact, of an urgent necessity of war till death, as the grand business and obligation of life, that, to the greater number of the persons to whom we offer illustrations of christian topics, no language sounds so idly, no figures appear so insignificant, no forms of common-place so "stale, flat, and unprofitable," as those which represent in a military character the exertions by which men are to evince themselves the servants of God. An appeal might safely be made to the consciousness of many hearers and readers, whether at the recurrence of these images in any religious reference, they have not a marked sense of insipidity strongly tending to disgust, caused in some degree, we may allow, by a too frequent iteration, but still more by the impression of unmeaningness and futility in employing such terms for such a subject.

It is striking to observe, at the same time, how some of the persons who are thus tired to loathing of these images in their moral and spiritual application, will feel their latent energy beginning to stir and breathe at similar language and figures coming before them in literal representation of war. Most of the excitable class of spirits, whether in youth or much later life, can be kindled to enthusiasm by the grand imagery of battles and heroic achievements. The terms of martial metaphor which, perhaps in a religious discourse, are inflicting dulness and disgust in a representation of the "spiritual conflict," "the christian warfare," may relieve them by suddenly turning to their literal sense, and diverting the mind away to an imagined scene of conflict; and it shall feel a proud elation in passing from the vapid story of a spiritual war, to the magnificence of the combats which are displayed in fire and blood to the eyes, and in thunder to the ears. The attention being wholly withdrawn from the strain which is perhaps still proceeding, in words no longer sensibly heard, to figure out the christian soldier, the imagination shall follow the track of some brilliant mortal, of history or fiction, through scenes of tumult, and terror, and noble daring; and shall adore him as beheld exulting unhurt in victory, or as expiring in the manner in which it is poetically graceful for a hero to fall. The enthusiast, while sitting still and abstracted, may be at moments enchanted into a kind of personation of the character, and glow with emotion in the mimic fancy of acting himself a part so splendid. And these scenes of fury and destruction, thus fervidly imagined, shall really be deemed the sublimest exhibitions of man, in which human energy approaches nearest to a rivalry with the "immortals,"—for the epic diction of paganism may naturally be the expression of sentiments fired by its spirit. "Immortal," may be also the word which he is silently pronouncing in his adoration of the personage whose career he is pursuing in reverie; conformably to that caprice of human madness, which has determined the special selection of such an epithet for bedecking the most active dealers in death, and whose exposure to be smitten by it is an inevitable condition of their inflicting it.

If, in this inflamed state of the mind, the idea were again presented of the christian warfare, of a contest against principalities and powers, and spiritual wickedness, it would be repelled with disdain of the impertinence or arrogance which could assume for *such* matters any of the lofty terms belonging, and, (it would be proudly said,) *deservedly* applied, to the transactions of Trafalgar and Waterloo. This contempt may be felt by persons to whom the glories of war are only a pageant of the imagination; but it would be a still stronger sentiment in most of the men who have actually witnessed and shared the terrors and triumphs of martial exploit, if they by accident should hear the figurative language in question, and lend for a moment attention enough to understand what it should mean. In short, between distaste for its insipidity, and almost resentful scorn of its impertinence of pretension, the metaphor would be, by most men of high-toned spirit, flung back on the imbecile religionists, as an inane fancy, in which they are seeking to make for themselves a compensation for their incapacity of any thing truly great. Let these wars, enemies, and heroes of vapour, they would say, busy the feeble souls that can make a mock reality of such matters.

But what shall we think of the sanity of the perceptions of minds thus capable of being enchanted away into such imaginary scenes, proudly sympathetic with the ardour of battles and triumphs, and bereft of all cognisance of their own nearest, deadliest, mightiest enemy, Moral Evil? And if our thoughts go from those who are thus fired with the imagination of martial scenes, to those who are in the temper for the reality, how deplorable it is to behold moral agents, whom we are to call rational, prompt in hostile pride, vigilantly quick to see or suspect an enemy, burning with heroic spirit, inflated with notions of glory, but who would turn away with slight or scorn at the representations, by which divine or human admonition is attempting to alarm them to a sense of their danger from that foe compared with which all others are but shapes of air! That creatures should be thus maddened with fancies of the glory of destructive combats with one another, and insensible of the presence and quality of that destroyer which is invading them all, is truly a sight for the most malignant beings in the creation to exult over; a phenomenon of as dark a character as the frightful spectacle sometimes exhibited in a shipwreck or a dungeon, where a company of men have fallen with demoniac fury to mutual destruction, when through the disaster of their situation they were perishing by one common calamity; or as that which would have been presented by opposed armed parties or legions, gallantly maintaining battle on the yet uncovered spaces of ground, while the universal flood was rising.

Alas for the stupified intelligence of those minds which can regard as idle extravagance this language which would arouse their attention to what is as certain a reality as their own existence, and will infallibly make the most fatal proof of its power on the spirits the least aware that the destroyer is at hand! What a renovation of perceptive faculty is necessary to that being who would ask, either in levity or ignorant surprise, What and where is that foe, so malignant and powerful?—while there is exposed in full view the mighty mass, and force, and operation, of all that deceives, and depraves, and ruins the souls of men! This spiritual obtuseness would itself betray the intervention of the very enemy described. Let a thoughtful man survey the world of mankind, and see what there is universally among them to excite the sad exclamation, "Wo to the inhabitants of the earth!" Let him deeply consider *what it is* that he is beholding, while he observes this power of evil assailing, and committing grievous mischief upon, every human being, his experience testifying that himself is not exempted He is to form his judgment of the gloomy fact under his view, on an estimate of the injury done to each one, and of the number so injured, including in the account the generations of all past time. And let him try whether an earnest and protracted attention to the dire exhibition will detect a fallacy in its dreadful aspect, so that his last sober judgment shall be like the relief of recovering by the aid of reason from a superstitious terror. No; he will find, uniformly, that the evil reveals itself to him in still more substantial and deadly character, the longer he fixes an unshrinking inspection on any of its innumerable forms. The impression thus reinforced by stronger demonstration might become too aggravated to be borne, if there were to be suddenly imparted to him a great addition of religious light and sensibility, through which he should receive, while contemplating this vision of evil, a brighter manifestation of the holiness of God, and the perfection of his law. And even such a view might still be but a faint apprehension compared with the perception of some superior pure intelligence looking on this world; and how much more so in comparison with the thought and feeling with which the Redeemer beheld the error and depravity of our race! No language or images for communicating information in any world, can ever represent *his* estimate of the scene. But *that* was the only adequate apprehension of it. In whatever degree, therefore, its portentous quality is manifested to the view of a religious observer, he will always be certain that there is in it a depth of evil still beyond the capacity of his thought; while in that which he does apprehend he perceives a magnitude and atrocity which can be but feebly expressed by borrowing terms from circumstances the most odious and dreadful in material existence, and saying, that the multitude of human souls are invaded, robbed, polluted, chained, tormented, or murdered.

Sometimes we contemplate, perhaps, the mighty progress of destruction, as carried over a large tract of the earth by some of the memorable instruments of the divine wrath, such as Attila, Jenghis Khan, or Timour.

We behold a wide spreading terror preceding, to be soon followed by the realization of every alarming presage, in resistless ravage and extermination. Numberless crowds come tumultuously to our view, in all the varieties of dismay, and vain effort, and suffering, and death; a world of ghastly countenances, desperate struggles, lamentable cries, streaming blood, and expiring agonies; with the corresponding circumstances of fury and triumph, and the appropriate scenery of habitations burning and the land made a desert. And while one general character of horror is spread over the immensity of the scene, the imagined forms and aspects of individual victims, frequently marked forth from the confused aggregate, and presented to the mind in momentary glimpses, as vivid points, standing out to verify that dreadful character, give an effect of reality to the visionary spectacle of misery and destruction.

When a man of ardent imagination has dwelt upon such a scene till it almost glows into actual existence in his view, let him be assured it is the language of truth and soberness that affirms this spectacle to form but a faint and inadequate image, to typify that other invasion which is made on the spirits of all mankind; that invasion of which, indeed, all these horrors are themselves but a few of the exterior signs and results. And yet creatures assailed and in danger of destruction by this more awful calamity, surveying in fancy, and shuddering while they survey, these furies and miseries of remote times or regions, shall bless their good fortune that *they* are not exposed to any persecution of evil a thousandth part so formidable!

When following in thought those perpetrators of devastation and carnage, we have the consolation of foreseeing its end. The Cæsars and Attilas were as mortal as the millions who expired to give them fame. Of Timour, the language of the Historian, kindling into poetry, relates that "he pitched his last camp at Otrar, where he was expected by the Angel of Death."* But the power that wages war immediately on the souls of men, the power of depravity and delusion combined, has continued to live and destroy while all these renowned exterminators have yielded to the decree that sent them after their victims. It is perpetually invigorated by the very destruction which it works; as if it fed upon the slain to strengthen itself for new slaughter, and absorbed into its own every life which it takes away. For it is in the nature of moral evil, as acting on human beings, to create to itself new facilities, means, and force, for prolonging that action. From the effects there is continually reflected back an augmentation of power to the cause; a circumstance explained by the fatal aptitude of the subject operated upon to give its own strength to aid the pernicious agency. The injured subject,—the corrupted nature,—still less and less, at each return of the injurer, thinks of suspecting or resisting; still more and more effectively contributes that the malignity may not be frustrated. So that the power of sin acquires over those who are surrendered to it a more decided predominance in each stage of their progress, and makes confirmed assurance of what they will be in the next, unless prevented by something foreign to their own moral nature. And since the majority of human beings have always been under this power, what a security it has possessed for prolonging its empire of destruction! What a security, in the principle by which, in every period, the greater number of all mankind were, as individuals, incessantly growing worse! And to what a dreadful perfection

* Gibbon.

of evil might such a race attain but for Death, that cuts the term of individuals so short, and but for the Spirit of God, that converts some, and puts a degree of restraint on the rest.

And now, if there really is thus in action against the souls of our race, such an enemy as all these epithets and images can but inadequately figure, can a professed servant of God look round, and felicitate himself on having an extremely easy test of his fidelity? Where does he find his privileged ground of immunity and indulgence, while this mighty force of evil drives and sweeps and rages, against God, and truth, against goodness and happiness, his own spirit and all men's spirits, as really as ever he that was named the Scourge of God ravaged the countries of Asia and Europe? In seeking such exemption he must abandon all the objects and interests against which this hostility is directed; must therefore compromise and in effect co-operate with the enemy. Let him consider what scheme it is possible to conceive of true service to the King of Heaven in this bad world, which should not commit him in conflict at every point of its execution. Against *every* good he can think of, he will find an appropriate antagonist evil already in full action, an action that will not remit and sink into quiet when he approaches to effect the intended good. Nay, indeed, in what way is it that the servant of God the most readily apprehends the nature of his vocation but in that of seeing what it is *against?* And when he puts the matter to experimental proof, does he ever find that those apprehended adversaries are nothing but menacing shadows? Let him that has made the most determined, protracted, and extensive trial, tell whether it be idle common-place and extravagance when we say that all Christian exhortation is in truth a summons to war.

There are many modes of the action of this grand enemy, moral evil, which press so immediately on a man's own personal concern, that a habitual conflict with them is an essential condition of the Christian character: a practical question of hostility or acquiescence is implicated with the ordinary course of his self-government. There are other forms, of great magnitude and hatefulness, existing in the world, which do not so directly force themselves into the question of his being a Christian or not. In judgment and feeling he must be, of course, their implacable enemy. But since they throw no temptation in his way, have the sphere of their malignant operation at a great distance, leave a very wide space clear for Christian exercise, and may seem also, by their vastness and consolidated establishment, to be placed the very last of all things that individuals can account themselves competent to attack,—to be as enormous mountains limiting their field,—it may be acknowledged a matter of somewhat less definable obligation in what degree he shall actively expend his animosity upon them. The exhortation to supply a share of his efforts in that direction, may be considered as partly an appeal to those higher sentiments of the religious spirit which aspire to the full magnanimity and zeal of the christian character. It is an admonition to the professed adherents of Him who came on earth with a design extending in hostility, without limit or exception, to *every* thing adverse to goodness and pernicious to the human soul, that if all the moral evil in the world is not acting immediately against *them*, it is against *Him*; and that it is most reasonable that one of the laws of their devotion to him should be, to identify themselves with him in the practical warfare to the *widest scope* which is really open to their enterprise. It is an incitement to their ambition, not to leave it to be ever said again, with respect to any part of his operations against evil among men, that he trod the winepress alone, and that of the people there was none with him.

When animated to this high and adventurous spirit, a good man may wonder that the Heathenism prevailing over large tracts of the world should so little have been, in this country or other Protestant nations, till a comparatively recent time, accounted as comprehended within the sphere of required Christian exertion.* One most amiable fraternity, indeed, whose gentleness at home involves a principle by which it glows into energy and heroism in proportion to the remoteness of the distance, and the barbarousness and ruggedness of the field of action, to which it is voluntarily exiled, have made missions to the heathens an essential part of their institution. But in general the friends of religion seem to have regarded those great maladies of the moral world, the delusions and abominations of paganism, with a sort of submissive awe, as if, almost, they had established a prescriptive

* The indifference of Protestants was not for want of examples, such as they were, of activity in this department. It was very well known that there had been various missionary enterprises under the appointment of the Romish Church. And certain individuals employed in those missions were held worthy of perpetual remembrance for their invincible perseverance, and for a share, it was fair to believe, of a truly Christian principle in the motives which actuated them. But when these undertakings were viewed in their general character, it was so notorious that they were, as to the prevailing motive, projects of hierarchical ambition, and that, in their mode of prosecution, they accommodated, with the corruptest policy, to the paganism they professed to convert, and introduced a great deal of what was no better than paganism of their own, that Protestants could hardly regard them as *Christian* projects; and therefore felt no stimulus at the view of their activity, and derived nothing to excite hope from the boasts, or the facts, of their success.

right to the place they had held so long ; or as if they were part of an unchangeable, uncontrollable order of nature, like the noxious climates of certain portions of the globe. Or at least, when these religious men have looked on these mighty forms of darkness and iniquity, as destined to vanish at some time from the scenes of which they have been so long the curse, and have prayed for that time to be hastened on, they have found themselves anticipating and invoking, with undefined conception, some entirely unwonted and even properly miraculous mode of Divine interposition, and have felt as if it should be for men to stand off and see what God can do ; in this very feeling perhaps admitting on their minds the imposition, through which a defect of faith and zeal may be mistaken for humility and devotion.

Within a later period, however, (within that, chiefly, which has shown on so vast a scale the availableness of human agency, for overturning things of ancient, and wide, and commanding establishment,) many good men have begun to regard with much less prostration of feeling those gigantic "dominations" which have so many ages held so many nations in the debasement of superstition. It came to be questioned why a servant of Christ should shrink from looking any of the powers of darkness in the face, from defying them in his Master's name, or from making the experiment of an application of heaven's own fire, to the munitions of that realm of deceit and cruelty in which the souls of men are destroyed. In proportion as the imaginary defence around these tyrannies over the mind was in any part seen ready to fall, in proportion as the reputed guardianship of fate or infernal power which had seemed to render them impregnable, was breaking up, the idea of such an experiment on them assumed a less visionary appearance. It took a character of evident practicability; and then it grew to a conviction of duty, in some of those to whom the cause of heaven was the object of highest concern on earth.

This impression was strongly felt by the first movers of the project of that Mission to India, which we regard as one of the most worthy enterprises of the enlarging Christian ambition to make war on the greatest and most inveterate evils of the moral world. When awaked, as it were, to behold an ampler view of the world as a field of activity for the zealots for the best cause, they were struck with surprise at seeing so few adventuring into the distance against the most ancient and vast dominion of paganism; and they thought it high time that an end should be put to the quietude of sentiment, the antichristian tolerance, toward what was standing in defiance of that cause, with such proud impunity.

The quality and the strength of this possessor of so wide a region and so many slaves, were evident enough under a very imperfect exposure, to place the meditated experiment of hostility greatly out of the common calculations of Christian daring. It could not but appear so far beyond those ordinary presumptions, as to provoke the contempt of those who have no notion of the interference of the Divine power in aid of such projects. Yet the information possessed at that time, by even the intelligent part of the nation, had been too superficial or deceptive to give anything approaching to an adequate idea of the superstition and corruption of the people of Hindoostan. It has been chiefly during the period since this Mission was commenced, and in a considerable degree in consequence of the discussions and the exposition of evidence occasioned by animosity against it, that a rapidly increasing knowledge has brought the general opinion to that judgment of the character and condition of the Hindoos, which the translations made from their sacred books by the missionaries and other eastern scholars, and the reports of travellers reduced at the last to the necessity of keeping to the truth,—are fast contributing to place beyond all honest controversy. If there was in so old and well examined a thing as human nature no undetected perversity, for these disclosures to bring to light as a new principle of evil, they have, however, shown some of its known evil principles inhering and operating in it with such an absoluteness of possessive power, and displaying this despotism in such wantonly versatile, extravagant, and monstrous effects, as to surpass our previous imaginations and measures of possibility.

There is much in the Hindoo system that is strikingly peculiar; but as it is the substantial greatness of the evil, rather than its specific modifications, that requires to be presented to the view of Christian zeal, much of the stress of our brief observations will be laid on properties which are common to this with the other principal modes of paganism. The object is rather to display the system in its strength of pernicious operation, than to attempt any explanatory statement of its precise materials or construction. There needs no great length of description, since the communications of missionaries, and the depositions of inquisitive observers less liable to the suspicion of prejudice, have made, within the last few years, all who take any interest in the subject familiarly acquainted with the prominent features of the heathenism of central Asia. As for the possible attainment of anything like a complete knowledge, it may defy all human faculty; which faculty besides, if it might search the universe for choice of subjects, could find nothing less worth its efforts for knowledge. The system, if so it is to be called, appears, to a cursory inquirer at least, an utter chaos, without top, bottom, or centre, or any dimension or proportion belonging either to matter or mind, and consisting of materials which deserve no better order. It is a world of crude vanities, endlessly sporting into monstrous conformations and dissolving them; much resembling the bustle of tragi-comical creations in a dream of delirium. It is the most remarkable exemplification of the possibility of degrading a grand idea by conjunction with meanness; that of immensity becoming here contemptible by combination with the very abstract of worthlessness.

But, deserving of all contempt as the superstition is in itself, regarded merely as a farrago of notions and fantasies, it is a thing for detestation and earnest hostility when viewed in its practical light, as the governing scheme of principles (so to call them) and rites to a large portion of our race. Consider that there is thus acting upon them, as religion, a system which is in nearly all its properties that which the true religion *is not*, and in many of them the exact reverse. Look at your religion, presented in its bright attributes before you, reflecting those of its Author; and then realize to your minds, as far as you can, the condition of so many millions of human spirits receiving, without intermission, from infancy to the hour of death, the full influence of the direct opposites to these divine principles,—a contrast of condition of which we should have but a faint emblem in that between the Israelites and the Egyptians, in beholding on the different sides the pillar, in its appearance over the Red Sea. It is as in passing on toward another world, that we have to make the comparison between the respective systems of religion under the guidance of which we and they are in the progress thither. While ours has, as its solar light and glory, the doctrine of One Being in whom all perfections are united and infinite, theirs scatters that which is the most precious and vital sentiment of the human soul and of any created intelligence, that is, the affection which regards Deity, to an indefinite multitude and diversity of adored objects;* the one system carrying the spirit downward to utter debasement through that very element of feeling in which it should be exalted; while the other, when in full influence, bears it upward through all things that combine to degrade it. The relation subsisting between man and the Divinity, as declared in the true religion, is of a simple and solemn character; a few plain important propositions define it; whereas the Brahminical theory exhibits this relation in an infinitely confounded, fantastic, vexatious, and ludicrous complexity. While in the Christian system the future state of man is declared with the same dignified simplicity, the contrasted paganism, between some dream of an aspiring mysticism on the one hand, and the paltriest conceits of a reptile invention on the other, presents, we might say sports, this sublime doctrine and fact in the shapes of riddle and whimsey. Ours is an economy according to which

* It is acknowledged that the most ancient authorities of Hindoo faith retain a trace of primeval truth, in the doctrine of a Supreme Spirit, distinguished from the infinity of personifications on which the religious sentiment is wasted, and from those few transcendent demon figures which proudly stand out from the insignificance of the swarm. But this idea reduced to inanity by time, superstition, and ignorance, feebly apprehended by the general mind, a mere *nebula* in the Hindoo heaven, is inefficacious for shedding one salutary ray on the spirits infatuated with all that is trivial and gross in the superstition.

religion, considered as in its human subjects, consists in a state of the mind instead of exterior formalities; the institutes of the Hindoos make it chiefly consist in a miraculously multiplied and ramified order or disorder of ritual fooleries. It is almost superfluous to notice in the comparison, that while the one enjoins and promotes a perfect morality, the other essentially favours, and formally sanctions, some of the worst vices. It may suffice to add, that while the true religion knows nothing of any precedence in the Divine estimate and regard, of one class of human creatures before another, in virtue of nativity or any mere natural distinction, the superstition we are describing has rested very much of its power upon a classification according to which one considerable proportion of the people are, by the very circumstance of their birth, morally distinguished as holy and venerable, and another more numerous proportion, as base and contemptible, sprung from the feet of the creating god, that they might be slaves to the tribe which had the luck and honour to spring from his head.

Such is this aggregate of perversions of all thought, and feeling, and practice. And yet, the system, *being religion*, acts on its subjects with that kind of power which is appropriate and peculiar to religion. The sense which man, by the very constitution of his nature, has of the existence of some superhuman power, is one of the strongest principles of that nature; whatever, therefore, takes a really effectual hold of this sense will go far toward acquiring the regency of his moral being. This conjunction of so many delusions does take possession of this sense in the minds of the Hindoos, with a mightier force than probably we see in any other exhibition of the occupancy of religion, on a wide scale, in the world. But to the power which the superstition has in thus taking hold of the religious sense, is to be added that which it acquires by another adaptation; for it takes hold also, as with more numerous hands than those given to some of the deities, of all the corrupt principles of the heart. What an awful consideration, that among a race of rational creatures a religion should be mighty almost to omnipotence by means, in a great measure, of alliance with the evil that is within them! What a melancholy display of man, that the two contrasted visitants to the world, the one from heaven, the other deserving by its qualities to have its origin referred to the world below,—that these two coming to make trial of their respective adaptations and affinities, upon human spirits, the infernal one should find free admission, through congeniality, to the possession of the whole souls of immense multitudes; while the one from heaven should but obtain in individuals, here and there, a possession which is partial at the best, and to be maintained by a conflict to the end of life against implacably repugnant principles in the soul. Well may a Christian be affected with most humiliating emotion, both for his race and himself, while he reflects,—I have a nature which might have yielded itself *entire* to a false religion, but so reluctantly and partially surrenders itself to the true one, as to retain me in the condition of having it for the chief concern of my life and prayers that the still opposing dispositions may be subdued.

The fact is too obvious to need illustration in particulars, that this superstition, while it commands the faith of its subjects, completes its power over them by its accordance to their pride, sensuality, and deceitfulness; to that natural concomitant of pride, the baseness which is ready to prostrate itself in homage to any thing that shall substitute itself for God; and to that interest which criminals feel to transfer their own accountableness upon the powers above them. But then think what a condition for human creatures! they believe in a religion which invigorates, by coincidence and sanction, those principles in their nature which the true religion is intended to destroy; and in return, those principles thus strengthened contribute to confirm their faith in the religion. The mischief inflicted becomes the most effectual persuasion to confidence in the inflicter.

Observe, again, the power possessed by this stupendous delusion in having direct hold on the senses, in so many ways, even exclusively of the grosser means, (the grossest possible, as you are apprised,) of which it avails itself to please them. It has attributed an inherence of something representative of the properties of deity to numberless visible objects, whence it emanates in a continual influence on the mind through the senses. All the vain notions of the superstition thus stand embodied before its devotees in material phenomena, which are informed with a significance that seems to look at them and speak tc them. Presented to them in these sensible types, those delusive ideas occupy their faculties sooner, almost, than they can think, more constantly than they think, and in a mode of possession stronger than mere thought. Indeed it is a mode of possession which, (after faith has grown into the habit of the mind,) may be effectual on the feelings though direct thought be wanting; for we may presume that in India, in other places, when external objects have been admitted as symbols of things believed but unseen, they may preserve in the people much of the moral habitude appropriate to that belief, even at times when there is no strictly intellectual apprehension. The Hindoo is under the influence of this enchantment on his senses, almost wherever the christian remonstrant against the dogmas and rites of his superstition can approach him.

seeking access to his reason and conscience. The man thus attempting may have read idle fictions of magical spells, which obstruct the passing of some line, or preclude entrance at a gate; but here he may perceive a *real* intervening magic, between the truth he brings, and the intellectual and moral faculties into which he wishes to introduce it. In his missionary progress among the people, perhaps he shall address them where there is in sight some gigantic idol, some holy river, some votive object, some consecrated relic, or the tomb of some revered impostor; things which being connected, in their apprehension, more closely with religion than their garments are with their persons, will impress the assurance that the religious power (the *numen*) whose emblems are present, is present itself; that it is a reality, of which every thing adorable or fearful is at that instant impending in menacing authority over them. A thing inconsiderable in itself, firmly associated with an invisible greater thing as its sign, may have the effect not only of reminding of that greater, but of aggravating the sense of both its reality and importance.

His next address may be uttered in the vicinity of a temple, which, if in ruins, seems to tell but so much the more impressively, by that image and sign of antiquity, at what a remote and solemn distance of time that *was* the religion which they feel to be the religion still; if undilapidated and continuing in its sacred use, overawes their minds with the mysterious solemnities of its unviolated sanctuary; while the sculptured shapes and gestures of divinities, overspreading the exterior of the structure, have nothing in their impotent and monstrous device and clumsy execution to abate the reverence of Hindoo devotion, toward the objects expressed in this visible language. The missionary, if an acute observer, might perceive how rays of malignant influence strike from such objects on the faculties of his auditors, to be as it were reflected in their looks of disbelief and disdain on the preacher of the new doctrine. What a strength of guardianship is thus arrayed in the very senses of the pagan, for the fables, lying doctrines, and immoral principles, established in his faith!

Or we may suppose the protester in the name of the true God to be led to the scene of one of the grand periodical celebrations of the extraordinary rites of idolatry. There, as at the temple of Jaggernaut, contemplating the effect of an intense fanaticism, glowing through an almost infinite crowd, he may perceive that each individual mind is the more fitted, by being heated in this infernal furnace, to harden in a more decided form and stamp of idolatry as it cools.

The very riches of nature, the conformations and productions of the elements, co-operate in this mighty tyranny over the mind by occupancy of the senses. Deity, while degraded in human conception of it in being diffused through these objects, comes, at the same time, with a more immediate impression of presence, when flowers, trees, animals, rivers, present themselves, not as effects and illustrations, but often as substantial participants, or at least sacred vehicles, of that sublimest existence, and the whole surrounding physical world is one vast mythology, an omnipresent fallacy. In praying that the region may be cleared of idol gods, the missionary might feel the question suggested whether he be not repeating Elijah's prayer for the withholding of rain, since that would certainly do the most toward vacating the pantheon, by the destruction of the flowers, trees, animals, and streams.

This great enemy, against which we are wishing to excite christian zeal, is "mighty" in the strength of venerable antiquity. Antiquity is, all over the world, the favourite resource of that which is without rational evidence; especially so, therefore, of superstition; and the Brahminical superstition rises imperially above all others in assumption of dignity from the past, which it arrogates as all its own, but emphatically that where amazing remoteness appears to confer a character of solemnity on time. Other dominations over human opinion are under the necessity of acknowledging an origin at a particular period, and in comparative insignificance; and have had to attain their due honours by a slowly enlarging progress downward through ages. But this proud imposture, disowning every thing like an infancy, disdaining all idea of having ever been less and afterwards greater, and defying all computation of time, makes the past, back to an inconceivable distance, the peculiar scene of its magnificence. And it teaches its devotees to regard its continued presence on earth, not as the progress of a cause advancing and brightening into greatness and triumph, but merely as something of the radiance reaching thus far, and with fainter splendour, from that glory so divine in the remote past. Its primeval manifestation was of such power as to prolong the effect even to this late period, in which the faithful worshippers have to look back so far to behold the glory of that vision it once condescended to unfold on this world. The grand point of attraction being thus placed in a past so stupendous as to assume almost a character of eternity, the contemplations, the devotional feelings, and the self-complacency, are drawn away in a retrospective direction, and leave behind in contempt all modern inventions of faith or institution, as the insignificant follies sprung from the corruption of a heaven-abandoned period of time. The sentiments excited in them by the many signs of decay in the exterior apparatus of their system, such as the ruined state of numerous temples, will rather coincide with this attraction in carrying the homage and the pride to the glory that was once, than lead to any suspicion of a futility for which the system deserves to grow out of use. This retrospective magnitude, this absorption of all past duration in their religion, this reduction to insignificance of whatever else has existed, (if, indeed, all that has existed have not been comprehended in it,) cannot fail to produce a degree of elation in the minds of the Hindoos, notwithstanding their incapability of genuine sublimity of conception and emotion.

And again, however inanimate their affections toward their contemporary relations, the idea of an ancestry extending back through unnumbered generations, all having had their whole intellectual and moral existence involved inseparably in their religion, and surrendering in succession their souls to become a kind of guardians or portions of it, must add a more vital principle of attraction to the majestic authority and sanction of such an antiquity. Generations of little account in their own times may acquire, when passed away to be contemplated as ancestry, a certain power over the imagination by becoming invested with something of the character of another world,—a venerableness which combines with and augments the interest which they hold in our thoughts as having once belonged to our mortal fraternity. This combined interest going wholly into the sentiments of religion. in the pagans of whom we speak, they will feel as if a violation of that would be an insult to each of the innumerable souls of the great religious family departed, all worthier of respect than any that are now living in the world from which they have vanished. This habitual reference to their ancestors, with a certain sense of responsibility, is maintained by various notions and rites of their superstition, expressly contrived for the purpose; as well as by the pride which they can all feel, in a still much greater degree than the more refined and poetical tone of sentiment, in thus standing connected, through identity of religious character and economy, with the remotest antiquity.

Nor can the influence be small, in the way of confirmed sanction and cherished pride, of beholding that which has been the element of the moral existence of an almost infinite train of predecessors, attested still, as to its most material parts, by a world of beings at this hour coinciding with the devotee in regarding it as their honour, their sanctity, and their supreme law. Let the Hindoo direct his attention or his travels whichever way he will, within the circuit of a thousand leagues, he meets with a crowding succession, without end, of living thinking creatures who, notwithstanding many capricious diversifications of their general faith, live but to believe and act as he does with regard to the most revered of its impositions. And what, in effect, do they all think and act so for, but as evidence that he is right? The mind can rest an assurance of its own rectitude of persuasion on this wide concurrence of belief, without therefore acknowledging to itself a degrading dependence. Its mode of seeing the matter is, not that the faith of a large assemblage of other minds is therefore *its* faith, but that its faith is *theirs*; not—I think and act as they do, but, They think and act as I do. This sort of ambitious expansion outward, from the individual as a centre, saves his pride of reason from being humiliated by the consideration of the sameness of his notions with those of the great mass. The sense of community in human nature is strongly and complacently admitted, when agreein multitudes corroborate a man's opinions without depriving him of the *self*-complacency of believing, that he holds them in the strength of his own wisdom.

This corroborating influence of the consent of contemporary multitude in the most essential points of the system, has, as we have hinted, its effect among the Hindoos independently of social affection. Never did any where a great number of human creatures exist together with such slender bonds of attachment to one another. It is a striking illustration of the tendency of their superstition, that it nearly abolishes these interests, keeping the whole population in the state of detached and most selfish particles. This seems indeed to be foregoing one of the strongest means of power, since a system of notions and moral principles might find the greatest account in so combining itself with the affections of nature as to engage them for auxiliaries. But then what a triumph of this bad cause, that while, instead of enticing these charities into its service, it tramples on and destroys them, it can notwithstanding make this assemblage of dissocial selfish beings act upon one another in confirmation of their common delusion, with an effect hardly less than that which might have arisen from friendly sympathy. Of little worth in one another's esteem as relations, friends, and fellow-countrymen, it is as things which the gods have set their stamp upon, and located their essence in, that they have their grand value. They have the effect of the sacred figures sculptured on their temples, or of leaves of their books of mythology. The seal or brand of the deities set upon them does not indeed *dignify* them all, but it makes them all vouchers to the religion. They all in conjunction personify, as it were, that system which as much requires the existence of Soodras to verify it as of Brahmins. The "miry clay" of the feet is as essential a part as the royal material of the head.

Thus the vast multitude are made to serve just as surety to one another, and all to each, for the verity of the superstition. And as the existence of any of them on any other account had been impertinent, their existence in such prodigious numbers must needs seem to demonstrate a mighty importance in that, for evidence and exemplification of which it was worth while for them to be so many.

With so despotic a command over the people's minds, it would have been strange if this empire of delusion had forborne to assume the advantage and security of those temporalities, which no other spiritual tyranny was ever unearthly enough to forget, and which, indeed, it would have been a foolish impolicy to forego. Indirectly, it possesses this mode of strength in having for its subjects the princely and opulent persons of the community; who render it double service, at once by profuse expenditures on its temples, celebrations, and priests; and by the homage of acknowledging all mere secular superiorities, of wealth, rank, and power, to be intrinsically subordinate to the highest of the distinctions founded in religion. There must be constant tokens of recognising, as paramount, whatever belongs or is kindred to the divinities. But those divinities have also their direct revenues, in the shape of fixed, and many of them ancient appropriations; with the addition of an undefined right of exaction, enforced by priests and consecrated mendicants upon the religious charity of the people. This charity is in one sense voluntary; but when it is considered with what lofty pretensions these applicants make their demands, (not unfrequently even assuming some mode of identity with the gods themselves,) and what benefits or curses are declared, and by the people believed to depend infallibly on their surrendering or withholding the tribute required, it is easy to judge how much these offerings and their quantity are left to free will.

Their own rights and those of their idols might be trusted, for the power of maintaining them, to men whose demands of a share of the superstitious cultivator's produce are to be resisted at the believed hazard of a blast on the whole. As if, however, both such endowments, and such force of requisition, had left cause to fear that this infernal hierarchy should become deficient in the substantial resources for preserving its dominion of delusion and iniquity, the Christian Government over India has sought the honour of being its auxiliary; in which capacity it is at once accepted and despised by the descendants of Brahma. The aid has been afforded not simply in the way of securing, in observance of the principle of toleration, the pagan worship and means of worship from violent interference, but in the form of a positive active patronage. The administration of the funds for the ceremonial and abominations of idolatry, has been, to a very great extent, taken under the authority and care of the reigning power, composed of persons zealous on this nearer side of a certain extent of water for the established christian religion, which establishment has also been recently extended to that further side,—with what effect toward exploding, or even modifying, this very marvellous policy, or whether deemed to be perfectly harmonious with it, we must wait to be informed.* In the mean time, the religious

* The writer has been told, that certain readers have taken offence at something in this passage. He cannot well understand why; and perhaps those readers would not be much

public are amply informed of a course of measures having been deliberately pursued tending to support and prolong the ascendency of paganism. It has been disclosed to their view that the highest authority has taken upon itself the regulation of the economy of idols' temples, has restored endowments which had lapsed, and has made additional allowances from the public revenue, where the existing appropriations have been judged inadequate to preserve to those establishments the requisite dignity and efficiency;—requisite for what, but to prevent any relaxation of the hold which the imposture has on the people? And, be it remembered, the revenue which is to afford this aid is constantly pressing heavily for its means of competence on the distressed resources of this Christian country.

We cannot presume to conjecture how much sooner this accessional mean of power will begin to fail, than those ancient ones, which the system was possessed of when none of its gods or sages could have foreseen a reserve of assistance in such a quarter. Nor do we

disposed to explain. The two facts are, that the English Government have adopted a policy of superintending and patronising the idolatrous establishments in India; and that, while systematically pursuing this policy, they have also appointed and endowed a Christian Ecclesiastical Establishment there. Now, they do, or they do not, consider this measure of establishing a Christian national church there as compatible, consistent, harmonious, with that policy of sanctioning and promoting idolatry. Do they, or do they not? Which part of the alternative to assume, it may not be very easy for candour to decide.——As to the fact of the systematic policy in question, it has been formally stated, or incidentally mentioned, in several publications relating to India. But whoever may wish to see it exposed in its full extent and evidence, may find it in a long, and very able and important article in the 12th volume of the *Christian Observer*, (the numbers for October and November, 1813.) We do not hear of any change having taken place in the system.

pretend to know what oracles of the "lying spirit," once before trusted in by a government, have given assurance against all alarm respecting the judicial notice which the Governor of the world may take of the Christian supporters of a system which he has doomed to destruction.

If we add to all these modes and causes of the mightiness of this superstition, the indefatigable activity of the powers of darkness, meaning literally infernal intelligences, believed to be by sufferance busy in this world, it might be readily admitted, we should imagine, that there is nothing in it worthier to have sprung from the inspiration, or to be kept in force by the craft, of such a malignant agency. If there are theologians who deny the intervention of such a cause in this enormity of evil, is it that their laying it all to the account of man alone will serve the argument for that other favourite opinion of theirs, which denies the radical corruption of his nature?—What new hopes, or consistencies or facilities, for the prosecution of this warfare, might be afforded by their view of the matter, which makes the human nature to be so excellent, and yet makes all this to be its spontaneous product, it would be of no use for us to stay to inquire; since it is our destiny to proceed in the contest under the notion, that such magnitude of evil can be no less than the leagued depravity of *two* bad natures. Those who can ascribe it all to one, and at the same time lavish their adulation on that one, would seem to make no contemptible approximation in point of rationality, toward the superstition we are speaking of, which acknowledges unreservedly what wickedness is committed by the gods, but insists that they are not the less to be adored.

Now, can a system of intellectual and moral perversion, of which the demoniac strength is but slightly developed in this brief description of some of its characteristics, shew itself in the view of the adherents of the true religion, without conveying a provocation to their conscience and zeal to come forth, in aid of any reasonable project for carrying a new power into attack on what has maintained, through so many ages, its character of a defier of the living God, in spite of all that might have been supposed to operate toward its destruction from time, and Nature, and the vaunted reason of man? Those who partake of the spirit of Elijah, and are "very jealous for the Lord of Hosts," will wish that good men might be moved to conspire in a hostility, which shall be carried into effect through being first sent up as a devout service and appeal to heaven, to be thence returned, (for it is in this reflected power that Christian zeal has its efficacy,) to be thence returned, as in burning rays, to scorch and blast, here and there, the extended array of idolatry, and at length to annihilate it. But, in thinking of such a conspiring zeal, thus reflected with an intensity not its own, to consume the mass of abomination, it is for each one to ask within himself, Is there not in that system, made up of so many depravities, some small part, some poisonous atom, some serpent vehicle of an evil principle, which *I* may be, through the same divine force imparted in its measure to the humblest individual's effort, the means of destroying? And that minute portion of active principle, which noxiously works on in consequence of my not crushing it,—may it not be accounted to work in my name, making my contribution, real however diminutive, and though only by way of omission, to the deadly mischief of that system which I *might* contribute just so much to abolish? But even though the state of the matter were, that no actual effect at all should result, none discernible by Him who discriminates every thing in the total of things, still, might I not be required, in mere proof of my fidelity to him, to give some demonstration of hatred, to fling some practical salutation of war, against an infernal monster that, in character of a constellation of gods, arrogates the worship of a large portion of the human race, and repays it with perdition? Can I hope to go, without some sense of dishonour, to that higher empire of the Almighty where every *possible* sentiment of devotion is in *actual* excitement, from a region where I have been nearly at peace with such an odious usurpation?

But even this state of peace with it has not been enough for some of our countrymen to maintain; and we think the partiality, arising in some instances almost to fanaticism, which, both at home and abroad, they have manifested without reserve for this grossest paganism, may serve to enforce our demand on Christian zeal. It may do so, partly, by the illustration thus afforded of the quality of the design, since that may be presumed to be greatly excellent which has had the exact effect of irritating out by contrariety the worst vice lurking in profane minds; and it may additionally do so by the consideration, that if a peculiarly odious kind of depravity, of the existence of which there was perhaps no previous suspicion, suddenly discloses itself in a nation, there should be an extraordinary effort to promote a counterbalancing good. Such an effort, besides that it is due to the honour of God, would seem to be called for in behalf of the *character* of a Christian people. It may also involve somewhat of that policy, in reference to their welfare, which sober men would not easily pronounce superstitious as exemplified in the parallel case of a ship, in which, if several of the passengers were expressly and ravingly insulting Omnipotence, any others, fearing the "God of the sea and the dry land," would consider an extraordinary degree of homage rendered to him on their part, in direct contravention, a matter not altogether foreign to the safety of the vessel. If their very devotions had been, in the first instance, the cause of bringing out this malignant impiety, they would be certain, on the exhibition of it, rather to double than remit the earnestness and frequency of their prayers.

The promoters and immediate experimenters of a christian attempt on the pagans of the East naturally expected, in spite of the pretended amiable mildness of the Hindoo character, to encounter a strenuous and perhaps malicious opposition from idolaters. But it was hardly within their calculation that a considerable number of persons of some note in England; men enjoying the advantages of education; of repute in the legislation, the mercantile interest, and the literature of the country; belonging to its respected classes and professions; and pretending, for the most part, a veneration for the religious establishment; would be provoked to join in a violent outcry against a scheme for imparting the gospel to the people of India. Still less was it anticipated of what strain the only music in this clamour was to be; that the virulent invective against the "pernicious fanaticism" of missionary enterprise would ever and anon be heard modulating itself to an expression of indulgent partiality toward the execrable superstition threatened by that enterprise. We were not distinctly enough aware of the fact, that men who hate the intrusion of a divine jurisdiction have a natural inducement to be favourable to a mode of pretended religion which they can make light of, as devoid of all real authority The inducement is, that it helps them to make light of religion altogether. The idolatrous superstition is recognised as of the generic nature of religion; and it comes with great pretensions to authority,—high antiquity, reported miracles, learned priests, and an immense number of believers: it may nevertheless be disbelieved with reason and most certain impunity. Under the encouragement of this disbelief with reason and impunity, the mind, impatient of acknowledging any express manifestation of a divine will, ventures to look toward other religions, and at last toward the Christian. *That* also has its antiquity, its recorded miracles, its priests, and a multitude of believers. There is an exterior, though in part very fallacious, appearance of similarity. And though there may not be assurance enough to assume formally the equality of pretensions in the two cases, there is a successful eagerness to evade the evidence and the conviction, that the apparent similarity is superficial, the real difference infinite; and the irreligious spirit springs rapidly and gladly, in its disbelief, from the one, as a stepping place, to the other. But that which affords such a convenience for surmounting the awe of the true religion, will naturally be a favourite, even at the very moment it is seen to be contemptible, and indeed, in a sense, *in consequence* of its being so. Complacency mingles with the very contempt for that from which contempt may rebound on Christianity.

These partisans of paganism when it can be turned to such an use, it were in vain to warn of a time, when the summons to them will be, in effect, to "come forth *against* the Lord," if they dare then repeat their well remembered words of homage to idolatry;* a time

* The most furious and raving of them, a person under a military designation, is dead since this was written. The most

when their impious affectation of liberal respect for all "religions," as proper and useful for their several parts of the world, (meaning that none of them is true,) will give place to the insufferable conviction of having insultingly rejected that infinite good which one, certainly and exclusively, had to offer; and when their contemptuous disallowance of any higher rule of judging and proceeding with respect to a people's religion, than the consideration of how it may affect government and commerce, will come to be estimated and pronounced upon, in a scene where all worldly policy will be at an end—excepting in its retribution; and where so many millions will be awaiting that consignment, whatever in the equity of the Almighty it may be, for which they will have grown to a fitness as subjects of a false and depraving religion. Then will such men meet their account with the fabricators and imposers of false religions to serve their ambition, with apostates, and whatever other enemies of Christ will hear with despair the sentence, "Behold, ye despisers, and wonder, and perish." It can be of no use, we repeat, to admonish *them;* but we may urge it on the friends of true religion and the illumination of the world, that to this phenomenon of a zealous avowal and effort in favour of paganism,

jocular, vulgar, clever, and far enough from least malicious, of the revilers of the design for converting the idolaters, a person with the ecclesiastical prefix to his name, still lives, amply prosperous in the emoluments assigned by the church to excite and reward faithful labours to promote the christian religion in the world. The coarse revilings, of which the chief objects were the senior missionaries at Serampore, were expended on men who, between the direct efforts to communicate the Bible and teach its doctrines to the idolaters, and the more secular labours to create pecuniary means purely for application to that great purpose, were exerting themselves, amidst innumerable difficulties, and in an oppressive climate, to the utmost stretch of human ability and patience; as the now ancient. survivors of the fraternity have continued to do for twenty years longer.

in this christian country, in this stage of its knowledge, their contrary zeal and exertion should be what the living rod of Moses was to the serpents of the magicians.

It is at the same time to be acknowledged, that there is a great abatement of the public manifestation of this disposition to vindicate idolatry, and this animosity against all attempts to reduce its dominion. However unallayed the rancorous sentiment may remain, it has been found that its unqualified exposure is a little incommodious on the score of character. Indeed, in the season of its most virulent eruption, some of the persons in whom it raged thought it worth while, (others were more bold or honest,) to endeavour to give it a disguised appearance. It was made to inspirit some argument of pretended political expediency. It was vented under the form of a representation, urged with every seeming of a most sincere and wrathful earnestness, that missionary proceedings, permitted but a very little while longer, would infallibly work the destruction of the British empire in Asia; although it is probable that some of these malignants laughed in private at such as might be simple enough to let themselves become, upon this representation, affected with this panic. Such assertions were hazarded in a sanguine confidence, for which it is a lamentable reflection on our country that there should have been no slight grounds, that the matter would not be suffered to proceed to the trial. But a power from heaven interposed, acting partly by the instrumentality of the zeal of the religious part of the community ; the Government were decided to prolong the impunity of the reviled missionaries, which authority in their favour has silenced many that were incapable of feeling any restraint from the fear of God; and time and experience have brought contempt on all their rant of prognostication.

We have alluded to such men only to gain from them a service for which we shall owe them no thanks. Religion should keep pace with physical science in the art of making noxious things contribute to salutary operations. No bad moral force, if it cannot be annihilated, should be left free from attempts to cheat it into a contrary action to what it naturally intends; and we wish to make the force of evil, emitted from these men's minds, act in coincident impulse with the motives which should carry the servants of God into a closer and still more animated conflict with the powers of heathen darkness.

This good cause has prevailed on the judgment, and obtained the practical aid, of the religious public, to an extent which we are willing to regard as an omen from heaven, of great effects to be accomplished in its progress. But it is not improbable there may still remain, among a minority of good men, some feelings not quite reconciled to schemes of such wide scope, such interminable demands of assistance, and such a distant field of execution; schemes, too, at the naming of which we may still seem to hear an echo of the numberless voices that pronounced them chimerical and fanatical; schemes but partially emerging from the effect of that general ridicule which leaves such marks upon an object that most men are long ashamed to entertain it.

There is much difference of mental constitution for receiving the impression of such projects. There is a class of good men naturally formed to be exceedingly sober, and cautious and deliberate, and anxious for all things to be kept in right proportions and manageable compass. Excellent qualities when themselves in right proportion; adapted specifically to some departments of duty, and of great use in a certain measure of interference in all. But let it be suggested to their possessors, that there is perhaps no class of men so apt to overvalue their peculiar endowments, in contradistinction to those of a different order ; and no class more needing to be warned of the faults akin to their virtues, and into which those virtues are liable to be insensibly transmuted. Nor, while they are in an especial manner ready to take credit to themselves for independence of judgment, are there any good men whose feelings and opinions are more at the mercy of those from whom they differ ; no class being liable to be driven further on one side the middle line, in a concern of duty, by what appears to them an extreme on the other. And in their own extreme, when they have once taken their position there, they will maintain themselves with an air and pride of that strong-mindedness which, to deserve the name of firmness or independence, ought to have kept them out of it.

It may be conceded to these worthy men, that the advocates of missions have not always avoided extravagance. Especially when under the influence of a large assembly, supposed to be animated by interests which extend to the happiness of a world, they may have been excited into a language which seemed to magnify these interests, and the projects in which they were embodied, at the expense of all other duties and concerns ; insomuch that some of those extra prudent friends of ours, in the auditory, have been wondering, and not without reason, what, at that rate of devotement of time, exertion, and money, we are to do, not only with the other claims of religious duty, but with the whole ordinary economy of life, pressing on us as it does with so many peremptory demands. But allowance must be made for a little excess in the pleader of such a cause. Its importance, of which he is at all times soberly certain, expands into a kind of dazzling magnificence before him, when a multitude of minds seem to be contemplating it in sympathy with him. It appears to him as bright with a reflection of all the complacent regards which those minds are fixing upon it. Under such a temporary animating influence, all the topics and arguments which he has previously accumulated in favour of the selected subject, become as it were dilated and on fire, without any intentional exaggeration; and unless he had a capacity, like Bacon, of keeping all subjects within his view almost at once, in their relative proportions as in a map, he will naturally represent the claims of the selected one in terms partaking too much of ambition and monopoly. We cannot wonder that our calculating friends should be making, in their minds, a strong protest against this excess; but they are aware how little they need entertain any apprehension for its consequences; as well knowing that the persons addressed are never betrayed into such prolonged enthusiasm, as to forget to take the practical standard of their duty at a sufficient reduction of the requirement made or implied in the hyperbolical language of the advocate.

While, however, some concession is thus made to the cautious good men, who are more afraid of extravagance than of all other errors in designs for promoting religion, they must be told, that it would have been an ill fate for Christianity in the world, if Christians of their temperament could always have held the ascendency in projecting its operations. If they would for a moment put themselves, in imagination, in the case of being contemporary with Wicliff, or with Luther, and of being applied to by one of these daring spirits for advice, we may ask what counsel they can suppose themselves to have given. They cannot but be instantly conscious that, though they had been Protestants at heart, their disposition would have been to array and magnify the objections and dangers; to dwell in emphatic terms on the inveterate, all-comprehensive, and resistless dominion of the Papal Church, established in every soul and body of the people; on the vigilance and prompt malignity of the priests; and on the insignificance, as to any probable success, of an obscure individual's efforts against an immense and marvellously well organized system of imposture and iniquity,—even were it not the extreme of self-delusion to expect that those efforts themselves could be of any long continuance, when so easy and apparently certain to be cut short by the *ultima ratio* of his provoked enemy, in the form of tribunals, dungeons, and death. In a word, if in those instances such counsel had been acted upon as they would have given, that zeal which was kindling and destined to lay a great part of the mightier Babylon in ashes, would have smouldered and expired in a languid listless hope, that the Almighty would *sometime* create such a conjuncture of circumstances, as should admit an attempt at reformation without a culpable and useless temerity. And so we might, for Wicliff and Luther, have been worshipping waxen toys, and trusting our most momentous interests on the strength of masses, penances, absolutions, and ceremonial antics, at this very day.

And to descend to the undertaking now under consideration;—all that has been accomplished by it in India, and is now accomplishing, as introductory, we trust, to a religious change not less glorious or extensive than the Reformation, may be regarded by its active friends as a reward, in some sense, for having refused to be controlled by the dissuasive arguments and desponding predictions, of many worthy deprecators of rashness and enthusiasm.

It is from such a quarter that we may hear disapprobation conveyed in the question, What can *we* do against an evil of such enormous magnitude, and so consolidated? It may be answered, (as it has been already suggested,) What you can do, if the expression mean what precise quantity of effect a severe calculation may promise from a given effort, is not always to be the rule of conduct; for this would be to deny the absolute authority of the Divine Master. We refuse to obey him for his own sake, if we assume to place the governing reason for all the services we are to render in a judgment which we think we can ourselves form, whether they will accomplish an end worth the labour; and therefore to fix their limit at the point beyond which we cannot with confidence extend our calculations. Such an arrogant principle, carried to its full length, would at last demand of him that he should require *no* service without placing clearly within our view all those consequences of it on which his own just reasons for exacting it are founded. That is, it would become a demand to be exempted from all services whatever, of a higher order than the secular business of life.

It is the very contrary spirit to this of restrictive parsimonious calculation that has been the most signally honoured; inasmuch as some of the most effectual and of the noblest services rendered to God in all time, have begun much more in the prompting of zeal to attempt something for him as it were at all hazards, than in rigorous estimates of the probable measure of success.

Let it be observed also, how all history abounds with great ultimate consequences from little causes; in which fact it only declares and exemplifies a prevailing law in the constitution of the world; a law by which the diminutive grows to the large, sparks flame into conflagrations, fountains originate mighty streams, and most inconsiderable moral agents and actions are made the incipient points whence trains of agencies and effects, proceeding on with continual accession, enlarge into results of immense magnitude. Some of these great results, now forming most important circumstances and modifications in the state of the human race, bear on them a peculiarity of character which will hardly allow us to look at them without a reference in thought to the points whence the progression began. They appear, notwithstanding their extension, with a certain prominence and distinctness by which we are reminded of their history; while others are become so diffused and blended into the general conformation of things, that their own distinguishable colour, so to speak, does not remain obvious enough to excite readily or necessarily any thought of them as effects which may be retrospectively traced to precise points, where their causes first sprung into action. Much of the actual condition of our part of the world consists of a number of these grand results of enlarging trains of effects, progressive from the smallest beginnings at various distances back in the past. And were not these now wide-spread consequences so combined into one order of things and familiarized around us, and were not, besides, their history from their origin so deficient and confused, it might very often be a pleasing employment, for both the philosophic and the devout mind, to trace them backward to the diminutiveness in which they began. A mysterious hand threw a particle of a cause, if we may express it so among the elements; it had the principle of attractic" in it; it found something akin to it to combine wi

.nts

obtaining so an augmentation, to be instantly again augmented, of the attracting and assimilating power, which grew in a ratio that became at length stupendous; and it exhibits the final result, (if any result yet attained could be called final,) in something, perhaps, which now forms the most important distinction and advantage of a nation, or of a still larger section of the world. What was the commencement of the true religion in this land, and of those several reformations which have partly restored it from its corruptions? And what would be the term of proportion, according to our principles of judging, between the object as seen in the diminutiveness of the incipient cause, and in its present extent of prevalence?—between the germ in the acorn, and the majestic oak?

A result thus growing to an immense magnitude from an original cause apparently so insignificant, is the collective consequence of a great number of causes progressively starting and multiplying into consentaneous operation, each of them having in the same manner its appropriate enlarging series of consequences, still uniting in the one great process. And in looking to the future progress of an undertaking for diffusing Christianity in India, is it not rational to presume, that many small means and little events will be, in their respective times and places, the commencements, and in a sense the causes, of trains of consequences interminably advancing and enlarging?

For example, we may imagine the destiny of some particular copy of the Bible or New Testament, in one of the native languages; and such a volume would be looked at and held in the hand with a strange interest, could there be any sign to indicate this destiny, at the moment of its issuing from the repository. It may be supposed to come into the hands, in a way much like casualty, of a heathen somewhat more thoughtful than his companions. Disgust or indignation at the first aspect of what he finds there may prompt him to throw away the book, which he may perceive to be virtually an impeachment of his religion, his gods, his priests, and himself. But a certain disquiet, of curiosity mingled with a deeper sentiment, shall have seized him, and shall impel him irresistibly to that book again: he shall feel as if the eye of a spectre had glanced upon him, and stricken him with a fascination that compels him to follow whether he will or not. A rising suspicion that all within him, and around him, may have been wrong, shall be aggravated, by repeated perusal, to full conviction; while the dawn of the true light and of a happier state is breaking on the night of his soul. Communications and discussions with his relations and neighbours may accompany the latter part of his process; and his finally complete persuasion will be followed by zealous exertions to impart what he will deem the greatest good on earth. The vast majority will obdurately resist; but within a year he shall find one or two, and in the next several more, surrendering to the same convictions, and then, as it were instinctively, unfolding their new faith as a net for proselytes. Who shall presume to say what the consequence may not be in fifty or in thirty years? Which of our *christian* deriders of the madness of missionary hopes, would venture to pledge his fortune for the inviolateness, half a century hence, of those shrines and idols, at present frequented and adored in the district where such a man is perhaps at this hour beginning, by the intrusion of the supposed Bible, to be disturbed in his "unchangeable" notions and rites, as these christians have so often pronounced them?

We may without extravagance suppose these events

to happen in a great number of instances, here and there in that realm of darkness; and we might add many other diminutive incidents and agents. The possible effects of a few tracts, conveyed in a manner appearing at first unaccountable, to a great distance from the place where they may have been put into pagan hands, by good men little apprised of the dignified appointment with which those humble gifts left their own, have been remarkably exemplified in some of the rather recent accounts of this mission. Among the little causes thus having a destiny to great consequences, will be presented to our fancy some images of the infantine countenances of the pupils now taught, and hereafter to be taught, in those numerous schools brought into existence by the mission, not indeed contrived for proselytizing, as the immediate purpose, but certain to contribute to it indirectly in the course of years.

You are glad to admit how reasonable, how sober, it is to expect that many such apparently inconsiderable things will thus grow to magnitude, in the progress of their effects contributary to the success of the good cause. But it will occur to you that, in this fiction of great things from little beginnings, we have not begun *quite* at their beginning. It is a pleasing thing to see, in the hands of the supposed pagan, the book or tract which may thus explode his superstition, and perhaps be the cause of ultimately setting his temple and idols on fire; but how is that formidable substance to come, gratuitously, into his hands? Think what must have preceded. Think of the complicated process of its preparation, involving so many kinds of workmanship. And this brings the train of the operation up to its originating matter in your own hands, a commencement so long antecedent to the pagan's receiving the supposed book, the event from which we have dated such pleasing consequences, but on which consequences we are not to be indulging our anticipative gratulations as if the book were to fall from the sky. The little cause, then, which we may follow onward in thought to such noble effects,—see it deriving itself from a still less,—a piece of money; which may have carried its image and superscription, in the insignificance of ordinary service, through many hands, at each transit very harmless, in one or other of them possibly subsidiary, to the cause of Evil, till it has come into the hand that has devoted it to produce a Bible, which may have the effect at length of a thunderbolt on an idol's temple. Here is an answer to the question, perhaps querulously asked, What can *we* do?

But it will be said, that such fanciful fictions, even supposing a certainty that they will be realized, bring no lively incitement, because, the contributions being thrown into a common sum of means, no one's quota can have any *distinct* operation, no individual can please himself with the idea that *his* particular contribution may be made the point of origination of one or these happy trains; which would thus be merely so many streams sluiced from a reservoir of collective contribution; rather than springing from distinct original fountains, at each of which an individual might place some mark or inscription to signify that it is his. Well then, the question is, whether the *share*, which the individual shall have in originating whatever trains or progressive good shall take their rise from the general receptacle of christian liberality, shall be deemed not worth the purchase. A share belonging to him, though not distinguishable, will really be there. While this union or the means so contributed makes those who supply them sharers of the *loss* in all those bibles, those little books, and those cases of the tuition given to juvenile heathens, which shall fail of producing the intended good, it makes them participators also in all those happy and noble consequences, of which it may be assumed as certain that *some* of the bibles, *some* of the tracts, *some* of the instructed heathen children, will be the cause.

This confidence, that in the prosecution of the enterprise now under consideration, there cannot fail to be some striking instances of particular and apparently diminutive means thus originating a succession of important movements, enlarging as it advances,—this confidence is authorized (independently of all other reasons,) by the fact, that such instances *have* occurred in every recorded scheme of christian enterprise which has been prosecuted on a wide scale, from right motives, and with indefatigable perseverance. Not that in all of them there have been such magnificent ultimate effects from little causes as we have been describing; not that in every province of benevolent activity a rill from some little obscure source has swelled into a Nile, and fertilized a whole region; but in all of them it may be safely asserted that there have been instances, of a magnitude to throw contempt on frigid, indolent, and irreligious calculation.

It is not improbable the chief strength of whatever reluctance may still remain, among the friends of christianity, to yield their full cooperation in projects for sending that religion to supplant the delusion and idolatry of the heathen world, consists in a kind of Religious Fatalism, which would make the objection in some such terms as these;—If that Being whose power is almighty has willed to permit on earth the protracted existence in opposition to him of this enormous evil, why are *we* called upon to vex and exhaust ourselves in a petty warfare against it?—why, any more than to attempt the extirpation of all the venomous reptiles of India, or the immediate demolition of all the idols' temples? If it were his will that it should be overthrown, we should soon, without having quitted our places and our quiet, in any offensive movement toward it, feel the earthquake of its mighty catastrophe; and if such be *not* his will, then we should plainly be putting ourselves in the predicament of willing something which he does not will, and making exertions which must therefore infallibly prove abortive.

We may question such an objector as to the real length to which his opinion or feeling goes. May it approach to a sentiment like this,—that, the thing contemplated being permitted by him who is infinitely good and powerful, it is therefore *not* of a spirit hostile to him, *not* of a nature directly the reverse of that of his attributes, *not* of deadly malignity to his creatures; that, in short, the brand of divine reprobation stamped by both revelation and reason on idolatry, and on each of its deceits and depravities severally, is itself, in truth, but a deceit of another kind, a mere accommodation to a certain superficial and conventional theory, the real fact being, after all, that God is at peace with the thing thus reprobated?

We may presume he will instantly reply in the negative, and say, that he holds this mass of error and turpitude to be intrinsically and immutably opposite to the divine goodness and holiness, and pernicious to man,—any other judgment of the matter being, according to all fact, and all scripture, utterly and impiously absurd; and that therefore the divine permission of this great evil, being no sanction of it, is simply an impenetrable and awful mystery.

Then, we immediately say to him, there are two

views, according to one of which you are to form your scheme of conduct; on the one hand, a mystery in the divine government, a permission infinitely inexplicable to you; and on the other, the most glaring manifestation of the quality of the thing so permitted, as hateful in itself and in the sight of God. Consider from which of these two it is the most rational for you to take your rule of action; from that where your understanding is profoundly lost, or from that where all is demonstration or self-evidence. You have light given you on the nether tract where you are placed, beneath the awful mystery in the heaven above, which interposes darkness between you and the reasons and counsels of the Almighty. By this light you have an infallible manifestation of the infinitely odious nature of an object that stands before you. What can this light and this manifestation be for, but that you might not have need to look up into the darkness for an authority, from reasons unknown, to determine your sentiments and action? And is it rational, and can it be safe, that the clear evidence which has thus been given, in order to define for you a scheme of duty with the advantage of being independent of the mystery, should be rejected that you may revert to that very mystery for a determination of your duty,—or rather for an authority to conclude that you have none? Or would you, both despising this light and defying that darkness, aspire to surmount the region of mystery itself, ascend into the light around the throne of heaven, and, sharer of Sovereign Intelligence, enter into God's own reasons for permitting the evil? But even *that* transcendent illumination would not authorize the principle of action that because God suffers the continuance of an evil, *you* shall abstain from hostility against it. For there would be a further expansion for that light to reach, namely, an understanding also of his reasons for *requiring* from his rational creatures an active enmity to all evil, notwithstanding his sufferance of it, and an apprehension of the consistency between that requirement and that sufferance. Your presuming, therefore, in contempt of that consistency, and on a pretence of homage to one part of his reasons to contravene another part of them,—that part from which his injunction proceeds, — would be a flagrant impiety; and would convict you of a virtual alliance with the evil to which those reasons and that injunction could not move your hostility.

But perhaps you will say, that far from any tendency to such an alliance, you are, as an indispensable part and proof of your fidelity to God, a mortal foe of this foe to him, in every estimate of your judgment and every sentiment of your heart; and that the only exemption sought, on the plea of the divine permission of the evil, is, that you may be excused, at least for the present, from active measures that would but expend and waste your feeble strength, on that which the almighty strength spares.

Now in the first place, there seems to be a groundless assumption implied here, namely the *continuance* of this permission indefinitely into futurity; whereas, for any thing that can be known to you, hostile means put in action at this period may coincide with a divine decree to hasten the termination of that mysterious sufferance: and then, whatever were the natural inadequacy of those means, they would seem to have caught the fire of Gideon's lamps, and be made to flame out with supernatural power of rout and confusion to the host of pagan gods.

But in the next place, you cannot consistently acknowledge that the circumstance of the divine permission of this dreadful system of delusion affords no particle of ground for conciliation to it, but leaves you under the full obligation of a mortal enmity,—and at the same time claim from that circumstance an exemption from practical efforts against it. What indeed is its permission but simply its existence?—in virtue of which there can be no exemption from the duty of attacking it which would not be equally an exemption from all duty whatever in the form of opposition and conflict; which therefore would not confer an universal inviolability on evil, and end practically in the maxim, that the more evil there is in the world, the less there is for the servants of God to do. And yet you are saying, their *feeling*, in this state of exemption, should be the same as if they *had* a great deal to do, and a mighty host to fight. While, with respect at least to the giant evil at present in view, you would plead that they may remain in inaction, they ought nevertheless, you will say, to glow with the actuating principle. But then of what use is that principle except to disturb their repose? That they should be inflamed, as you acknowledge they should, against what is working infinite mischief and misery to a large portion of the human race, and yet should in point of action remain at peace with it, would not only be an inconsistency and absurdity, but would also be an uneasy and mortifying state. Vain passion of christian zeal! illusory and almost penal fire from heaven! animating the heart but to consume it, if there should be no practical mode and machinery for conveying outward its energy to strike against the hated object. To have the mind beset and filled, as by main force, with the revolting images of pagan abominations, and to know that this infernal usurpation triumphs in the slavery of millions of our common family, and yet, the while, to submit to be unfurnished with expedients of devout revenge; to have no arrows, no power of throwing reflected convergent sunbeams, no missiles charged with the elements most noxious to a malignant nature; would be felt as a hard *imposition* by a man of zeal, who would dread to have his soul, in reference to the service of God, in the condition of a hero in chains. What shall we think, then, of a servant of God desiring as an *exemption* and a *privilege* to be allowed thus to expend away the vital force of his spirit without action? We cannot believe that he *has* any of that zealous emotion which he pretends. No, you must not profess to feel and fulfil a duty of enmity in spirit against the permitted evil, and at the same time acknowledge no duty of offensive exertion. The true animosity would be so intent on some means of action, that it is certain the state of feeling which persuades to decline such means is far too placable toward what is insulting God and destroying man.

But it is still more plainly to our purpose, as against this religious fatalism, to allege the matter of fact, that though it has been the mysterious will of the Supreme Governor to permit such great evils in the earth, it has as evidently been his will to maintain, in his own proceedings, a continual war against them. Why have there been so many vindictive interpositions of his among the inhabitants of the world? Let the memorials of cities, and tribes, and nations, and in one instance a world, destroyed, testify whether he has set men the example of peace with irreligion and iniquity. What is the inscription on the monuments of beings that his vengeance has smitten? What has been the interpretation required to be put on all the formidable signs held out to deter, and all the plagues that have followed when those signs warned in vain? The victims of those plagues, and the witnesses of their infliction, could not say that the denunciations had been lying signs and oracles, in demanding to be heard as heaven's protest against the evils to which the will of man had been permitted to abandon him.

Thus we have the *action* of the Divine Being giving a rule for that of his rational subjects, in respect to the moral evil that infests the world; or rather impressing an awful sanction on the laws in which he has commanded their resistance to it. Each of these commands is against something which his unsearchable wisdom has withheld his omnipotence from preventing or instantly exterminating. But his servants are to obey in silence. Well indeed might they feel an alarming sentiment at hearing so very many things recounted for them to be committed in deadly strife against; but what would be the piety, or the prudence, or the consequence, of a remonstrance to him against so severe a vocation, on the plea that himself had permitted, and could have prevented, every thing that he was thus imperatively involving them in painful conflict with over every step of ground till they should fall into the grave?

We repeat, that the whole course of the extraordinary divine interference among men has been in the direction, and has commanded human spirits, on their allegiance, to concur in the direction, which we are endeavouring to give to your zeal. In visions and oracles sent to patriarchs; in deliverances and avenging judgments; in the miraculous suspensions of the laws of nature; in institutions of religion; in the illuminations of prophets and apostles; in the excitement of the best men to the most invincible pertinacity of warfare; in the mission of angels; and, transcendently above all, in the "manifestation of the Son of God to destroy the works of the Devil,"—in all these forms of the divine dispensation, and in all the operation that has been in progress from them to this hour, one spirit breathes, one perpetual emanation of divine will and agency against that which will, nevertheless, be permitted to retain, but with lessening power, an existence on the earth till a very late period, when the "Lord shall consume it with the breath of his mouth, and destroy it with the brightness of his coming."—Such has been the spirit of all the Divine Intervention. The sun is not more conspicuous by his own light, than this character of the religious economy.

Now then for a professed servant of God to refuse acting in conformity to this entire tendency of his cause, and to justify himself on the ground of the divine permission of that which the cause is directed against, what is it but, in effect, to say to the Supreme Governor,—I behold two views of thy government; there is thy sufferance of an awful array and amount of evils; and there is a system of thy dispensations constituted to work in most direct and absolute opposition to them. The impossibility of apprehending the unity of principle of these contrasted parts of thy government throws a dark mystery on the one of them. But with me, unlike my fellow-mortals, the mystery rests on the latter view, on the economy of interpositions, enactments, and mandates for resistance to the evil; whereas the reason for its permission is so plain to me, that I can, in dissent from all thy faithful servants since the world began, adopt it as my rule of conduct. In pursuance of this adoption, I dare to believe thou art, in truth, *not* so much the enemy of this same Evil, as is pretended, even in thy own revelation; and that I shall, upon a certain secret understanding, please thee fully as well by declining to join in an attack upon it, as by devoting to the utmost my active forces to cooperate against it, in a war which I do at the same time perceive clearly that thou thyself, for what reason of state I cannot conjecture, hast raised and maintained with a palpable and continual interference.

Let us suppose him to act in this spirit toward his own soul. When he looks there, he sees there is a proportion, a lamentable one, of "that abominable thing" which has rendered the world so horrid a scene. But the Almighty power has *permitted* its existence there. What then? Can he on that account remain quiet, while it is poisoning the essence of his being, and feel as if it were a homage to God to second, if we may so express it, that permission? With plain sad proof of the very active quality of the malignant infester, which seems also to become, even while he is looking at it, (if under a suspension of resistance,) sensibly stronger, by the force of a principle of augmentation altogether indefinite if left to its own action, and which tells him, as with a demon's voice, that his soul is the intended victim, can he calmly contemplate this permitted state and operation, just as an inexplicable phenomenon of the divine government? And if he were to pretend reverential submission, what manner of god could he deem himself adoring, that would be pleased with such a sacrifice? Unless his pretensions to religion are false, and his soul is actually surrendering to perdition, he will, at the sight of this mournful predicament of his own spirit, be ardently intent on an application of the means of resisting the destroyer. And he will be at once alarmed and indignant if he should perceive his mind admitting, under some influence of the consideration that God has not prevented the pernicious fact of sin within him, any slighter estimate of the required energy and promptitude of the resistance, than that which should be commensurate to the evil itself, viewed absolutely, in all its atrocity and activity.

But now let him revert to the heathen slaves of darkness and sin.—If it would be cruelty to his own soul, to make the lighter of the invasion, or the means of expulsion, of its deadly enemy, because God has not precluded nor exterminated it, he may be reminded, and all the friends of christianity may be reminded, of the obligation implied in the second great commandment, "Thou shalt love thy neighbour as thyself."

Try once more how strongly you can bring upon your minds the reality of an immense multitude of spirits, of your own nature, existing on a remote continent. You can by an effort of thought come to as realizing a sense of being placed amidst the countenances, the vital warmth, the talk, the worship, the infelicities, of people at the distance of some thousands of leagues, as of the inhabitants of an adjacent part of your own country. With as absolute an assurance of fact as if you were at this hour in India, and were just now descrying a tyger crouching to spring on one ill-fated person, or a serpent throwing its folds round another, you can behold the prodigiously numerous tribe of actual living immortal essences, images and counterparts of your own, as it were watched for, fascinated, sprung upon, grappled, by things arisen in fearful eruption from the bottomless pit. Look at them involved in the power of the Old Serpent.—If we might enforce the representation by a simile, suppose the case, that a professedly benevolent man sojourning in that country, happened to be in a spot where he saw a tyger, eyeing with deadly glare the intended but unapprehensive victim, or a serpent in the very act of contracting itself to dart on an unwarned human object; and suppose, too, that this spectator had an advantage of position which exempted him from danger, and also that he had in his hands the most efficient means for striking the monster with death or sudden fright; or that at the very least he could alarm the person in peril. Now what sort of philanthropist shall we represent if we next suppose, that while looking at this creature of living flesh and blood, who is perhaps approaching every instant nearer the spot where death is lurking, he coolly thinks what a hopeless and fearful plight; muses why the God of nature should suffer beasts of prey and serpents in a world made for man; takes time, if there *be* time, for the conclusion that, at all events, since God *does* suffer them, men must of course be devoured by them; and so, quietly awaits and witnesses the catastrophe, highly self-complacent, perhaps, in the sort of selfish piety with which he goes away blessing the Providence which had not doomed *him* to be the victim.

We need not make the application. We will only suggest whether, since the whole accountableness for all the error and wickedness of paganism must rest somewhere, the alleviation obtained before the Supreme Judge by the heathens who have been denied the means of deliverance from so wretched a condition, may not be at the expense of those who shall have refused to try those means upon them; and then whether, in the solemn time of adjudgment, these latter will dare to reflect off this accountableness for omission on the Judge himself, in the allegation that the evil was of his own permission,—when they will have the consciousness that he gave them means of at least attempting its destruction.

This torpedo kind of fatalism, from the dominion of

which we should be glad to see the active powers of all good men rescued, may somewhat change its tone; still, however, aiming to elude the requisition to come forth in the activity of the cause. It may affect to recover from the kind of hopeless dead prostration of feeling at the awful fact of God's permission of so dreadful an evil, into adoration of his power as almighty to destroy it. And how magnificently that power shall be glorified, and how emphatically man shall be degraded, when it is hoped that some exemption from service may be suborned from the contrast! Feelings of indolence combined with ideas of the sovereignty of God will form a state of mind prolific of such reflections as these: Of what consequence can be the trivial efforts of such insignificant creatures, as cooperating or not with the energy of an almighty power? What signify, in a great process of nature, some few rain-drops or dew-drops the more or the less? What are we, to be talking, in strains of idle pomp, of converting the people of half a world? How reduced to contempt, how vanishing from perception, will be the effects of all our petty toils, when mightier powers shall come into action; as the footsteps of insects and birds are effaced and lost under the trample of elephants. Were it not even temerity to affect to take the course where the chariot of Omnipotence is to drive; as if we would intrude to share the achievements proper to a God, or fancy that something magnificent which he has to do, will not be done unless we are there? No, let our text be, as best becomes the humility of mortals and sinners, "Be still, and know that I am God." If he wills the conversion of the heathen nations, he has such powers and means for accomplishing his purpose, as may well allow a sabbath to the hands of all his servants, while their souls may adore him in his triumphs.—All very true; and so in the literal warfare referred to in scripture cited at the beginning of our discourse, there were means of overthrowing the heathen invaders without the assistance of the people of Meroz, or any other people; for the stars in their courses were to fight against Sisera. It was not because he *needed* them for combatants, that the God of armies had required their presence in battle.—After what has been already said of the employment of feeble means to produce a triumphantly disproportionate effect, it is superfluous to make any other answer to this indolence, or indifference, or pride, or all of them together, pleading under the semblance of humble piety, than an admonitory suggestion, that, as it has been hitherto God's usual method to employ human instrumentality in his great works of beneficence, his now declining to do so would but be the alarming expression of his judgment, that the human agents are now not worth being employed on earth, nor being translated to heaven. Well might a dread of the fatal privilege of exemption under such a judgment suppress the disposition to seek, and the willingness to accept, such a privilege on any ground whatever.

The religious fatalism, in a still further modification, somewhat distinguishable from these preceding descriptions, will make professions of anticipating with great delight the certain accomplishment of the glorious revolution in question, *when God's selected time shall arrive.* Then, too, as in former great changes, there will be noble work, and enough of it, for such humble instruments as men to perform: meanwhile, beware of premature attempts, and wait for the signs that the time is come. Language like this has been within the memory of many of you, among the common-places of our christian communities. If there be still some cautious christians who cannot willingly let it grow obsolete, we might ask them whether they have exactly figured in their minds in what manner the expected grand process is to begin, or what appearances they could accept, as signs that the period is come when their efforts would not be like a vain attempt to constrain the fulfilment of a divine purpose before its appointed time. Are there to be extraordinary meteors, significantly passing eastward as they vanish? Are they to hear that the temples of Seeva are sunk suddenly in ruins at the stroke of thunder? Or, still more of prodigy, are all the chief statesmen, and mercantile men, and military men, especially concerned in the affairs of the east, to become with one accord inspired with a fervent zeal for the christianizing of Asia, perhaps impelled literally to a spiritual crusade against Hindoo idolatry?

Perhaps they will, after all, disclaim the expectation of any extraordinary signals from heaven, when it occurs to them that they are in danger of the impiety of demanding a *specific* change in God's manner of declaring his mind to men. And probably they will profess that they wait for no other tokens than such as may afford a rational presumption, according to the rules of judgment commonly admitted amongst wise men. Then we may venture to ask why they should not accept, as something like the required signs, certain of the circumstances that have attended, thus far, this christian enterprise in India. Is it to be taken as a rebuke from Heaven, on a rash anticipation of Heaven's designs, that our missionaries have been kept in their positions and their work with a general impunity and freedom, notwithstanding that during many years of the time there prevailed against them a systematic unrelenting hostility of spirit, in authorities which in all human appearance might have crushed them in a moment, and were subject to no visible cause of restraint on their will,—a preservation reminding us of that of Daniel in the lions' den? Or, that the inactivity of fanatic malice, and the considerable favour, experienced among the natives, have seemed to betray some divine coercion put for their sake on the lions and the furies of direct paganism itself, to the disappointment of the *christian* paganism? Or, that they have been preserved in the excellence of the christian character in a scene presenting many temptations to forfeit the distinction, and while bearing the moral responsibility of an undertaking in which that forfeiture would have been fatal? Or, that by the multiplicity and extent of their labours and attainments they are sometimes recalling to our imagination the hundred-handed giant of fable? Or, that between the produce of their own exertions and the supplies from the religious public, pecuniary means have never failed for the constantly enlarging prosecution of the design,—even a very great disaster having operated as if the fall of an edifice should bring a concealed treasure of gold to light?* Or, that while the sacred scriptures have been spreading with rapidity among the nations of the East, the undertaking which has given them this range of mischief to the gods, has produced several marked benefits in our religious societies at home; especially in the point of helping to break up, by the introduction of so many new subjects connected with religion, the *monotony* which too much prevailed in their religious services, topics, and feelings?

What is the interpretation which our soothsayers of

* Alluding to the fire which, some years since, reduced to ashes the printing office at Serampore, with its large literary stores and other materials for the service of the mission.

the colder religious climate put on these signs, conjoined, as we are gratified to view them conjoined, with the enlarging missionary exertions and successes of our brethren of other religious denominations? Or will they sagely observe to us that, in the great concourse of casualties it is at any time possible enough for a sanguine spirit to descry and bring into conjunction a number of things which may be delusively converted into intimations, that a favourite project of its own is also the intention of Heaven? When they have said this, they may consider whether they should not, in their solicitous veneration for Heaven's appointment of times and seasons, abet the gods and their priests in an appeal to the Lord of the world against these missionary intruders, as guilty of insubordination to *Him*, in having presumed to "come to torment *them* before the time."

It has been the lot of several of the persons who have believed themselves to be obeying the will of the Supreme Authority, by leaving this country in prosecution of the christian enterprise in Hindoostan, to die in the service. They had devoted themselves so to die, and rejoiced in the confidence that they were also devoted by a superior decree. In what manner may we believe that their departing spirits have been received by their great Master? Has it been *qualified* "Well done, good and faithful servant," that they have heard?—as if he should say,—Feeble in judgment, rash in temperament, but honest in intention, you are pardoned through a peculiar extension of mercy; and are admitted now to a state of illumination in which you may cultivate the humility that was so defective on earth, and see, in the progressive disclosure of your Lord's designs, how long his servants ought to have repressed the presumptuous forwardness of their zeal.

No, this could not be their reception in a world where they were soon to be joined by the first-fruits of that very zeal, those converts from idolatry who, subsequently to some of their teachers, have died in the faith of Christ; and carried demonstrative living proof to heaven, that the true religion had not in a premature and officious zeal been conveyed sooner than the divine appointment had commissioned it to go, sooner than the divine power was ready to accompany it, to a region whither some of its professed friends would not have contributed to send it. And if we may imagine the nature of the emotion in the great assembly, at the arrival of these spirits from the dominions of idolatry, we shall not believe it to have been the repressed felicitation which should welcome them as but solitary exceptions to a destiny, regarded as still permanently to abide on the immense division of the human race whence they came. Repressed, we say; for we could not conceive of an unmingled delight in receiving them as translated thither chiefly to exemplify that sovereignty of God which he will manifest in every department of his government, by suspending in rare, and only rare instances, his most general appointments; as two individuals have been exempted from the general law of mortality. The sentiment without which the joy would be languid, must have been that which should hail them as signs that a decreed change of dispensation, a new aspect of the divine sovereignty, is beginning or approaching to shine on a dark hemisphere of the world; that death is becoming incomparably more tributary to heaven; and that the ancient barrier between the realms of Asia and the kingdom of eternal glory is beginning to break down.

This indulgence of thought in representing to ourselves the feelings experienced in an invisible and superior world, is quite within the just range of our contemplation of the subject. It is a noble distinction of religion, that (once admitted as true) it affords a rational substance to bear out the most imaginative exercise of thought. It is a ground on which our ideal excursions may venture, without offence to reason, such a length as they could not on inferior subjects without abandonment to poetical extravagance or mere vanity. It verifies to us as a reality a solemn relation between us and another economy of existence; and constitutes a vital intermedium through which we have the sense of a real interest in beings and a state beyond the sphere of this world. Thus religion, believed and felt, is the amplitude of our moral and intellectual nature. And how wretched an object therefore is a mind, especially of thought, sensibility, and genius, condemned to that poverty and insulation which infidelity inflicts, by annihilating around it the medium of a sensible interest in the existence, the emotions, the activities, of a higher order of beings! Our Lord tells us of great and happy intelligences in the invisible world who rejoice over a sinner when he repents. It is quite rational, then, to have indulged our imagination for a moment in ideas of the reception, in that scene, of those first converts from paganism, in the course of our Mission, who have been followed in death by some of the persons whose labours were crowned with this success. And we are especially warranted in the most vivid imagination which it is possible to form, of the emotions of these proclaimers and these converts of the truth, in their mutual recognition, when thus reunited and in communion with the preceding believers, apostles, and confessors. If but a comparatively faint apprehension of the emphasis of those congratulations could be brought, by some momentary illapse, on the souls of the most neutral or even the most hostile spectators of the attempt which has been the cause of such emotions in the happiest society, might it not instantly turn to grief at the thought that those felicities had owed none of that rapture to *them?*

And let us remind those professed christians, whose coldness toward a great project of evangelization would justify itself under a plea of reverently awaiting the disclosure of the divine purposes, that by their profession they aspire to join ere long that company to which departed missionaries and their converts have been added. It may be the destination of some of them to leave this world at nearly the time appointed for the removal by death of other of these indefatigable labourers, and of their proselytes. In the reflections which may be excited by such an idea, will there be no sentiment partaking of apprehension? No mortifying anticipation arises at the thought of entering the other world in company with an angelic being, the different rank of his nature precluding all comparison, or all painful humiliation at the difference if comparison were made. But methinks there is something to cause great displacency, and even a degree of intimidation, in the thought of approaching the most illustrious society in the universe in the company of spirits of our own nature and our own times, trained under nearly similar privileges and instructions, or possibly the very same, but who through superior zeal shall have left us in a great disparity. Think whether it be possible that, even on the passage to the superior kingdom, there might be an unwelcome sense of contrast. Supposing the transition to be contemporary and mutually witnessed, it were inevitable there should be a perception of a signal difference, between those passing from the conclusion of a course of devoted enterprise to extend the kingdom of their Lord into the regions of inveterate cruel superstition, by efforts whose commencing success is attested by redeemed spirits of heathens gone before or accompanying them,—and those persons who, though having been in circumstances little different from theirs in early life, and having professed the same devotedness to the christian cause, shall yet be conscious of having scarcely made an effort for its advancement; of hardly having given their cordial good wishes to this undertaking in its service; of even having, possibly, been almost pleased that the small number, as yet, of conversions from heathenism should seem to afford some advantage to the imputers of enthusiasm to the project. May not the thought of the feelings possible to be excited at such a time by such a contrast, suggest to christians whose faculties seem more readily applicable to the exercise of finding objections to animated schemes of christian experiment, than to that of devising means for their success, a new topic for solicitude and perhaps for prayer, namely, that they may be permitted to enter the superior state in a way that shall not immediately bring them in communication or comparison with their brethren ascending from the war against idolatry?

We may be allowed, at the least, to suggest, that in order to be entirely free from the anticipation of any reflections, tending to throw a shade over the joy of passing into the great Master's presence at nearly the same time as those devoted spirits, there must be the testimony of conscience that *in some other manner* his service is zealously prosecuted. The man indifferent or opposed to the enterprise in which these men are to die, but who yet professes to take an interest in the advancement of religion and the general good, can avoid the apprehensiveness of such a future comparison only by having evidence to himself that, though projects which seem to him to partake somewhat of enthusiasm are not exactly adapted to seize his mind, he is diligently intent on promoting the cause of God in plainer, less adventurous, and let him call them, if he will, soberer methods. But, in truth, experience is not in favour of our expecting a very active zeal for extending christianity in *any*, even the ordinary methods, from those who are prompt to impute enthusiasm to the extraordinary ones.

For ourselves, when we think of those who are thus appointed to fall in the immediate conflict with the powers of paganism, shall we not earnestly desire and pray, that we may be so animated to promote the christian cause in *every* practicable way, that we may never have reason to wish, as what would have saved us from any such pain of a close comparison at the time of going to the great account, that these men, instead of being our contemporaries, and fellow-countrymen, and neighbours, no more privileged originally than ourselves, had been in the number of those distinguished agents in the christian service of other times and countries, whom we can look at and venerate in the distance of history, without having our attention and conscience so directly forced on a comparative estimate between them and ourselves?

To return, but for one moment, to the repressive influence on some good men's principles of action and hope, from the idea of the sovereignty of the divine appointments, we may observe, that the most assured belief in the divine decrees, as comprehending all things, has not *necessarily* the effect of paralyzing the active powers. There is no denying that such is its tendency in cold, inanimate, indolent spirits, that are really indifferent to the objects demanding their exertion. And so with respect to *any* doctrine of religious or moral truth, there is a possible state of mind which is apt to take from it an injurious impression. But let there be an earnest interest about the objects in question, and then the zeal and activity will be incited rather than repressed by the faith in all-comprehending and absolute decrees. Accordingly it has been, we think, for the greater proportion, by decided predestinarians, that the most ardent and efficient exertions of religious innovation have been made upon the inveterate evils of the world. That they were not checked and chilled by this article of their faith, is the least that their conduct testified of its effect. Not only were they not withheld from driving impetuously against the hated thing before them by any surmise whether it might not, for the present, be guarded invisibly by the shield of a decree. Not only did they dart their weapons, when the enemy appeared to be within their reach, without being stopped by any suspicion of an optical deception in this seeming nearness, this possibility of striking it. This is only supposing them not to be *the less* energetic in consequence of their predestinarian faith ; it is what they might be, supposing them the while to *forget* it. But it was not as forgetting their principle, and being actuated, for the time, solely by the independent force of different ones, that they so nobly exerted themselves. No, they acted in the full recollection of it, as a source of invigoration no less indispensable than for Antæus to touch the earth. It was in the element of this doctrine of decrees that they felt their impetus the mightier, their weapons the sharper, their aim the surer,

And while their opponents in belief might be wondering at the phenomenon of such a glow of life, and play of strength, in an element which they had been constantly pronouncing the most mephitic in the whole world of opinion to moral energy, the persons on whom the faith had this influence could have shown how explicable and how far from absurd was such a practical effect, in the case of men in the prosecution of plans for the destruction of what was opposed to the kingdom of God. The first consideration in the matter was the trite and general one,—they were certain that the Almighty will make very great use of human agents in what remains of the course of his dispensations in this world. Next, whatever concealment may rest on the precise nature of his more special determinations, which constitute, so to speak, the divisible portions of his one grand design, there can be no question, with believers in revelation, whether that grand design be a progressive demolition of the dreadful tyranny of evil over the human race. Now *that* was what *they* were intent upon; and they were putting themselves directly into his hands as willing instruments to be applied to that use. And was it not (they thought) most reasonable to entertain a general assurance that willing agents, offered to him for a purpose which he is determined to accomplish, would have their appointment for effective service? If so many would be required that even repugnant or undesigning ones would be made to contribute and cooperate, by his constraining and over-ruling Providence, the willing and zealous ones might in all reason be sure of being put to such an use. The disposition itself was inspired, they thought, for the very purpose of adapting them, and the adaptation given with the intention of employing them. Thus, on the certainty of their coincidence with God's intention, considered generally, they justified a confidence that they had a *general* appointment to do something in his great work,—an appointment, that is to say, to promote it *in some way or other.*

But no man who is powerfully actuated can stop in generals. Those devout predestinarians, those *genuine* adorers of the God of decrees, were earnestly attentive to the manner in which his general and comprehensive design was seen, in his revelation, resolving itself into defined parts, and taking the form of several great purposes, distinguishable from one another, while all combined in the entire design. Of these several purposes, thus distinguished and announced, there was probably one which was of a nature more specially to interest their feelings, and draw to this particular direction the zeal and cooperation which were in devoted readiness to coincide with the divine intentions as regarded generally. And when they felt their general coincidence of spirit thus determined to one marked division of the divine plan, they acquired a still more animated assurance of their appointment to a practicable and successful service, in proportion as they thus came more distinctly to see *how* they might cooperate in that design.

Nor was this all; for when they thus saw one particular part of the scheme of the divine intention manifested with considerable definiteness, they felt an irresistible tendency to make it more definite still, by resolving this also into particulars. For example; if revelation has declared the destruction of superstition to be one leading object comprehended in the great general intention, their zeal has impelled them to regard this declaration as bearing with special emphasis on those particular forms of superstition which they were most intent on destroying. Those particular forms, they have said, so eminently hateful, cannot but be very marked objects of the exterminating intention of the supreme will. It has seemed to these men as if the whole force of the general decree were converging to strike just where *they* wished to strike. And as the principle of destruction is to be conveyed through the means of human agents, who so likely to be employed, they said, as we that are already on fire to destroy? Beyond all doubt it is exactly here that we have our decreed and unalterable allotment. Exactly here it is, that our will and the supreme will coalesce to a purpose which therefore defies all chance and all created power.

But their assurance that their intention, as fixed on a particular selected object, was decidedly identical with that of the Almighty, did not authorize itself solely by thus giving to those declarations which express the divine purpose in comprehensive terms, a more determinate bearing on a special object. For some inspired declarations were found which were themselves of special import. They evidently pointed out, by their own terms, with much definiteness, certain distinct parts and special processes in the general scheme which Providence will execute. These appeared as departments or sections, within wider divisions of operation, which are still themselves but parts of the grand scheme; as, for example, the foredoomed destruction of the Popish superstition, though a thing of such magnitude, is only a portion of the divine plan for the destruction of superstition in general, which is yet but a part of the entire scheme announced for accomplishment. The devout men who have sought their incitement and their strength in the decrees of heaven, have often believed that they saw, in some of these more defined and special portions, in these comparatively distinct representations of movements which are to fulfil on earth the purposes of heaven, the very image of such designs as the genius of their zeal was shaping forth. It was quite certain at least that those appointed operations must at any rate involve such as they were projecting; and the predicted success of the whole must be the success of the included parts. But, they said again, there are predestined *agents;* and who still so likely as men who shall be ready with their life and their death for precisely that service? The inference was not far off;—These very plans and proceedings of ours are decreed, as portions of the sovereign scheme; we and our work are a part of eternal destiny.

By this short process, through a general confidence of some predestinated appointment into a determination to one special service, we may believe that some of the distinguished actors in a good cause have gone into their career. At the same time it is to be acknowledged, as probable in respect to others of them, and possibly the greater number, that they have had no process to pass through, no need to verify their commission by speculative inferences from the general designs of the Almighty, no waiting and deliberating to know their destined vocation. It came on them by the immediate force of circumstances and events, that provoked them to action. Their attention was seized, and their ardour excited, at the sight of some one great evil to be combated, or good to be achieved; and that ardour itself, combining with their predestinarian faith, created the assurance of their destination. This is the very thing, they said, which we came into the world for; and this, unless accomplished sooner, we must prosecute till we go out of it.

We are not here called upon to suggest the cautions against the possible excesses and dangers of this confident assurance in good men that their designs are *specifically* identical with the divine purposes. Our object was to show, that the consideration of sovereign decrees, which cold unwilling minds are so ready to allege for their inertness, and which is so commonly asserted to have necessarily that consequence, may, on the contrary, become one of the mightiest forces for action. It is this that can make, but under a far nobler modification, the man that the poets have delighted to feign, who would maintain his purpose though the world fell in ruins around him. A missionary against the paganism of the Hindoos may feel an animation specially appropriate to the service, in this assurance that his intention is the intention of God. Those people fortify themselves in the notion, or the pretence, that they are immediately actuated by some deity, and therefore fulfilling, under a law of necessity, his determinations: the missionary will feel peculiar invigoration in advancing to the assault of a superstition with such a principle in its front, in the force of a principle analogous in form, but of heavenly essence. While they will have it, that he may as well spare the efforts on *them* which it were his more proper business to level at the gods, if he could reach them, the energy of his soul will reply, that he accepts the challenge so made for those enthroned abominations, for that he verily believes himself and his confraternity to be an *Avatar* for their destruction.

We have dwelt too long on this topic of religious fatalism, a term we have employed to signify a perverted application, in reasoning and feeling, of the doctrine which acknowledges God's sovereign and unalterable predestination of events. Our excuse must be, that these reasonings and feelings are peculiarly apt to suggest themselves in contravention to such claims as those we are at present wishing to exhibit. And besides their own direct force, they lend strength to other objections and repugnant feelings not arising from so speculative a source. The meanest of the passions, that can make an opposition to a worthy project, or withhold from it the necessary aid, are very ready to find an excuse, a justification, or even a merit, in a pretended waiting submission to the decrees of heaven.

Many causes of a nature not implicated with these obscure speculations, are operating to prevent or lessen the assistance to such an enterprise. We may briefly notice one or two.

If we just name Party-spirit, it is not in order to indulge in any accusatory complaints that our particular undertaking has materially suffered by it.* Doubtless we may be somewhat the worse for it; but we have as little the inclination as the means for calculating how much. And even were a calculation made and verified of that proportion of pecuniary and other modes of aid which a perfect christian liberality would have awarded to this project, and which party-spirit

* The Baptist Mission; of which the primary establishment, at the beginning of 1800, was fixed in the small Danish settlement of Serampore, in consequence of the menacing indications that the British Government would not tolerate, within their own dominions, an attempt to introduce Christianity among the pagans.

may have withheld from it, we should still please ourselves with the persuasion, that the greater part of what may have been so averted has probably been devoted to other excellent designs to which we wish all possible success. The history of this portion of the general christian operations of the age, will have little to say of convoys intercepted by selfish allies. We are too confident of the prolonged favour of Providence on our work, and too much pleased at seeing that Providence favouring the exertions of the same tendency made by other sects of the great christian community, to regret not having obtained any one particle of the means which have availed to good in their hands. And we think we have too systematically avoided giving any just cause of jealous reaction to our friends of the other denominations, to be debarred in modesty from denouncing, with unrestrained censure, the spirit which cannot see the merit of a noble object when there is some point of controversy with its promoters, and which would almost rather wish it might be lost than aid *them* to attain it: a spirit which, in promoting an interest professedly as wide as the world, as liberal as the sun, would enviously account success, or the means of success, conferred on a different class of labourers in the same general cause, so much unjustly subtracted from our own connexion and project; and would avenge on the grand catholic object the petty offences of party or affronts to individual vanity.

If the christian communities, most liable to feelings of competition, were asked in what character they conceive themselves to stand the most prominently forward before the world, as practically verifying the exalted, beneficent, expansive spirit of their religion, it is not improbable they would say, it is as conspirers to extend heavenly light and liberty over the heathen world. But if so, how justly we may urge it upon them to beware of degrading this the most magnificent form in which their profession is displayed, by associating with it littleness which may make it almost ridiculous. Surely, in thus going forth against the powers of darkness, they would not be found stickling and stipulating that the grand banner of the cause should be surmounted with some petty label of a particular denomination. Such mortals, had they been in the emigration from Egypt, would have been incessantly and jealously busy about the relative proximities of the tribes to the position of the cloudy pillar. A shrewd irreligious looker-on, who can divert himself at the expense of all our sects, and despises this their common object, might indulge his malicious humour, in saying, All this bustling activity of consultation, and oratory, and subscription, and travelling, is to go to the account, as you will have it, of a fervent zeal for christianity: what a large share of this costly trouble I should nevertheless be sure to save you, if I could just apply a quencher to so much of this pious heat as consists of sectarian ambition and rivalry.

We cannot too strongly insist again, that a sense of dignity should spurn these inglorious competitions from the sections of the advanced camp against the grand enemy. Here, at all events, the parties should acknowledge the Truce of God. If they have, and must have, jealousies too sacred to be extinguished, let their indulgence be reserved for occasions and scenes in which they are not assuming the lofty attitude of a war against the gods. But the great matter, after all, is to be solemnly intent on the object itself, on the good to be done, compared with which, the denomination of the instrument will appear a circumstance vastly trivial. Let all the promoters of these good works be in this state of mind, and then the modes in which the evil spirit in question might display itself will be things only to be figured in the imagination, or sought as facts in the history of former and worse times. For then we shall never actually see a disposition to discountenance a design on account of its originating with an alien sect, rather than to favour it for its intrinsic excellence; nor an eager insisting on points of precedence; nor a systematic practice of representing the operations of our own sect at their highest amount of ability and effect, and those of another at their lowest; nor the studied silence of vexed jealousy, which is thinking all the while of what it cannot endure to name; nor that laboured exaggeration of our magnitude and achievements which most plainly tells *what* that jealousy is thinking of; nor that manner of hearing of marked and opportune advantages occurring to undertakings of another sect which betrays that a story of disasters would have been fully as welcome; nor underhand contrivances for assuming the envied merit of something which another sect has accomplished and never boasted of; nor excitements to exertion expressly on the ground of invidious rivalry, rather than christian emulation; nor casual defects of courtesy interpreted wilfully into intentional hostility, just to give a colour of justice to actual hostility on our part, for which we were prepared, and but watching for a pretext; nor management and misrepresentation to trepan to our party auxiliary means which might have been intended for theirs.

While we would earnestly admonish all the promoters of our object to display an example in every point the reverse of such tempers and expedients, we will assure ourselves of the favourable dispositions of christians in general toward a design which has its own sphere of operations, in which it has both the happiness and the merit of interfering with no other. It has not, by either interference or ostentation, given any provocation to party jealousy; and we may add, that we trust it is grown to a strength and an establishment beyond the power of that unfriendly spirit, were it excited, greatly to injure.

When we mention the Love of Money, as another chief prevention of the required assistance to such a cause, we may seem to be naming a thing not more specifically adverse to this than to any and every other beneficent design. A second thought, however, may suggest to you a certain peculiarity of circumstance in the resistance of this bad passion to the claims of a scheme for converting heathens. By eminence among the vices which may prevail where the true God is not unknown, this of covetousness is denominated in the word of that God, Idolatry. Now as it is peculiarly against idolatry that the design in question is aimed, the repugnance shown to it by covetousness may be considered as somewhat on the principle of an identity of nature with its enemy. One idolater seems to take up the interest of all idolaters, as if desirous to profit by the warning, that if Satan be divided against himself his kingdom cannot stand.

Or rather it is instinctively that this community of interest is maintained, and without being fully aware; for the unhappy mortal, while reading or hearing how millions of people adore shapes of clay, or wood, or stone, or silver, or gold, shall express his wonder how rational creatures can be so besotted; shall raise his eyes to heaven in astonishment that the Almighty should permit such alienation of understanding, such dominion of the wicked Spirit: and there is no voice to speak in alarm to his conscience, Thou art the man!

As this unhappy man may very possibly be a frequenter of our religious assemblies, and even a pretender to personal religion, he is solicited, in the name of Jesus Christ, to bring forth something from his store in aid of the good cause. He refuses perhaps; or, much more probably, just saves the appearance and irksomeness of formally doing that, by contributing what is immeasurably below all fair proportion to his means; what is in such disproportion to them that a general standard taken from it would reduce the contributions of very many other persons to the smallest denomination of our money, and would very shortly break up the mechanism of human operation for prosecuting a generous design, throwing it directly on Providence and miracle, with a benediction perhaps uttered by this man, (for he will be as liberal of cant as parsimonious of gold,) on the all-sufficiency of that last resource: Yes, God shall have the glory of the salvation of the heathens, while he is happy to have secured the more important point—the saving of his money.

How much it were to be wished, that the fatuity which this vice inflicts on the faculty which should judge it, (herein bearing one of the most striking characteristics of idolatry,) did not disable the man to take an honest account of the manner in which it has its strong hold on his mind. If, when his eyes and thoughts are fixed on this pelf, regarded as brought into the question of going to promote the worship of God over the earth, or staying to be itself worshipped, he could clearly feel that he detains it from fervent affection to it as an absolute good, he would be smitten with horror to find his soul making such an object its supreme good—for supreme it plainly is when thus preferred to the cause of God, and therefore to God himself.

But perhaps he thinks his motive regards the prospects of his family. Perhaps he has a favourite or an only son, for whom he destines, with the rest of his treasure, that portion which God is demanding. In due time that son will be put in possession by his father's death, and will be so much the richer for that portion. That this wealth will remain long in his hands, a prosperous and undiminished possession, may not seem very probable when we recollect what has been seen of the heirs of misers. But let us suppose that it will, and suppose, too, that this son will be a man of sensibility and deep reflection. Then, his property will often remind him of his departed father. And with what emotions? This, he will say to himself, was my father's god. He did, indeed, think much of me, and of securing for me an advantageous condition in life; and I ought not to be ungrateful for his cares. He professed also not to be unconcerned for the interests of his own soul, and the cause of the Saviour of the world. But alas! it presses on me with irresistible evidence, that the love of money had a power in his heart predominant over all other interests. It cannot be effaced from my memory that I have often observed the strong marks of repugnance and impatience, an ingenuity of evasion, an acuteness to discover or invent objections to the matter proposed to him, however high its claims, if those claims sought to touch his money, which he contemplated, and guarded and augmented, with a devotedness of soul quite religious. But whither can a soul be gone that had such a religion? Would he that acquired, and guarded even against the demands of God, these possessions for me, and who is thinking of them now as certainly as I am thinking of them, oh would he, if he could speak to me while I am pleasing myself that they are mine, tell me that they are the price of my father's soul?

If the rich man in either of the parables which exhibit the curse of wealth without benevolence, (parables being for a moment taken as literal facts,) *might* have been permitted, as one of them petitioned, to send a message to his relations on earth, what might we imagine as the first thing which the anguish of his spirit would have uttered in such a message? Would it not have been an emphatic expression of the suffering which the wealth he had at once adored and abused inflicted on him now, as if it ministered incessant fuel to those fires? Would he not have breathed out an earnest entreaty that it might not remain in that entireness in which it has been his idol; as if an alleviation might in some way arise from its being in any other state and use than that in which he had sacrificed his soul to it? Send away some of that accumulation; give some of it to the cause of God, if he will accept what has been made an abomination by being put in His stead. Send some of it away, if it be but in pity to him of whom you surely cannot help sometimes thinking while you are enjoying it. Can you, in the pleasures and the pride which that wealth may impart, escape the bitter thought, that for every gratification which it administers to you, it inflicts a pang on him by whose death it has become yours, and by whose perdition it is so much?

How different the reflections of those inheritors, who feel in what they do *not* possess a delightful recognition of the character of their departed relations; who feel that they possess so much the less than they *might* have done, because those relations have alienated to them nothing of what was sacred to God, and to charity; and who can comprehend and approve the principle of that calculation of their pious predecessors, which accounted it even one of the best provisions for their heirs to dedicate a portion of their property to God. How different therefore the feelings of a descendant of such a person as that late most excellent christian and philanthropist of your city, whose name the present topic has probably recalled to the minds of most in this assembly.*

We cannot be unaware how many wellwishers to our cause must feel a severe limitation put on their means of aiding it by the pressure of the public burdens, those burdens which oppress the energy and the resources of every scheme for doing good. How often does the thought of such designs present itself to a benevolent man, at the moment of his being accosted with the peremptory demands on the public account, and make him look wishfully and regretfully at the sums he is thus surrendering, to be speedily followed, he knows, by more sums surrendered, from the profits of his laborious industry, or the produce of his little property. How many implements for the holy war, he says to himself, how many bibles, or tracts, or school-manuals, in the languages of Asia, might have sprung from even my share of this forced sacrifice; but this all-consuming monster, denominated the State, seems to know instinctively whatever good men are devising

* Reynolds.

of gratuitous service to the welfare of their fellow-creatures, and to delight in frustrating their designs, by making spoil of their means,—as if in revenge that they should seem to reproach the national power by presuming to apply their little individual means to worthier purposes than those on which the grand public resources have been expended without limit.

We cannot make the odious vision pass away from our view. A great christian state, with every conceivable mode of beneficence offered to its sight and within its powers, has throughout half an age been stimulated to almost miraculous exertions, to an expenditure surpassing all the dreams of the golden empires of romance, a consumption of forces and of materials which might seem to have been adequate, under some imaginable forms of application, to give a new character to the moral world ; and when, after all this, the christian philanthropist looks to see the condition in which this triumph of its astonishing capabilities has left it, he finds that, excepting some hopeful commencements, made quite apart from the public system, and in spite of its insatiable requisitions, that which *was* to be done remains still to be done, with a frightful addition of evils to the account ; and to be done by the efforts of individuals, and those individuals suffering, from the course of national affairs, a lamentable diminution and alienation of their means.

In any large assembly, nevertheless, there may be a number of persons who rather approved than condemned, while it continued, that headlong, rampant, and devastating career, of which they would plead the now oppressive consequences in excuse for contributing but slightly in aid of a concern like that under our contemplation. Without making it our business to arraign them for such approval, we may suggest that they should be discreet in using this plea. They should think again before consequences which, as resulting naturally from a certain order of public measures, they were required in reason to foresee, at least to a con siderable extent, when they deliberately gave their approbation to those measures, shall be alleged by them in exemption from assisting a better cause than any that has absorbed their subsidies. If they have been the professed servants of that Prince of Peace whose kingdom is not of this world, but nevertheless demands tribute from the worldly resources of its subjects, it must have been their acknowledged primary obligation to look to the advancement of that kingdom; in practical conformity with that prayer, of which the very first petition is in this reference—unless they could think it enough to *say* that prayer. This sacred obligation they had to keep in memory, while considering what other expenditures of their property they should take the responsibility of approving: the responsibility, we say; for to abet and sanction a proceeding is to incur the accountableness as completely as if the manifestation of an opposite opinion would *prevent* that proceeding; and it were an idle evasion to plead that the course of measures in question would have been pursued, all the same, though disapprobation instead of coincidence had been avowed by these individuals. With this obligation resting on memory and on conscience, they could not, one should think, without alarm for their christian principles, give their sanction to what must inevitably create speedy and large demands on their property, unless they had very solid ground for assurance of being left still competent to meet the claims peculiarly authoritative on them as christians. They had to consider then what, in sober calculation, it was probable or possible there should at length be spared to them, by the voracity of such a gulf as they saw swallowing up, year after year, the means of the community. We will presume that they *did*, as a matter of conscience, seriously consider this question, and that through the progressive stages of experience they were still satisfied, as remaining constant in the assurance that their approval of the policy which caused such a tremendous consumption, did not involve their consent to an alienation from the cause of Christ of any thing honestly belonging to it. But then we must tell them, that they will now come with a bad grace to say they have been deceived, and that the cause of Christ must pay the forfeit of their miscalculation. Surely against the claims of a service to which their best strength was put under the prior and paramount obligation acknowledged by their profession, they will hesitate to plead that they have been lamed in their willing adherence to another, of such widely different character.

To those who are not liable to this sort of *argumentum ad hominem*, while deploring the disability inflicted by the consequences of national conduct, it may be suggested as at once a consolation and incitement, that the most unequivocal omen of an amendment of the national condition, even in a temporal respect, is the very circumstance of this recently arisen zeal and activity, in missionary and so many other ways of operation, for extending the prevalence of the true religion in the world. From what has been seen thus far we may affirm, that the Almighty has indicated this as the part of the world whence he is determined to draw, in the outset at least, the chief human means of accomplishing his most glorious designs fôr its many nations; that here he has his mines, and his assembling camp; that here is the part where lie the sinews of the sacred war.* But if so, and if that war is to be on so great a scale as appears to be prefigured in the visions of his prophets, may we not venture to say that he will, that he must, protect the stores applicable to his approaching campaigns, from the renewal of such dreadful depredations as we have witnessed, and from the unmitigated continuance of such as are suffered now? We may assure ourselves that he will in due time warn off the sacrilegious hands of the plunderer. And what a glorious change of the national condition, when God shall, as it were, place his angel between what shall remain after all the ravage of ambition, war and corruption, and the re-approach of these spoilers. And how gratifying to behold too, in the contrasted operations, the different rate of cost in proportion to the respective results; to see that, whereas an astonishing and unparalleled expenditure in the vulgar kind of war has resulted in—leaving men, relatively to the objects of that war, not far from where they were, the grand spiritual power, which we behold entering into action, will require an incalculably less amount of material means for its consumption in the whole extent of its operations to transform the moral world.

You will not, my brethren, feel it a damp on the pleasure of anticipating the gradual retreat of the spoiler, that the temporal means so rescued will still not be held in entire and absolute property by their possessors, but will still be in part under a foreign and authoritative

* Our American brethren have given worthy pledges of a willingness to make themselves tributaries to the same imperial cause.

claim. For, besides that it is pleasing to devout minds to hold and regard all things as belonging to God, and as to subserve whatever purpose he pleases, they may be very confident that he will make it to be the better for the community itself, in a temporal respect, whenever there shall prevail in it a disposition to apply its means to promote his cause. Indeed this very spirit will involve a principle of counteraction to all such things as we have seen most miserably destroying the temporal welfare of the nation.

For the present, while many friends of religion are labouring under the grievous pressure, we may suggest it to them as a consideration not unfit to accompany the exercise of their prudence, that the offerings to God from what calamity has left have a peculiar value in his esteem, and in the feelings of the sufferer may contribute to exalt adversity into piety. Should we go back in thought to that period of the world when sacrifices, literally, were appointed for the expression of homage to Heaven, we might imagine the case of a devout man whose harvests, or plantations, or flocks, had for the greater part perished by some destructive visitation, as by tempests, or fire, or locusts, or disease. Let us suppose him, nevertheless, in looking pensively over the desolation, to consider whether yet some small portion of the remainder might not be spared for God, as a token of humble resignation to him that gave and had taken away. Would not that probably be the most acceptable sacrifice that had ever burnt on his altar, and offered with the most affecting emotions of religion? Nor would it seem to him to lessen what was already so little, but rather to augment it in value by bringing a divine benediction upon it. Or suppose a pious man, in that ancient time, to have been cast, by shipwreck, alone, on a desert coast. If his religion, predominant in all scenes and over all feelings, inspired the wish to make a burnt-offering to his God, his only means might have been something of the little store he had saved from the wreck, and fragments of his ship for fuel. But in the solemnity of bearing toward heaven the expression of a sublime devotion, this would surpass all other sacrificial flames he had ever kindled or beheld. It might appear to his faith, amidst the gloom of the solitary shore, as a symbol of that presence which was in the fire that Moses saw in the desert.

Perhaps it may be justly thought, that the notions, dispositions, and circumstances, above recounted as adverse to the spirit for christianizing the heathens, and as intercepting the desired assistance to a mission actually at work among them, did not require to be commented on at such length. We gladly leave them to become harmless under the progressive ascendency of unfettered thinking, experience, benevolent zeal, and that better aspect which we hope that a good Providence will ere long give to the times, if it were only for the purpose of replenishing the resources of schemes for extending the dominion of divine truth. We shall hasten toward a conclusion by briefly suggesting a few ideas tending to animate the piety of persons already inclined in this way to "come to the help of the Lord."

And surely there is something very captivating in such an expression itself, combined with numerous sentences in the Bible, less bold and striking in phrase, but of the same spirit. It is strange that we are not oftener surprised and delighted at the condescension shewn by the Almighty, in expressing the dictates of his will to his servants in terms and images which permit them to regard the performance of their duty, their mere duty, in the light of cooperation with him. The thought of being authorized by him to entertain so sublime an idea of their vocation, might bear them up in their deepest distresses and most arduous labours; might animate them though a world were against them. So ennobled a character of their service, however, which it would have been profaneness for them to have arrogated without such a sanction, is fit to be dwelt upon in its full magnitude only when their minds are the most elevated in devotion, when consequently their humility is the most profound. In the usual tenour of their religious feelings, it should be honour enough to inspire complacency and activity in their work, that they can regard themselves in the humbler capacity of mere instruments; that the Supreme Agent chooses to effect by means of them what he could accomplish with infinite facility without them.

Apply the consideration to the matter now before us. He could by a simple act of his will cause an instantaneous disappearance from the globe of that enormous system of mythological delusion, with all its rites, iniquities, and guardian evil spirits. It might vanish like a vapour of the morning, and leave but its wreck and monument in fallen temples and shivered idols, thenceforth a harmless mass of matter, dispossessed of that property which had breathed poison into men's souls. And indeed, if we were regarding the extermination of that monstrous superstition in no other view than that of the advantage of its being the soonest out of existence, we might be tempted to desire so illustrious a catastrophe. If such a thing might be, a servant of God would be willing to forego the honour of his share in the destruction. But when he finds it so evidently a principle in the beneficent designs of the divine administration of the world, that they are not directed solely to the accomplishment of one ultimate object, but are intended and adapted to be, in their execution, an employment, a discipline, and an honour, to human agents, he will feel (if his spirit be attempered to the great purposes of his Master) a generous impatience that these agents may be prompt to seize the honour thus brought within their reach. With fire-brands and torches put into their hands, can they be content, he exclaims, to stand still and let them burn out, while the huge fabric inhabited by demon gods, and filled with pestilent abominations, spreads wide and towers aloft in security and defiance before them? Let them advance and prove who has sent them, and whence the fire came that they bear. Let them go and demonstrate upon the proud assemblage of possessors of a region not their own, that the decree of expulsion coming on them at last is not the less armed with authority because He, whose own approach when on earth was always the imperative signal for infernal audacity to retire, seems now only to send his servants to execute his will. That his will should pass into effect through such an agency, may well excite the wonder of those who find such a commission offered to them. It must be the highest distinction which he has to confer on mortals, to be thus, by him, in the sight of far nobler mightier intelligences, ("a spectacle to angels,") accounted worthy to act a part in the grand scheme and process for the enlargement of his kingdom. It will also be a religious triumph as against the principalities and powers of evil, that it should please him to accomplish his victory by the means, in part, of creatures who. in thus serving their God, should be avengin their race; that these powers should see, that when the irresistible might was at last to be put forth, it was to be through the instrumentality of beings of that order, in whose debasement and misery they had so long maintained a direful evidence on the face of the creation that they were not yet consigned to the rigour of their prison-house.

It is a still further cause of delight, that this putting forth of strength under the external form of weakness, is analogous to the one greatest manifestation of vindicating and redeeming energy.

As an incitement to christians to throw a measure of their activity into enterprises aimed at such an object, they may be reminded that, while enjoined to preserve moderation in their own demands upon this earth, they are entitled to be ambitious, shall we not say arrogant, on behalf of their Lord. In their view, the worst usurpation beyond all comparison, in the world, must be that which any where presumes to withhold an inhabited tract from his actual dominion. On whatever it is that does so presume, let them expend the animosity which might otherwise find its meaner exercise against the boundaries that obstruct their own projects of acquisition. And in this nobler direction it will not be the passion which frets itself against what is immoveable and then subsides or recoils in despair. For they have reason to be assured that those limits against which this more consecrated ambition is impelled in hostility, will at length be carried away. They can descry through the gross darkness that covers the pagan regions, a mystical signature by the finger of God, on every spot, to indicate its assignment by that covenant which has given to the Messiah the heathen for his inheritance, and the uttermost parts of the earth for his possession. That declared decree in heaven, that substance of the thing hoped for, is brought down to the earth in the confident anticipations of the faithful, and beheld in foresight as become accomplished in the actual spectacle of an universal kingdom.

They see among leading mortals an ardent competition for dominion over spaces of territory, with angry controversy about titles and usurpations, and an incessant resort to the expedient which wastes the contenders and the subject of contention. They loathe and abhor this spectacle of a world with its unnumbered myriads continually made a sport and a prey of the bad passions of those predominant mortals, by their power of exasperating and directing the bad propensities of subservient multitudes. The contemplators of the scene, if they believed it must be always thus, might well be affected with passionate longings for omens of its approaching dissolution. An oracle that should tell them, in the plainest meaning of the words, that "the end of all things is at hand," might delight them more than ever a pagan mover of an ambitious enterprise was elated by voices or signs from the fane of his deity assuring him of conquest. But they have a better consolation in the faith that amidst all these tumults of conflict, amidst all these destructive competitions of transitory potentates, there is gradually unfolding itself a cause destined to grow to a dominion which will leave no province or tribe of the earth to be contested by the rivalries of an insane ambition.

In the mean time, if they observe any state making a great progress in power and occupancy of the face of the world, it will well become their character to show an animated concern that the kingdom which has their peculiar allegiance may be as evidently advancing, and that to this progress that enlargement of the temporal dominion may be made in some way to subserve. And here you will all be reminded of the wonderfully rapid extension of the British acquisitions in Asia, where we cannot help interpreting it as a sign in favour of a higher cause, that a lying spirit should have betrayed so many pagan and Mahomedan powers to provoke their own destruction. In this view of such vast conquests, we can thank the contrivers and the heroes, whose contempt would at any stage of the career have been excited at the notion of its being the real cause of their success that they were preparing the way for christianity.

It is of course for men of counsel and of war to scorn this fanatical mode of estimating splendid conquests. But we can see little on any other ground to console good men for the heavy addition made by conquests so splendid, to those public burdens which leave them such scanty means of doing good, of their own choice and in their own manner. Should national glory be talked of, we could have no fear of making the appeal to every one within hearing, whether he, as an individual of the nation, and one of the owners therefore of the glory of these eastern acquisitions, would not most willingly surrender his share of it on the terms of receiving back, were that possible, so much as it may fairly be calculated to have cost him. Especially this would be a safe appeal to a man who is thinking what a valuable contribution that sum would be to projects for diffusing christianity through any part of the world. It has not been left him for such disposal. But still, let him hope in Divine Providence that even to that object it has not been altogether lost. And here is a project which seeks to *redeem* to that very purpose what has been taken and expended in a spirit infinitely foreign to it, and what, unless so redeemed, may be truly accounted, for the greater portion of it, lost in the most absolute sense. But *this* enterprise too is a concern of serious expense. The advocates of this design have no way of avoiding the confession, that it seeks to impose a little more cost for India on persons to whom that country has, independently of their will, cost too much already; but it is an addition somewhat of the nature of an insurance for christianity on the ultimate effect of the expenditure. It is, like the prophet's action, casting something into the deep to cause that miraculously to float which were else irrecoverably sunk.

The object is, that the true religion may advance—too slowly, at first, it is true, but with a continual movement, to be accelerated in Heaven's good time—on the track of our victorious armies; may plant stations on the fields of their encampments and battles; may demolish, in the moral sense, as many strong-holds of superstition as our artillery has reduced fortresses; may, in short, carry on operations corresponding to the wars in all the points esteemed the most glorious. And what a delightful thing, if thus a Power never thought of by any of the parties in the long conflict, shall come in and take the best of the spoils; and assume, in a better sense, the dominion which so many potentates have been compelled to resign; showing the one people how they had, in truth, been beguiled through expenditure and exertion, for an object for which they would have scorned to make, knowingly, a hundredth part of such a sacrifice; and the other, that they had lost their political independence but as a prelude to their deliverance from their tyrant gods.—But how is a design which looks to such consequences to be supported in the early stages of its prosecution? It is evident there is no way but that in which the friends of religion may, if they will, decline to afford their aid.

Among the many reasons to be pleaded why they should not so decline, we may suggest the certainty that all the pecuniary aids received by our brethren in India will be faithfully applied, so as to return the best equivalent, in labour and the results of labour, that can be insured by that careful economy of expenditure which has hitherto been one of the most uncontested merits of their proceeding. It is impossible to conceive a stronger pledge for that faithful application, than the fact of their having many years generously devoted the product of that portion of their own indefatigable labours, which they undertook and have prosecuted for the sole purpose of creating their own means for their christian enterprise. *This* warfare therefore, in Hindoostan, is in no danger of incurring a charge which has been constantly and heavily laid on the conduct of our other wars there. We may be assured that all the supplies afforded to *this* service will go into the effective apparatus, and will be felt in the enemy's camp.

While we pay the tribute of our grateful admiration to the devotedness, the disinterestedness, and the most extraordinary performances, of the fraternity at Serampore, we cannot help being reminded that the chief of these labourers are advanced in life, and the leader of the band verging fast, in point of age, to the decline. We will not dwell on the irreparable loss which the cause sustained by them with so noble an energy is one day to suffer. But it does seem highly desirable that the remaining portion of the lives of these veterans should be turned to the utmost account. A few spirits so long and severely disciplined, who have mastered so much difficulty, that nothing which can remain appears formidable to them, and who habitually, and now as it were mechanically, labour at the extreme pitch of their labouring power,—and that power indefinitely increased by practice,—a few such men, and those also acting in concert, are to be estimated at many-fold their numerical force, even considered in reference simply to the amount of work they can perform. The valuation, therefore, of whatever may remain to them of life is to be according to what these acquired powers and habits have added to the ordinary efficiency of industry and ability. Now, while there is no adding to the *length* of these invaluable lives, it is possible to make, if we may so express it, an addition to their *breadth.* That is, it is possible for these men's minds and their system to be carried, by means of larger supplies, into action on a wider extent. And our argument is, that such ampler supplies during their life would be means put in action, over that extent, not to produce an effect merely according to what may be deemed their ordinary rate of operation, but in proportion to the advantage, which is temporary and may be short, of being employed by such excellently disciplined agents: such enlarged aid would serve the cause in the magnified proportion of these men's peculiar qualification to make them effectual to serve it.

Nor is it any disparagement, by anticipation, to the zeal and talent which we are confident the Supreme Head of the church will appoint in long succession to this work, when we represent the special importance of aiding it in this particular stage, on the ground that a combination of men uniting the advantage of a patriarchal priority in time, with individual endowments so adapted, such diversified exercise and experience, such difficulty surmounted, and such duration of faithful, firm conjunction, can hardly ever be equalled in the power of making the most efficient application of whatever means shall be supplied.

The right policy, in this case, is the same as that which would impel a State, engaged in some ambitious enterprise, to push its military operations most earnestly, and with every practicable reinforcement, during the last campaign in which those operations could probably have the advantage of being directed by an unbroken band of veterans trained in conjunction to victory in the service.*

* It may not be amiss, with respect to persons but slightly acquainted with the missionary portion of the history of our age, to add a few sentences to the mention, in a preceding note, of the three men who formed themselves into a fraternal union at Serampore, between thirty and forty years since.—The rule of their institution was, that as soon as possible (and it was soon actually attained) they should support themselves, and devote to the christian service all they should gain, beyond what was strictly necessary for that support, by combining with their directly missionary employments certain other occupations, literary and connected with literature, as expedients for raising an income.—Not long afterward there were stationed in the same place and neighbourhood other missionaries of the same religious denomination, in a certain degree associated with them, but not of the union in which these three had voluntarily constituted their own independent system, of deliberations, measures, support in common, and mutual accountableness, exclusively of all other authority.

Within a very few years after the time the references to them were made in this discourse, one excellent member of that union, Ward, was removed by death. The remaining two, one of them now past seventy, and subjected at last to a pressure of bodily infirmity which indicates the approaching conclusion of his labours, the other but few years below that age, both having been remarkably favoured in point of general health during the third part of a century, in a climate so inauspicious to Europeans, have continued to prosecute with unremitting exertion to the present time (1833), with a gradual accession of assistance by the active

And even as regarding these men themselves, willing, like St. Paul, to forego, if it might be put at their

zeal of younger cooperators, the undertaking to which they so long since devoted themselves for life and death. Their missionary operations have been continually extending to a wider compass, though sustained by pecuniary resources far less in proportion than the ordinary cost of similar undertakings. But, their own means for creating those resources having been gradually reduced, by various circumstances in that country, almost to nothing, they have now to depend chiefly on such aid as shall be supplied to them from those in this country who cannot be willing that such workmen should be disabled by any thing but death, or that so important a work should fall to the ground in the presence of the idolaters and their gods.—Through good report and evil report they have proceeded on, actuated by the same invariable determination, to their great object; not surprised that they have had to experience, what must be reckoned on by all who surpass their fellow-mortals, in the service especially of christianity, an ample visitation of malice, misrepresentation, and calumny; partly from the undisguised enemies of religion, and partly from such as claim to be accounted its friends. But they will stand most worthily and eminently conspicuous in christian history, ages after the calumnies and their authors shall have sunk in oblivion.

Mere justice to them requires an observation to be here made, on what was said in the discourse in the way of urging a somewhat extra liberality, on the consideration of the too probably short remainder of the lives of men so peculiarly qualified to apply the contributed assistance to the best advantage. The writer, (or discourser,) never having had the least curiosity to inquire into the official affairs of societies or committees, was really not aware that no part of what was contributed, then or long before, to the general missionary purposes, went in aid of the Serampore fraternity; who sought no such assistance, but, during a very long period, more, probably, than twenty years, supported and extended their system on the sole strength of their own exertions and means; and were disinterested enough to be willing that this fact should be very little known, while their great reputation was availing so powerfully to obtain from public liberality supplies which went to missionary uses entirely distinct from their operations.—In the long course of those operations they have expended, for purely christian and philanthropic purposes, from the proceeds of their own various industry in ways secondary and subsidiary to their extensive gratuitous labours in missionary and bible-translation work, an amount which would have made them all rich; but which, in their honourable poverty, they are rejoicing to have so choice, a more speedy emancipation from their toils to the final rest, and to labour on to the last period of exhausted nature,—it seems due from our sympathy and gratitude to wish that, if death should not deny them the time, the christian public should not refuse them the other means, for advancing the introductory process of the great work to a point where they would be perfectly willing to bid it adieu. That supposed limit of their christian ambition is not altogether an imaginary one: not a chariot like Elijah's for their departure would inspire in them such joy, in quitting the world, as to know that the most important parts of the revelation of God had been brought to speak in *every* considerable language of Asia.

But at all events, they will depart with the delight of knowing, that their distinguished lot on earth has been to open the way, in an important sense, to the region whither they are going, for innumerable souls escaping from the kingdom of darkness in succession of time to follow them; while they will rejoice to have stayed long enough to see the evinced and completed

expended.—By the loss, in the recent dreadful commercial crash at Calcutta, of what small funds they possessed appropriate to the service, they are at present reduced to a situation of extreme difficulty for the means of continuing the support, on even the most restrictive plan of economy, of the missionaries whom they have placed at no less than *eighteen* different stations on the immense territory under the British government or influence. They have transmitted a plain statement of this situation, with an appeal to the liberality of the friends of religion in this country.

During a very long period they held an ostensible connexion, without dependence or accountableness on their part, with the Baptist Missionary Society; and, when toward the end of that period their resources had become greatly diminished, received pecuniary aid, for a few years, from that Society. But about seven years since the connexion entirely ceased; and from that time all assistance requested for them is expressly in their name as the Serampore Missionaries.

efficacy of their appointment as evangelists in some that are gone before them. They will know that by the cause in which they have lived and laboured, and are dying, a new mode of the divine attention, a greater measure of the divine interest, has been drawn and must remain fixed in benignant radiance on a formerly estranged and desolate tract of the world; inasmuch as wherever there are faithful witnesses to the truth, repenting sinners, and pagans making sacrifices of the idols to which they had offered sacrifice, and commencing in the name of Christ a new life, amidst prayers and praises in languages which never addressed the Almighty before, there is (speaking reverently) something to necessitate toward that spot a far more special emanation of favour and providence from heaven, than when that moral waste contained nothing spiritually related to God. If there were but one particle there of such new and sacred existence, heaven *must* continue in communication with the spot where there is something so much its own, till it became extinct, or were resumed to the sky. How happy then if there shall be there an augmentation, every day, of what thus bears a special relation to God, to become a continually stronger attraction of the divine benignity thitherward; till at length the language of prophecy shall be fulfilled, "Behold, the tabernacle of God is with men, and he will dwell with them, and they shall be his people, and God himself shall be with them, and be their God."

In a confidence of a progressive prevalence of the gracious dispensation of which we think we see the commencement, it might be permitted to indulge for a moment in the contemplation of India as in a future age, in which distant period we can in a measure conceive what will be the reflections of a devout observer, regarding the scene in reference to the past. With the picture on his imagination of India as the missionaries had found it, and as many preserved authentic descriptions will agree with them in representing it, he may look over the ample region, to wonder what is become of that direful element, which was once perceived pervading and corrupting the whole wide diffusion of mental and moral existence; betraying in a darkness visible the character of the people's souls through their less sable exterior. The dusky visages, the attire and the structure of habitations perhaps, and the grand features of Nature, will be seen the same; but a horrid something, composed of lies, and crimes, and curses, and woes, that did rest in deadly possession over all the land, will be broken up and gone. Where has a place been found for what occupied for ages after ages so many cities, and villages, and houses, and minds? What tempest has driven it away? What presence has been here which *that* presence could not abide? Was it that Spirit in awe of which eternal night vanished at the creation of the world?

He may look from the southern and western shores toward the sublime mountain-boundary of the region on the north, and reflect what a scene it was to confront heaven, in all this breadth, with deities and worships, institutes, dogmas, and licensed morals, hostile and hateful to God; each individual of unnumbered millions being infatuated with notions, and perverted to habits, which exemplified to what depth a rational nature could fall. But how glorious for that reflecting observer to feel it verified to him that this is but a vision of the past, and that, departing like a dream when one awakes, it leaves him in view of a bright and blessed reality. How he will exult in the palpable evidence that the Son of God has spread his dominion from those shores to those mountains; that the oracles of truth have taken place of the most silly, and loathsome, and monstrous legends with which the father of lies ever made contemptuous sport of the folly of his dupes; and that the new religion admitted in faith as doctrine, has evinced its moral excellence in the virtues of its believers. When joining with them in exercises of worship to the true God, he may have short lapses of mind into a view of the past, presented in vivid images of the fantastic fooleries, and the detestable orgies, that had once elated superstition to madness on the very same spot, as attested by some monumental ruin of a temple; and he will recover from such brief alienation of thought to verify the fact, that he actually *is* among persons reverently calling on God in the name of Christ. That disease of the soul will be gone that exhibits itself in alternate lethargy and raving The charities of humanity, restored among them, will show why it was that their ancestors could look upon, or even cause, the death of relations and friends with stockish indifference. And finally, he will see the effect of that which missionaries are seeking to promote among them, in the manner in which the death of christianized Hindoos will differ from that insensate quiet, that stoicism without magnanimity, with which the pagan Hindoo submits to fate.

And if we might, for a moment, entertain so improbable an idea, as that this observer and comparer should be uninformed of the general course of means and operation, through which the Almighty Spirit had accomplished this great change, we can suppose his conjectures on the subject to be much too magnificent. How came thousands of temples to be surrendered to the decay of time or the shorter work of dilapidation, an infinity of idols to be demolished, a mythology and ritual, involving the whole life and being of the human multitude, to be exploded, the powers of Brahmins and priests to be annihilated, a whole intellectual and moral system to be supplanted by its opposite? Might not such questions put his mind on the effort to imagine the most extraordinary modes of divine interposition? He might fancy, perhaps, that some great convulsion of nature had contributed to the overthrow of so many structures forming the glory and the fortresses of superstition; that portentous phenomena, bearing a menacing aspect on the pagan rites, had been displayed in the heavens; or that a new dispensation of miracles, at once verifying the record of the ancient ones and surpassing them in magnificence, had expelled the fabulous monsters of the popular faith, as our Lord sent the demonized herd into the sea, and had brought the truth with the force of irresistible facts. Might there not also have been an eminently peculiar manifestation of providence for the temporal welfare of the converts, marking them out to the gross apprehension of the idolaters as exclusively the favourites of the Power that governs the world? And might he surmise in addition, that the foreign christian state, which had conquered Hindoostan, must have systematically lent, during the acquisition and possession, its whole influence arising from conquest and dominion, to promote christianity by every expedient short of force?

No, he might be told, you see, in this happy trans formation, nothing which is to be referred to any such causes. The work began in some of the humblest movements that ever pointed to a great object, movements in which the actors owed in part their toleration to the contempt felt for them by the people they adventured among. A train of ideas had been excited in the minds of some individuals respecting the prophecies relative to the heathen nations. Their conversations about these with their religious friends, had led to meetings, prayers, little arrangements of cooperation, and slender contributions of money. A gradual extension of these measures had resulted in the sending of several zealous men, by means of conveyance marked with the disfavour of the governing authorities, to begin the experiment. It was commenced under appearances very far from resembling Constantine's pretended vision of a cross in the clouds, inscribed as the sign of victory; or from recalling to mind what is said of pagan priests of other ages having been affrighted by a trembling of their fanes, and fearful voices from their recesses announcing the abandonment of the solemn abode by the deities. Had these servants of Christ taken up their design on any condition of the intervention of preternatural omens, or any presumption of a sudden revolutionary efficacy of their humble and ordinary instrumentality, the only dictate of their experience hitherto would have been to lay it down. But, wild as they were accounted, both the promoters in England, and the agents in the East, they had not been such elated visionaries in their expectations as that a less than moderate success thus far should deject them to a surrender of the resolution to persevere, and to enjoin on their successors an interminable perseverance, in the trial of what the Almighty should see fit to accomplish at length by means of the divine revelation sent into every region, a never tired repetition of missionary journeys, addresses, and friendly conferences, with the cooperation of schools and proforms of more immediate invasion of ourselves, that worst enemy maintains a powerful and dreadful presence. We require to be kept in a habitual and alarming sense of the fact, that the one thing in the creation which surpasses all others as an object for hatred, is here amidst us, and all around, in many diversities of malignant existence; and with all of them it is our vocation to be at enmity and war. It were in vain to seek to escape from the condition of our place in the dominions of God. A mind of wandering and melancholy thought, impatient of the grievous realities of our state, may at some moments almost breathe the wish that we had been a different order of beings, in another dwelling-place than this, and appointed on a different service to the Almighty. In vain! Here still we are, to pass the first part of our existence in a world where it is impossible to be at peace, because there has come into it a mortal enemy to all that live in it. Darkness and silence over the universe deny us all knowledge of the inhabitants of its innumerable worlds; but we would willingly believe that this may be the only region (except that of penal justice) where the cause of evil is permitted to maintain a contest. Here perhaps may be almost its last encampment, where its prolonged power of hostility may be suffered in order to give a protracted display of the manner of its appointed destruction. Here our lot is cast, on a ground so awfully preoccupied; a calamitous distinction! but yet a sublime one, if thus we may render to the Eternal King a service of a more arduous kind than it is possible to the inhabitants of any other world than this to render him; and if thus we may be trained, through devotion and conformity to the Celestial Chief in this warfare, to the final attainment of what he has promised, in so many illustrious forms, to him that overcometh. We shall soon leave the region where so much is in rebellion against our God. But we shall go where all that pass from our world must present themselves as from battle, or be denied to mingle in the eternal joys and triumphs of the conquerors.

THE END.

LONDON: PRINTED BY WILLIAM CLOWES AND SONS, LIMITED,
STAMFORD STREET AND CHARING CROSS.